Human Resources JumpStart

Human Resources
—— JumpStart™ ——

Anne M. Bogardus, SPHR

SYBEX

San Francisco ◆ London

Associate Publisher: Joel Fugazzotto
Acquisitions and Developmental Editor: Elizabeth Hurley Peterson
Developmental Editor: Tom Cirtin
Production Editor: Susan Berge
Technical Editor: Cynthia Erickson
Copyeditor: Nancy Sixsmith
Compositor: Chris Gillespie, Happenstance Type-O-Rama
Graphic Illustrator: Happenstance Type-O-Rama
Proofreader: Nancy Riddiough
Indexer: Nancy Guenther
Book Designer: Judy Fung
Cover Designer: Richard Miller, Calyx Design
Cover Photographer: Daisuke Morita, Photodisc

Library of Congress Card Number: 2004104229

ISBN: 0-7821-4344-X

Manufactured in the United States of America

10 9 8 7 6 5 4 3 2 1

About the Contributors

The following esteemed professionals contributed to this book by sharing their own real-world experiences, lessons, and know-how. Many thanks for their invaluable contributions.

Alice Elliott, SPHR   Alice lends over 20 years experience in HR and staffing to *Human Resources JumpStart*. Most recently, she was the vice president of human resources for IP Infusion, Inc., a software IP startup. Prior positions have included vice president of human resources at In League, a web-based Mohr Davidow Company; Staffing Manager at Network Appliance; and multiple positions with Synopsys.

Cynthia Erickson, SPHR   Cynthia, a seasoned executive, has 20 years of practical, cross-functional experience in financial services, high-tech, and healthcare. Her pragmatic solutions to business challenges are valued by both novice and veteran managers alike. She is a certified management trainer and skilled lecturer in the field of human resources. Based in San Francisco, CA, Cynthia is currently engaged on a global scale, partnering with managers and employees in the United States, Europe, Asia, and Latin America. Cynthia also collaborated with Anne Bogardus on the *PHR/SPHR Professional in Human Resources Certification Study Guide* by being the primary technical editor.

Marilyn Evans, Compensation Management Consulting   Marilyn is an independent compensation consultant with significant consulting and industry experience in designing total compensation programs that are consistent with and supportive of corporate strategies and objectives. She has technical expertise in state-of-the-art compensation systems, including variable compensation plans and broad-banded, competency-based and integrated human resources systems.

Rick Sherwood   Rick is a managing partner at Innovative HR Solutions, LLC, a management consulting firm specializing in the design, development, and implementation of internet-based employee opinion surveys. He is a facilitator for organizational change and has improved the productivity and financial results for numerous organizations. Prior to forming Innovative HR Solutions, Rick was the director of human resources for Stanford University Bookstore and West Coast Beauty Supply Co. Rick has also worked at Bechtel International and Bank of America. His 20-plus years of executive human resources management experience in a variety of industries offers clients a wealth of expertise. Rick is also member of the Society for Human Resource Management and the Professionals in Human Resources Association. He has a B.S. from Willamette University, Salem, OR, and an M.S. from the University of Southern California, Los Angeles, CA.

Phyllis A. Simmons, M.A., CSP   Phyllis is a board-certified safety professional with extensive consulting and train-the-trainer experience. As founder and president of the San Francisco–based firm Creative Safety Designs, she assists organizations with the development of injury prevention, training, and leadership programs. Simmons received her M.A. in Education from San Francisco State University and her B.S. in Safety and Systems Management from the University of Southern California.

For Linda and Robert with love and gratitude for their encouragement and support.

Acknowledgments

So many people participated in or supported this project, and it could not have happened without the contributions of each of them. To begin with, thank you to Elizabeth Peterson and Joel Fugazzotto for the opportunity to write another book for Sybex. Elizabeth, thanks for doing double duty on this one and putting up with me yet again—you are the best cheerleader. Joel, thank you for listening and for understanding.

The production team at Sybex was fantastic. Thanks particularly to Susan Berge for keeping everything (including me) on track, to Leslie Light for the backup support, and to Rachel Gunn for her patient tolerance of a stressed-out author. I'm grateful for the level of professionalism and expertise that each of them brought to the project. Thanks to the team of illustrators at Happenstance Type-O-Rama for translating my rough illustrations into polished graphics. Judy Fung's work on the book design is phenomenal—great job, Judy! Many thanks to Nancy Sixsmith for her copyediting contributions. I'd also like to acknowledge Tom Cirtin's contribution and thank him for teaching me some new Microsoft Word tricks.

I am grateful to all of the subject matter experts who willingly shared their expertise with readers. Phyllis Simmons, masterful trainer and safety expert, thank you for your clear explanations on those topics. You are a joy to work with. Marilyn Evans, you are clearly a master of the compensation field and your concise descriptions made an intimidating subject easier to understand. Rick Sherwood, my certification mentor and dear friend, thank you for your enthusiastic participation and clear explanation of the employee survey process. Last (but certainly not least), thank you to Alice Elliott, whose pointers for performance management were right on target. My heartfelt thanks to you all—it's been a pleasure.

I owe a huge debt of gratitude to the technical editor for this book, Cynthia Erickson. Considering everything else that has been going on for you this year, I am deeply appreciative of your enthusiastic willingness to jump right into another book with me. Aside from that, your words of support and encouragement always give me the boost I need to go forward. You are *still* awesome!

Thanks to all of my friends and family for their encouragement and support, and for still remembering my name after all the time I've spent holed up working on this book. I value all of you more than you know.

Contents

Chapter 4   Building the Compensation Plan   87

Chapter 5   Building a Safe and Secure Workplace   107

Introduction

Before we begin, consider these questions. Are you...

- Interested in learning more about the human resource (HR) field?
- Exploring different areas of business management prior to choosing a career?
- Being asked to take on human resource–related duties in your current job?
- Expanding your current HR duties to include functions you haven't worked in before?
- Working in another business function and looking for a better understanding of what to expect from the HR department in your organization?

If the answer to any of these questions is "yes," this book will inform you about the scope of human resource practice, answer your questions, and increase your understanding of how HR adds value to organizations.

If you ask 10 different people what human resources is or does, more than likely you'll get at least eight different answers. Depending on who you ask, HR is seen as an employee advocate, management advisor, recruiter, counselor, executive coach, trainer, event planner, or administrative expert—and these are just a few of the roles that are attributed to those who work in HR. If you are interested in entering this field and want to be successful, you'll want to understand what you are getting yourself into and get an idea of what day-to-day work might be like. The goal of this book is to clear up some misperceptions about the profession and inform readers about the evolving role of HR and how this important function contributes to organizational success.

Organizations are evolving to meet the changing demands brought on by globalization and advances in technology. As is true for all business functions, HR must evolve in order to meet organizational needs in this changing environment. Activities performed by human resource practitioners generally fall into one of the following six functional areas:

- Strategic Management
- Workforce Planning and Employment
- Human Resource Development
- Compensation and Benefits
- Employee and Labor Relations
- Occupational Health, Safety, and Security

Whether HR practitioners are *generalists* (with responsibilities in all these areas) or *specialists* (with responsibilities concentrated in a single function) depends to a large extent on the size and needs of individual organizations. HR practitioners work in organizations that vary greatly in size, from as few as 50 employees with a sole practitioner to as many as several hundred thousand employees with an HR department of several hundred practitioners. Larger HR departments often include a combination of specialists (in areas such as compensation, benefits, training, and organization development) and generalists (who are assigned to handle employee relations, staffing, and safety issues for specific departments or business units). Other large organizations might operate HR call centers to serve the needs of employees spread across the country or around the world. The structure of HR departments in different organizations depends, quite simply, on the size and needs of each organization. For this reason, many folks have trouble answering what exactly the human resources department does.

In the current business environment, practitioners need to fully understand traditional operational and administrative HR functions. In addition, successful practitioners increasingly are expected to function as full business partners in their organizations. This requires a broad understanding of other organization functions (such as sales and operations) and the ability to tie traditional HR functions to business needs and goals. This book provides you with basic information about traditional HR functions and provides basic explanations of how these functions are connected with the operating needs of organizations.

Reading this book will give you a jump start for understanding the practical application of human resource principles. You can build on this knowledge base by taking human resource classes; reading other books related to strategic management, compensation and benefits, employee and labor relations, and occupational health and safety; and networking with others in your organization or community involved in human resource work.

Who Should Read This Book

This book was written for those of you fairly new to human resources and lays the foundation for an understanding of the basic principles of good human resources methodologies. Even if you've had some experience in the human resources field, you'll find the detailed descriptions, key terms, and additional resources included in this book immediately applicable to your current endeavors.

The fact that you purchased this book means that you're interested in learning new things and furthering your career. Having a solid understanding of human resources practices and functions will help you increase your marketability. Your knowledge and practice of the principles outlined in this book will help assure employers that you understand the basic tasks associated with facilitating a human resources department. If you choose to take this endeavor further by acquiring hands-on work experience and then becoming certified, you will increase your chances for advancement and improve your odds for landing the higher-paying human resources positions. Potential employers will view your pursuit of human resources knowledge and certification as assertive and forward thinking, and they know that this will ultimately translate to success for their organization.

What This Book Covers

This book walks you through not only practical HR information but also how it is applied in daily operations. We've included many useful examples, tips, and hints that will help you solve common human resources dilemmas. Here's an overview of what this book covers:

Chapters 1 and 2 These chapters lay the foundation of human resources by providing an overview of workforce management and the evolution of the human resources profession. Also explored are the different types of laws that affect HR practice.

Chapters 3 and 4 In this section of the book you will learn about the elements that are necessary to effectively staff an organization with the right people at the right time. It also deals with the various elements of compensation used by organizations to attract candidates and retain employees. Last, these chapters describe how an organization's compensation strategies can further its strategic goals.

Chapters 5 through 7 These chapters walk you through benefits, the legal requirements of OSHA, and some of the related issues employers face in providing a hazard-free workplace. You will also learn how to build an employee relations program and develop a communication strategy.

Chapters 8 and 9 This section focuses on maintaining high productivity by building training and development programs and performance management programs. The aim of these programs is to enhance productivity, build relationships, and facilitate on-going communications among supervisors and their employees.

Chapter 10 The purpose of this chapter is to look at how the functions covered in previous chapters fit into the overall management strategy of an organization. Parallels and connections will be drawn to illustrate how the HR practitioner must be able to identify how the functions, programs, and activities they provide must contribute to its success.

Making the Most of This Book

At the beginning of each chapter you'll find a list of topics that the chapter will cover. You'll find new terms defined in the margins of the pages to help you quickly get up to speed on human resources–specific terminology. In addition, several special elements highlight important information:

NOTE

Notes provide extra information and references to related information.

TIP

Tips are insights that help you perform tasks more easily and effectively.

WARNING

Warnings let you know about things you should—or shouldn't—do as you perform human resources tasks and duties.

Also, throughout, you will find "Real World Scenario" sidebars. These sidebars have been written by a myriad of human resources experts especially for this book. Each sidebar is designed to give you a real world perspective about a particular human resources function.

 Real World Scenario

Real World Scenarios provide you with some practical perspectives and help you understand a task's or practice's real world relevance.

You'll find several Review Questions at the end of each chapter to test your knowledge of the material covered. The answers to the Review Questions can be found in Appendix A. You'll also find a list of Terms to Know at the end of each chapter that will help you review the key terms introduced in each chapter. These terms also appear in the Glossary at the end of the book.

Last, we've provided additional resources for you in Appendices B and C. Appendix B will provide you with up-to-date information on FairPay Exemption Regulations, which should be effective August 23, 2004. Appendix C provides you with internet resources as well as additional book resources. These will add dimension or different perspectives to the information presented in this book.

Chapter 1

The Human Resource Profession

So, you think you want to be a human resource (HR) professional? Or maybe your job requires you to perform human resource functions as part of more broad responsibilities within your organization? If that's the case, or if you're working as a specialist in one area of human resources and want to broaden your basic knowledge of other aspects of the profession, this book is for you. We'll be examining different aspects of the human resource profession to provide you with a basic understanding of the diverse functions that fall under the purview of human resource departments in different organizations.

This book combines theory with practical information about how the theory is applied in daily operations. Each chapter includes information from subject matter experts (SMEs), who write about topics they focus on in their daily work. These insights from specialists who have "been there, done that" are designed to help you better absorb the information presented in the chapter so that you may more easily apply it in your work as a human resource practitioner.

In this chapter, we'll start our examination with an overview of workforce management and the evolution of the human resource profession.

What Is Human Resource Management?

Human resource management (HRM) is the organizational function with responsibility for attracting, retaining, and managing the people who make up organizations. From the Chief Executive Officer to the worker on the production line, HRM is involved in the recruitment, selection, employment, and exit of employees from organizations. HRM includes all the following activities:

◆ Finding and interviewing candidates, and hiring the best-qualified person for the job

◆ Determining how best to compensate employees through salaries, wages, and benefits

◆ Providing a safe and secure workplace

◆ Understanding federal, state, and local employment laws and regulations; and ensuring that workplace policies comply with them

◆ Developing policies to build effective working relationships between organizations and employees

◆ Designing processes to enhance communication from the bottom up as well as from the top down

◆ Providing training and development opportunities that build employee skills

◆ Motivating and retaining employees

◆ Facilitating the exit process, whether it is voluntary or involuntary

HRM is one of the five basic functions that make up modern organizations. In addition to HRM, these functions include sales and marketing, information technology (IT), operations and manufacturing, and, of course, finance and accounting. The operations and manufacturing function supplies the products or services that are the source of income for the organization. The sales and marketing function, in conjunction with production, develops products or services that will be offered by the organization, seeks out customers, and sells those products or services. The finance and accounting function collects information about sales and expenses, and provides reports to management that summarize this information for use in managing the business. The information technology function is responsible for maintaining the systems that manage data for organizations, such as customer relationship management (CRM), human resource information systems (HRIS), e-mail, and, of course, the computer systems that connect employees with each other. Regardless of the size of an organization, all these elements are present in some form.

Each functional area plays a vital role in the operation of any organization. Without people, the organization could not exist. Without a product, there would be no jobs. Without sales, there would be no money to pay people or produce the product. Without financial reports, management would be unable to manage the business successfully. Without information systems, communication and information gathering would be less efficient. The following illustration shows the interrelationship of these organizational functions.

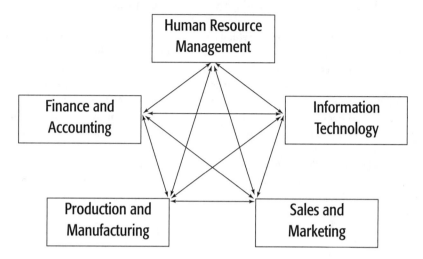

The organizational need to manage workforce requirements is a fairly recent one, developing as society evolved from one in which work was largely agrarian to one in which work was overwhelmingly industrial. Workers in agrarian societies had, for the most part, direct daily contact with their "manager," the farm owner. When jobs moved off the farm and into factories, the sheer size of the workforce precluded the business owner from having individual relationships with each employee, so this responsibility was delegated to supervisors and managers.

As organizations grew larger, the need to keep track of information about employees increased. It became necessary to hire workers whose only job was to keep track of all the workers: how many hours they worked and how much they were owed. The personnel department grew from this clerical function, and as labor laws were enacted, personnel, which already kept track of all the employees, was the natural function to assume responsibility for managing the new legal requirements. As the industrial age evolved into the information age, the personnel department evolved into the human resource function, with responsibility for managing overall employment relationships within organizations.

During this same period, changes in the work environment were taking place. The production needs on a farm were simple and tied directly to natural requirements that could not be manipulated. It was, after all, somewhat difficult to change the length of the growing season or to increase crop production by having the sun shine longer each day. With the advent of manufacturing processes, these natural constraints disappeared, and business owners could control conditions in a way that had not previously been possible by extending the workday to begin before dawn and end long after sunset. As business owners sought to increase productivity, experts with backgrounds in scientific measurement were brought in to identify ways to do so. This scientific management approach was popular in the late nineteenth and early twentieth centuries, but it focused on productivity to the exclusion of the needs of workers. This environment helped to create the union movement, in which employees banded together in an effort to improve working conditions as well as to address wage and benefit issues.

Because the personnel function was already involved with employee records and employment laws, it was also natural to place responsibility for managing employment relationships into this function. As these important responsibilities were added to personnel, the change in scope required businesses to look at this function in a different way and resulted in the function as it is known today: human resources.

The relationship between employees and organizations requires a balance between the need of the organization to make a profit and the need of its employees to have a work environment that is safe and satisfies basic human needs. During the last 30 years, the HRM role in organizations has evolved to become the function that finds solutions to satisfy these conflicting needs.

The Changing Role of Human Resources

Early in the twentieth century, the personnel function was focused on providing services (such as hiring employees); advising management on workforce issues; and ensuring that managers and employees complied with company policies, employment legislation, and government regulations. In the challenging business environment that exists today, HRM must play a more active role in ensuring the success of the business. To that end, the HRM role is evolving into one that is strategic, operational, and administrative.

strategic role
Identifies organizational goals and develops HR practices and programs that contribute to the achievement of those goals.

In its *strategic role*, HRM studies business goals to determine which human resources will be needed to achieve them and to develop legally compliant HR policies that contribute to the achievement of the goals. For example, if business leaders determine that they want to hire the most highly skilled employees available, HRM can further this goal by developing a compensation plan that leads the labor market for those skills (discussed in Chapter 4, "Building a Compensation Plan"). To do this, HRM must identify the demographic characteristics of candidates with the needed skills, find out what their competitors are providing in terms of compensation and benefits, develop a plan that exceeds what is being offered by the competition, and provide a staffing budget that demonstrates the impact of this plan on the bottom line. In this way, HRM demonstrates its ability to contribute to the overall success of the organization.

In another example, if business leaders determine that it is in the best interest of the organization to use a new form of technology in its production processes, HRM must examine the skills available in the current workforce to determine whether those skills are the ones needed to develop and implement the new technology. If not, HRM must do two things: develop a plan to train current employees in the new skill requirements and examine its recruiting methods to determine whether these methods can attract candidates with the desired skills. In this way, HRM ties a traditional function, recruiting, with the strategic goals of the business and also demonstrates its ability to contribute to the successful achievement of organizational goals.

In its *operational role*, HRM executes day-to-day tasks (such as recruiting new candidates or solving employee relations problems) in a manner consistent with the organization's needs and goals. In the area of staffing, for example, this role includes working with hiring managers to analyze jobs, writing job descriptions, creating recruiting plans for individual jobs, running ads, interviewing and evaluating candidates, administering pre-employment tests, and conducting background or reference checks on selected candidates.

operational role
Performs day-to-day tasks such as recruiting, counseling employees, and coaching managers—among many others.

In its *administrative role*, HRM maintains employment records and ensures compliance with federal, state, and local employment laws and regulations. In this role, HRM also ensures that company policies are fairly, equitably, and consistently applied throughout the organization. Many administrative tasks are managed with the use of an HRIS, an electronic system that collects and maintains information and statistics. HRIS systems have streamlined data collection and maintenance duties, freeing HRM professionals to spend their time on strategic and operational duties.

administrative role
Develops company policies that enhance the organization's ability to meet its goals and be in compliance with federal, state, and local employment laws and regulations.

To see how these roles work together, let's use the performance appraisal process as an example. The process begins strategically, with selection of a review process designed to improve employee performance and communications between managers and employees. Operationally, HRM trains managers to conduct appraisals and might coach them through difficult reviews. Administratively, HRM advises managers of the appraisal schedule, follows up with managers to ensure that the process is completed, and records the results in the HRIS system. In this and many other HRM responsibilities, practitioners may find themselves acting in all three capacities at different times to complete their assignments.

As you can see, the HRM function can be complex. In addition to what we do, we often must wear many hats in our organizations, moving from employee advocate to management coach to compliance advisor.

Professional Associations

As the personnel function evolved during the first half of the twentieth century, it became clear to practitioners, those who worked in the field on a day-to-day basis, that there was a need for a national association. This would provide them with a way to connect with others in the field and provide opportunities for professional development. They wanted to form an association that would enhance their ability to share information and be of benefit to all who worked in the field.

In 1948, 28 of these individuals formed the American Society for Personnel Administration (ASPA) to serve these needs. In 1989, to reflect the changing needs of business and the broader scope of responsibility of its members, ASPA became the Society for Human Resource Management (SHRM). SHRM has more than 175,000 members in 120 countries and is an influential voice on behalf of HR professionals, taking an active role in shaping legislation and government regulation of workforce activities.

This section describes SHRM and then touches upon several other organizations and forums that reflect developments in this rapidly changing field.

Society for Human Resource Management

The founders of SHRM and its early members were instrumental in developing the field as a profession. In 1964, SHRM (then known as ASPA) took the first steps to do so, beginning with a definition of what constituted a profession. They determined that the HR profession is defined by five characteristics:

- ◆ Common body of knowledge
- ◆ Code of ethics
- ◆ Ongoing research into the body of knowledge
- ◆ Certification program
- ◆ National professional association

body of knowledge (BOK)
A BOK defines the information that is common to the practice of a profession. The HR BOK requires knowledge of strategic management; workforce planning and employment; human resource development; compensation and benefits; employee and labor relations; and occupational health, safety, and security.

SHRM then set about to define the *body of knowledge (BOK)* that was unique to personnel, so a certification program could be developed. The ASPA Accreditation Institute (AAI) was created in 1975 to accomplish these goals. (AAI became the Human Resource Certification Institute, or HRCI, in 1989.) Over the years, the BOK has been revised to keep up with changes in the business environment and the impact of these changes on the practice of the profession. Today, the BOK consists of six functional areas:

Strategic Management   This area looks at the "big picture" in the organization and requires knowledge of the other operational functions (such as IT or marketing). When HR professionals can tie daily activities to organization goals, they are operating strategically.

Workforce Planning and Employment   This area covers operational responsibilities, including those needed to recruit, select, hire, retain, and exit employees from the organization.

Human Resource Development   This area refers to the activities performed to ensure that employees have the skills necessary to produce goods or services for the organization.

Compensation and Benefits   This area includes all the activities related to paying employees, including direct compensation they receive (such as cash and equity) and non-direct benefits the company provides (such as medical insurance and retirement plans).

Employee and Labor Relations   This area covers relationships between employees and each other and between employees and the organization, as well as issues related to union environments.

Occupational Health, Safety, and Security   This area covers the issues that involve the physical environment in which employees work each day.

The chapters that follow discuss aspects of these functional areas from the perspective of each of the three roles HR practitioners play in their organizations: strategic, operational, and administrative. Whether HR practitioners be entry-level, mid-career, or seasoned professionals, to be involved in the management of the organization and have the impact they desire on the workforce, every aspect of their practice must begin with an assessment of its strategic value or how it will contribute to the achievement of corporate goals. On top of that, to be seen as credible in their organizations, HR practitioners must ensure that HR programs run smoothly and deliver the services that management and employees expect. Chapter 11, "Strategic Human Resource Management" discusses how all the disparate elements of the HR profession come together for the benefit of organizations.

Other Professional Associations

As HRM functions became more complex, specialties began to develop, and practitioners in those areas began to form professional associations to meet their particular needs. The following organizations represent only a small number of those available to practitioners:

- American Society for Training and Development (ASTD)
- International Public Management Association for HR (IPMA-HR)
- International Association for Human Resource Information Management (IHRIM)
- WorldatWork
- National Association of Personnel Specialists

Most of these national associations have local chapters throughout the country. Members can meet, exchange ideas, look for jobs, and find qualified candidates for openings in their organizations. Most association websites provide contact information for local chapters and encourage members to participate at this level as well as at the national level.

Informal Networking Communities

With the advent of the Internet, opportunities for networking with other professionals have increased exponentially. Virtual HR communities provide camaraderie, information, and support from practitioners at all career levels. Each of these communities has its own personality, and many long-term members form close bonds. A major benefit of these groups is that their members can post questions and ask for advice on highly sensitive and confidential situations without breaching confidentiality or privacy requirements. Sometimes, just having someone else who has "been there, done that" can provide insights you may not have considered and help you to formulate a plan of action. It never hurts to get a variety of ideas and approaches for handling difficult situations. One of the best examples of this is the Human Resource Mentoring And Networking Association (HRMAN). The experience level of members of this community ranges from recent college graduates in their first jobs, to office or administrative managers who perform HR duties as part of their jobs, to employment law attorneys and senior HR executives.

Two other sites that provide useful information and an opportunity to ask questions are HRhero.com and AHIpubs.com. HRhero.com is an online community which provides a variety of information sources and services, including an online test, "HR I.Q.," that lets you test your knowledge. AHIpubs.com is another source for solid information and advice, and has an active community participating on its bulletin board.

You can access these sites at `www.hr-man.com.`, `www.hrhero.com` and `www.ahipubs.com.`

Professional Certifications

professional certifications
A professional certification indicates that an individual has met requirements established by a national certifying body for that profession.

There are a number of *professional certifications* available to HR practitioners. Some are awarded to specialists in areas such as staffing, compensation and benefits, and training; others are awarded to generalist professionals whose work encompasses multiple areas of human resource responsibilities. Let's begin with a discussion of the generalist certifications awarded by HRCI.

Generalist Certifications

The first HR certifications were earned in 1976; by May 2003, more than 68,000 HR generalists had earned professional certification. Today's certification process, which has evolved over time, consists of three levels of certification, Professional in Human Resources (PHR), Senior Professional in Human Resources (SPHR), and Global Professional in Human Resources (GPHR). According to the "HRCI State of the Institute Report 2003," the process of identifying the body of knowledge for a new level of certification, nonexempt and entry-level employees, will begin in 2004.

The certification process allows practitioners to demonstrate their mastery of the profession by meeting standards set by fellow practitioners who work in the field each day.

If you're a generalist who is seriously considering the certification path, I recommend that you pick up a copy of my book, *PHR/SPHR: Professional in Human Resources Certification Study Guide* (Sybex, 2004) to help you prepare for the exams. It has hundreds of sample questions, and many real-life examples that will help you apply what you've learned.

HRCI has set some requirements that must be met by candidates for the PHR, SPHR, and GPHR exams. You should check their site, www.hrci.org, for the most up-to-date information regarding exam requirements.

NOTE

Compensation and Benefit Certifications

Compensation and benefit professionals are certified by two different organizations: WorldatWork, which was previously known as the American Compensation Association, and the International Foundation of Employment Benefit Plans. WorldatWork certifies professionals at three levels, described as follows.

Certified Compensation Professional (CCP)   Candidates for CCP certification must demonstrate competence in nine areas, and the certification process requires candidates to pass exams in each of the areas. Six of the exams are designed to cover a wide variety of basic compensation knowledge, including the management of total rewards programs, knowledge of compensation and benefit regulations, fundamentals of benefit programs, job analysis, documentation and evaluation, and quantitative analysis methods. In addition to exams that measure basic compensation knowledge, candidates must select three areas of specialty, such as international benefits, mergers and acquisitions, or communicating with employees about total rewards (among others).

Certified Benefits Professional (CBP)   Like the CCP, the CBP certification requires candidates to pass nine exams to demonstrate their knowledge of various benefit programs.

Global Remuneration Professional (GRP)   Earning the GRP requires candidates to demonstrate their knowledge of remuneration techniques that apply to organizations with operations around the world. It consists of a series of exams focused on global application of compensation and benefit practices.

Information about compensation and benefit examinations is available on the WorldatWork website: www.worldatwork.org.

Employee benefits specialists can also earn certifications from the International Foundation of Employment Benefit Plans (IFEBP), in partnership with the Wharton School of Business at the University of Pennsylvania (for U.S. candidates) and with Dalhousie University in Nova Scotia (for Canadian candidates).

This organization recently revised its certifications to include four levels, described as follows.

Certified Employee Benefits Specialist (CEBS)   The CEBS designation is earned by individuals who complete coursework in eight areas and earn a passing score on a comprehensive examination that covers all aspects of employee benefits programs.

Other designations   The IFEBP recently revised its certification program by adding three new designations. The Compensation Management Specialist (CMS), Group Benefits Associate (GBA), and Retirement Plans Associate (RPA). These three designations are designed to acknowledge individuals who have mastered knowledge in each area of specialty. Information about these certifications can be found at www.IFEBP.org.

Staffing Certifications

Staffing professionals formed an association known as the National Association of Personnel Services (NAPS), which sponsors two professional certifications:

Certified Personnel Consultant (CPC)   Candidates for the CPC certification must pass a certification exam designed to measure knowledge of employment laws, government regulations, ethical standards, and best business practices.

Certified Temporary-Staffing Specialist (CTS)   The CTS exam covers topics similar to those on the CPC exam, but focuses on how they affect temporary service agencies.

In addition to these certifications, NAPS also sponsors a certification for recruiters who specialize in placing physicians, the Physician Recruiting Consultant (PRC) certification. Additional information about NAPS and these certifications is available on its website at www.recruitinglife.com.

Training Certifications

The ASTD is the professional association for training and development professionals. This association sponsors two certificate programs, as follows.

Certified Performance Technologist (CPT)   The International Society for Performance Improvement (ISPI) developed the CPT certification to measure candidates on 10 Standards of Performance Technology. These standards include the ability to focus on results, to analyze situations within the context of the larger organization, to add value to programs, and to collaborate with clients in developing programs, among others.

Human Performance Improvement (HPI)   The HPI certification is awarded to candidates who successfully complete six courses, covering topics that include analyzing and improving human performance at work;

selecting, managing, and evaluating interventions used to improve performance; and moving from a focus on traditional training techniques to performance improvement consulting.

Information about the ASTD certification programs is available on the ASTD website at `www.astd.org`.

Other Certifications

Although I could write an almost endless list of certifications with some relevance to HR practice, those mentioned previously are ones that will be most often encountered during the course of a career. Should you find yourself becoming a specialist in a different area of HR practice, it is worth your while to seek out a professional association that represents that specialty and investigate opportunities for certification in that field. Certification provides practitioners with many benefits and can be a useful career tool.

Professional Conduct

The different roles played by HR practitioners in organizations require flexibility. On the one hand, we represent management and contribute to organizational goals; on the other, we are charged with representing employee needs. There are many cases in which these roles are in direct conflict with each other, and balancing them can be rewarding and challenging—and often is the source of frustration. Ultimately, HR professionals provide the management team with strategies and tactics designed to improve and maintain productivity. The ultimate goal of any organization is, after all, to produce a product or provide a service, and employees are the people who make that happen.

In performing their duties, HR practitioners must operate within a *code of ethics* that allows them to maintain credibility in their organizations. The SHRM "Code of Ethical and Professional Standards in Human Resource Management" establishes guidelines for appropriate professional conduct and sets a high standard for dealing with daily conflicts that arise between the multiple roles required by our organizations. There are six core principles that guide practitioners in the performance of their duties, as described in the following sections.

code of ethics
A code of ethics establishes guidelines for professional conduct.

Professional Responsibility   HR professionals are responsible for setting and maintaining high standards of excellence, conducting themselves professionally during the course of their work, ensuring that their organizations comply with legal requirements, and advocating for employees.

Professional Development   Not only do employment laws change regularly, but business needs change rapidly as well. To perform professional work at the highest standards, HR professionals must engage in lifelong learning for continuous development of the knowledge and skills that further business goals.

Ethical Leadership   SHRM sets a high standard for ethical behavior, expecting practitioners to set the standard for ethical conduct within their organizations by conducting themselves ethically in all their duties.

Fairness and Justice   HR professionals are in a unique position to ensure that all individuals within an organization are treated equitably, and with dignity and respect.

Conflicts of Interest   It is crucial for HR professionals to exhibit a high level of integrity. For this reason, it is important that we refrain from activities that leave even the appearance of a conflict of interest and call the practitioner's credibility into question.

Use of Information   During the course of daily work, HR professionals are routinely exposed to sensitive and confidential information. Sharing information of this nature invades the privacy of the affected employee and can destroy an HR professional's credibility.

Visit the SHRM website at www.shrm.org/ethics/code-of-ethics.asp to read the entire code of ethics.

Although it is human nature to want to become part of the group, working in HR can place a strain on workplace friendships. It is one thing for a group of employees to gossip about work and complain about the boss; it is quite another when HR participates in such a conversation. Because HR plays dual roles as both a management representative and an employee advocate, HR practitioners who are made aware of activities involving any form of harassment or activities that could expose the organization to legal action have an obligation to advise management of serious situations. This may make it difficult to develop friendships with coworkers outside of the HR department because they may not be fully aware of your responsibility as a representative of management. At the same time, one of the functions of HR is to provide services for the employee population, so it is important to build relationships with these workers. We'll talk more about balancing these requirements in Chapter 6, "Building the Employee Relations Program."

Elements of Effective HR Programs

In the previous section, we identified the six areas of the HR BOK. This book examines basic aspects of each of these areas that are common to any organization employing people in its operations.

These basic elements are a part of any effective HR program, regardless of the size of the organization. In some very small organizations, they may not be identified specifically, but they are part of the employment process nonetheless. In very large organizations, these elements may be represented by separate departments staffed by specialists in each area; they may be combined in a single department and managed by a generalist in small and medium-sized organizations.

Let's take a look at each of the elements of effective HR programs, so you can better understand them:

Compliance: Employment Law and Organization Policy   Each of the other elements is subject to employment laws and regulations enacted by federal, state, and local legislatures, as well as to common-law practices. In addition, each organization establishes policies ensuring that employees are treated in a consistently fair and equitable manner regardless of which department they work in. An effective HRM program ensures that each element complies with these laws, regulations, and policies.

Staffing: Workforce Planning and Employment   Staffing refers to the process of acquiring and exiting employees from the organization. This process includes identifying the skills needed by the organization, the duties that need to be performed, and the level of experience necessary for success in a position. With that information, HR can recruit effectively, manage the selection process, hire, transfer or promote employees, and orient them to the organization. When employees resign, or must be laid off or terminated for other reasons, the staffing process identifies whether or not a replacement is needed and ensures that a smooth transition is made.

Compensation: Compensation and Benefits   Compensation is a critical element for attracting and retaining employees in an organization. Compensation comes in many forms: tangible, intangible, monetary, and non-monetary. Business goals are a crucial piece of a compensation program that attracts employees who possess the skills needed by the organization.

Safety: Occupational Health, Safety, and Security   Employers must provide a safe work environment for their employees.

Employee Relations: Employee and Labor Relations   Effective employee relations programs are a key element in retaining employees and avoiding unionization of the workforce.

Communications: Employee and Labor Relations   It is essential that employee communication programs provide avenues for "bottom-up" communication as well as "top-down." Giving employees the ability to influence their daily work aids retention and results in greater productivity.

Training and Development: Human Resource Development   Training provides skills that employees need to be successful in their current positions, such as new-hire orientation or training on the use of new software that is installed. Development prepares employees to take on increased responsibility within the organization, and may be achieved through academic methods, on-the-job, or by other means.

Performance Management: Human Resource Development   Performance management is an ongoing process that, when done effectively, provides employees with regular feedback. Performance appraisals, generally given on an annual basis, are one aspect of performance management.

As demonstrated in the following illustration, these basic elements form the building blocks of an effective HRM program:

The diagram shows two additional building blocks: Global HRM and Strategic HRM.

Global HRM   In today's business environment, even relatively small organizations might have global operations. When these operations involve employing workers in other countries, HR professionals must become familiar with employment laws and customs in the host country as well as ensure compliance with U.S. laws that apply to global operations.

Strategic HRM   It's a fact that HR professionals at all levels must operate strategically today. This means that programs must be scrutinized to ensure that they contribute to the capability of the organization to achieve its goals. After you learn the basics, we'll talk in practical terms about how to operate strategically in your daily work.

HR Practices in Different Employment Sectors

For the most part, jobs fall into one of two sectors: public or private. Jobs in the public sector include those in federal, state, and local government agencies. In the private sector, jobs exist in for-profit businesses and nonprofit organizations. An effective HR program in any of these organizations contains all the basic elements described in the previous section. Depending on the type of the organization, however, the combination of the elements and the importance placed on different elements can vary.

Public Sector Organizations

Jobs in the public sector have a number of unique characteristics that set them apart from the private sector, including the prevalence of unions, legal restrictions that govern employee relations issues, and mandated limitations on compensation and benefits. For many years, the reputation of the public sector was one of extreme bureaucracy and of being resistant to change, characterized by mountains of paperwork and red tape. Change, when it did take place, often occurred as the result of a lengthy process requiring the involvement of numerous committees and agencies, and approvals at multiple levels in the hierarchy. Today, in response to the need to reduce the cost of government, these practices are changing. At the federal level, change was spurred by the Government Performance and Results Act of 1993, which Congress enacted to provide federal agency managers with the tools necessary to improve services and reduce costs. Similar trends are occurring in state and local governments as well, as public officials struggle to make tax dollars go further.

For the HR practitioner, what this means is that, just as in the private sector, it is necessary to demonstrate the value of current and proposed programs and how they add to the achievement of public mandates—as evidenced by legislative actions or the initiatives of elected officials such as mayors and governors or, at the federal level, the president. It is no longer possible to justify programs based on the number of employees who participate in them; HR must now be able to demonstrate their effectiveness by showing how programs contribute to improved services or reduced costs.

A hallmark of public sector jobs is that they are often viewed as more secure than those in the private sector. Although this is true to a large extent, some job categories are unique to the public sector: those that are political appointments. These incumbents serve "at the pleasure of" the president, governor, or mayor who appointed them; and they are most often replaced when the administration changes. Public sector jobs are different from those in the private sector in that they are often subject to legislatively mandated employee rights with more legal protections and longer appeals processes. Although this makes it more difficult to terminate poor performers, it also serves to protect employees who are not political appointees from political pressures that change as the result of an election.

One aspect of jobs in the public service that hasn't changed very much is the level of compensation. It is still generally true that public sector jobs pay lower salaries than do those in the private sector. This differential is sometimes offset by more generous benefits such as more paid holidays and more generous leave-of-absence policies, for example. The larger employee base of most government entities usually means lower benefit costs to employees, as well.

The majority of those who choose to work in the public sector do so as a means of public service, with the desire to affect public policy decisions and improve circumstances for their neighbors, families, and friends. Public service jobs are available in widely diverse areas, including support staff for legislatures at the federal, state, and local levels; administrative and teaching positions in school districts, colleges, and universities; court districts; hospitals; libraries; and office work for government agencies. This diversity provides a challenging and interesting environment in which to practice human resources.

Private Sector Organizations

In the private sector, organizations can operate for profit or not-for-profit. Although both types of organizations are governed by the same laws, differences in the ways the organizations operate, and the motivations of the people who work in them have an impact on the way HRM is practiced.

For-Profit Businesses

Businesses operate for a profit. The owners of the business, whether they are single individuals or shareholders, invest in the business expecting to earn a return on that investment. For this reason, business decisions are focused on increasing the *bottom line*, or the amount of money the business earns after all the expenses have been paid.

There are many different industries within the business environment. The type of work done in different industries determines the skills that are needed to produce the goods or services for individual businesses. This affects HRM in many ways. For example, depending on the level of skill needed and the availability of individuals with that skill in the local area, a business may need to recruit nationally for new employees instead of running an advertisement in the local newspaper to find them.

Employees in different types of jobs have different needs and are motivated by different incentives, and HRM must be able to identify these motivators in order to retain employees.

Nonprofit Organizations

A nonprofit organization (NPO) is one that is funded by contributions, such as the National Wildlife Federation; or by government programs, such as some child-care centers. In either case, the funding is limited to what can be raised by those who work for the NPO. For this reason, salaries and benefits in NPOs are generally lower than those an employee could earn for doing the same job in a for-profit organization or in a public sector job. As a result, NPO employees are generally motivated by non-monetary reasons. Although this is good for the budget, it means that it is often difficult to attract employees with the highest skills, and it has an impact on operations. The limited funds present numerous challenges for HRM because the need to improve skills may not be supported by the availability of funds to provide adequate training.

Building the HR Department

Now that you have a better idea of the scope of the profession and the role played by practitioners at work, we can explore what it means to build an HR department. I've organized this book around the elements that are needed to build an HR department from the ground up because it allows me to explain the process in a logical progression, with each element building on previous elements. Let's talk a little about the general issues involved in building an HR department from scratch.

Understanding Organization Functions

As mentioned earlier in this chapter, HR is one of five basic elements common to all organizations. HR's function is to provide workforce management services to the other functions in the organization. Because of this interrelationship, HR practitioners must have a working knowledge of the needs of each of these functions, how they are unique, and what elements they have in common. In the technology sector, for example, individuals who work in highly technical positions, such as software engineers or scientists, are often characterized as being detail-oriented, highly intelligent introverts with poor people skills. One motivator that is extremely important to these "techies" is work that allows them to stay on the cutting edge of technology developments. It is important to HRM to understand this for several reasons, including the following:

- ◆ Promoting an employee who has been successful in a technical role might require the company to provide additional training in supervisory, management, and motivational skills.

- ◆ Advanced training on new technology is an effective motivator for technicians.

In contrast, employees in sales positions are often characterized as highly competitive extroverts with excellent people skills who find paperwork unnecessary and are often highly motivated by cash incentives. When HRM understands this, it is possible to develop reward programs for the sales team that concentrate on cash incentives that are tied to sales goals.

Understanding that like all human beings, employees are motivated when they have some control over their daily work allows HRM to develop management-training programs to improve the ability of managers and supervisors to empower employees. When employees take responsibility for their individual performance, increased productivity is often the result.

Tying HR Plans to Organizational Needs

I've mentioned several times the importance of tying HR activities to business goals. Each of the following chapters begins with a brief explanation of some ways to do this. Keep it in mind as you read the chapters, and give some thought to ways in which you can tie activities in these areas to your own organization's goals. In Chapter 11, I'll talk about how this all works along with some specific strategies that can be used, even when performing the most basic HR activities.

Terms to Know

administrative role	operational role
body of knowledge (BOK)	professional certifications
code of ethics	strategic role
human resource management (HRM)	subject matter expert (SME)

Review Questions

1. What is the role of human resource management in an organization?

2. What does it mean for HR professionals to "be strategic?"

3. How is HRM restricted in an NPO organization?

4. What sets HR apart as a profession?

5. What are some things for HR to consider when establishing operations outside the United States?

6. Why do HR professionals need to understand other organizational functions?

7. What areas of HR are subject to legal requirements?

8. Describe the administrative aspect of HRM.

9. Describe the operational aspect of HRM.

10. What is the difference between training and development programs?

Chapter 2

The Impact of Employment Law on HR Practice

Building an effective human resource management (HRM) program requires an understanding of the various federal, state and local laws and regulations that affect employment relationships. This understanding helps human resource (HR) professionals develop legally compliant programs that contribute to organizational goals. Programs that are built without this understanding can result in fines, penalties, or lawsuits, none of which achieve organization goals. Since it's not possible to discuss the particular laws of every state in this book, this chapter introduces those federal laws that affect HR practice.

The Sources of Legal Requirements

Much of HR practice requires compliance with a variety of laws and regulations that are the result of legislation enacted at the federal, state, and local levels; regulations created by government agencies; and court decisions that form the basis of common law doctrines. Although I am not an attorney, and this chapter is not intended to provide legal advice by any stretch of the imagination, as an HR practitioner, you must be aware of the employment laws with which your employer must comply during the course of its business operations. Legal requirements can be the result of any of the following types of laws:

Statutory Law   Statutory law is the result of actions taken by legislative bodies at the federal, state, and local levels. This chapter will talk mainly about federal laws because state laws vary widely. In a subsequent section, I'll provide some resources for you to use in locating information about state laws that apply to the states in which your business operates.

executive order (EO)
An executive order is issued by the chief executive of a federal, state, or local government entity (for example, the president, governor, or mayor).

Another type of statutory law is the *executive order*. Executive orders (EOs) are issued by the chief executive of a government: the president of the United States, the governor of a state, or the mayor of a city. In the case of a presidential executive order, the president issues a proclamation that is published in the Federal Register for 30 days, after which it becomes a law. Federal executive orders related to employment most often apply to federal government employees and private businesses with federal contracts. I'll talk more about them in the next section.

Regulatory Law   A regulatory law is one that is issued by a government agency at the federal, state, or local level. This type of legal requirement is also sometimes referred to as "government regulation." This type of law is made possible when a legislature passes a law designed to protect citizens in some way. The legislators (sometimes) realize that they do not have all the information necessary to develop the specific protections, so they delegate their rule-making authority to an agency of the government that has more experience with the specifics. At the federal level, Congress creates regulatory agencies such as the Occupational Safety and Health Administration (OSHA) or the Equal Employment Opportunity Commission (EEOC) to enforce a specific law. In the case of OSHA, for example, Congress created the agency and delegated to it the authority to create workplace safety standards designed to protect workers from specific hazards that were known to cause workplace injuries or death.

Common Law   Common law doctrines have developed as a result of court decisions over a period of time. There are several common law doctrines that should be very familiar to HR practitioners, including employment-at-will, constructive discharge, and defamation. I'll talk about these doctrines in more detail shortly.

Now that you know the difference between the various legal requirements that affect HR professionals in their daily work, let's talk about the impact of employment law on HR practices. Equal employment opportunity, immigration, compensation and benefits, safety, and employee relations are all areas of HR practice in which employment laws have an impact. In this chapter, I'll be introducing basic information about the most significant laws in each of these areas.

Equal Employment Opportunity

Most employers in the United States are familiar with the idea that they must provide equal employment opportunities for all applicants and employees. This area of employment law developed during the 1960s as a result of the civil rights movement.

The Civil Rights Act of 1964 sought to eliminate discrimination in many areas of American life, including housing, education, and employment. Title VII is the section of the act that addresses employment practices. It has been amended several times since it was first enacted; and for purposes of our discussion here, I will discuss what is currently required as a result of the initial legislation and the amendments. In addition to Title VII amendments, Congress passed several other laws to ensure that equal opportunities are provided to American workers

If you are interested in seeing how these laws developed over time, a complete description is available in the *PHR/SPHR Professional in Human Resources Study Guide* (Sybex, 2004).   — **NOTE** —

Congress included a provision for enforcement of equal employment opportunity requirements in Title VII by establishing the Equal Employment Opportunity Commission (EEOC). Title VII authorizes the EEOC to enforce its statutory requirements as well as to enforce other equal opportunity legislation. Title VII required the EEOC to promote equal employment opportunities, provide education and assistance to employers with regard to fair employment practices, and to report periodically on the progress of equal opportunity in the business community. As additional laws were passed, enforcement responsibility was increased to include them. The laws currently enforced by the EEOC are:

- Title VII of the Civil Rights Act of 1964
- Equal Pay Act of 1963
- Age Discrimination in Employment Act of 1967
- Americans with Disabilities Act of 1990
- Civil Rights Act of 1991
- Family and Medical Leave Act of 1993
- Uniformed Services Employment/Reemployment Rights Act of 1994

In 1972, Congress amended Title VII with the Equal Employment Opportunity Act (EEOA). The EEOA increased EEOC enforcement powers by authorizing the EEOC to initiate litigation with employers who did not agree to enter into conciliation agreements designed to eliminate discriminatory employment practices. The EEOA also established guidelines for the processing of discrimination complaints. These guidelines require the EEOC to notify employers within 10 days of the receipt of a complaint and to issue findings within 120 days.

Let's begin by discussing common terms and concepts related to equal employment opportunities.

protected classes
Protected classes are groups of individuals identified by equal employment opportunity legislation as having been subjected to discrimination in the past.

Protected classes   Title VII identified five classes of individuals who suffered discrimination in the past and prohibited the continuance of this discrimination. These five *protected classes* include race, color, religion, national origin, and sex. Subsequent to Title VII, Congress passed other laws that added to the list of protected classes. The following list identifies groups currently protected by federal equal opportunity legislation:

◆ National origin

◆ Race

◆ Color

◆ Religion

◆ Sex

◆ Age

◆ Pregnancy

◆ Disability

unlawful employment practice
An unlawful employment practice is any employment practice that has an adverse impact on members of one or more protected classes in any of the terms and conditions of employment.

Unlawful employment practices   Title VII also identified *unlawful employment practices*, or practices that have an adverse impact on members of one or more protected classes. According to Title VII, an unlawful employment practice is one that discriminates in recruiting, selection, hiring, compensation, benefits, access to training programs; or in any of the other terms and conditions of employment. Title VII recognized some exceptions to these requirements, including seniority, merit, and piece-rate systems used by many businesses to reward employees. These practices are allowable as long as they do not intentionally discriminate against protected classes.

bona fide occupational qualification (BFOQ)
A BFOQ is an exception allowed by Title VII when a business can demonstrate that a practice is necessary to maintain normal business operations.

Bona Fide Occupational Qualification   A *bona fide occupational qualification (BFOQ)* is another exception recognized by Title VII. BFOQs are allowed when a position requires that an employee be of a specific religion, sex, national origin, or age. Title VII specifically limits the use of this exception to circumstances in which the BFOQ is "reasonably necessary to the normal operation" of the organization. For example, it is reasonable to expect that a synagogue would require a rabbi to be Jewish, the Catholic church would require a priest to be Catholic, or a manufacturer of men's clothing would require that models of its clothing be men.

Disparate Treatment   Title VII addressed issues of discrimination that resulted in *disparate treatment* of individuals in protected classes. Disparate treatment occurs when members of a protected class are treated in a way that intentionally discriminates against them and is motivated by the fact that they are members of a protected class. Disparate treatment could occur, for example, if an employer required all female candidates for a position to pass a physical ability test to demonstrate that they could lift a 25-pound weight, but did not require male candidates to pass the same test.

disparate treatment
Disparate treatment occurs when members of a protected class are intentionally treated differently from other individuals.

Disparate Impact   The courts interpreted Title VII to include discrimination that resulted from *disparate impact*; actions that on the surface appear to be neutral, but result in a disproportionate negative consequence on a protected class. Disparate impact can occur whether or not there is an intent to discriminate against a protected class. One of the best examples of this is the *Griggs v Duke Power* case discussed in the following sidebar.

disparate impact
Disparate impact, which can be intentional or unintentional, occurs when an employment practice that is applied equally to all individuals has a disproportionate adverse effect on members of a protected class.

Sexual Harassment   Although Title VII does not contain a specific reference to "sexual harassment," court decisions have established it as an action that constitutes discrimination on the basis of sex. The courts have identified two types of sexual harassment: quid pro quo and hostile work environment.

Quid pro quo is a Latin term meaning "this for that." In the context of sexual harassment, *quid pro quo harassment* occurs when a supervisor or manager asks for sexual favors in return for a favorable employment action. The term "sexual favor" is broadly defined by the EEOC and can include actions that range from repeated requests for dates to other more explicit requests. Quid pro quo harassment is characterized by victims who feel that they must comply with these requests in order to remain employed or to receive promotions or other favorable treatment at work.

quid pro quo harassment
Quid pro quo is a Latin term meaning "this for that." Quid pro quo harassment is a term used to describe harassment in which a supervisor or manager asks for favors in exchange for favorable employment actions. It is usually used in reference to sexual harassment.

A *hostile work environment* is created when employees are exposed to taunts, comments, or physical conduct that would be considered offensive by a reasonable person. When that conduct adversely affects or interferes with the ability of those employees to perform their job duties, it becomes sexual harassment.

hostile work environment
A hostile work environment can be created by a coworker, customer, vendor, or visitor to the workplace as well as by supervisors or managers. It is an environment in which individuals are exposed to taunts, comments, or physical conduct that would be considered offensive by a reasonable person.

An important distinction between quid pro quo harassment and a hostile work environment is that quid pro quo harassment by definition is committed by a supervisor or manager who has the ability to make decisions that directly affect employee jobs. A hostile work environment, on the other hand, can be created by coworkers, customers, or vendors as well as managers and supervisors.

prima facie evidence
A Latin term used to describe evidence that clearly shows a violation of an employment law.

tangible employment action (TEA)
A TEA is any action taken by an employer that significantly changes the status of an employee.

Prima Facie In a legal context, when something appears to be true when it is first seen, it is known as *prima facie evidence*, a Latin term meaning "at first view." In HR practice, this term is used to describe activity that clearly violates the law. One of the court cases in the following sidebar, *McDonnell Douglas v Green*, provides an example of how this term is used in an employment context.

Tangible Employment Action A *tangible employment action (TEA)* is an action by an employer that significantly changes the employment status of an employee. This action can include any of the terms and conditions of employment, such as hiring, firing, promoting, compensating, or assigning an employee to unpleasant or undesirable duties.

Court Interpretations of Equal Opportunity Laws

Shortly after Title VII became law, workers who believed they had been discriminated against began filing lawsuits to enforce their rights. Many of these cases found their way to the United States Supreme Court, which interpreted how the law was to be applied. There are many interesting cases related to equal employment opportunities; the ones I have included here illustrate how these laws have been applied in different circumstances.

> **DISPARATE TREATMENT: *Weeks v Southern Bell Telephone Co.*** The result of this case was a ruling by the Fifth Circuit Court of Appeals, saying that practices restricting women from performing some job duties (by assigning weight lifting or other arbitrary requirements) that were not related to job performance were not legitimate BFOQs.
>
> Ms. Weeks worked for Southern Bell Telephone Co. in Georgia. As part of her union's contract with Southern Bell, there was a clause requiring seniority to be the deciding factor for selecting employees in the job-bidding process. When Ms. Weeks and one other employee, a man, applied for a job as a switchman, Southern Bell told her they had decided not to place women in the position and placed the man in the position, even though he had less seniority than did Ms. Weeks. Ms. Weeks filed a complaint with the EEOC and later filed a lawsuit against Southern Bell. Although the company admitted this was a prima facie violation of Title VII, it claimed that the requirement was a BFOQ based on a Georgia law imposing a weight lifting requirement of 30 pounds for women and children. The Fifth Circuit ruled that the company had not proved the requirement was a BFOQ and noted in its decision that the Georgia law had by then been repealed.
>
> *Continues*

DISPARATE IMPACT: *Griggs v Duke Power*   The result of this case was a Supreme Court ruling that an employer must show that job requirements are related to job performance.

The case was brought by a black man, Willie Griggs, who worked in the Labor Department, the lowest-paid of five departments at a power station in North Carolina. For many years, the company operated without any particular education or testing requirements. In 1955, it began requiring a high school diploma, however; and in 1965, it began to require a passing score on two aptitude tests to move out of the Labor Department. Mr. Griggs was able to show that because many white employees who had transferred out of the Labor Department before these requirements were implemented were performing their duties successfully, neither requirement was related to the ability of an individual to do the work.

DISPARATE IMPACT: *Washington v Davis*   The result of this case was a Supreme Court ruling that a test is lawful if it is a valid predictor of future job success.

This case was brought by two applicants for the police-training program in Washington, D.C., who claimed that the written test given to applicants for positions as police officers adversely affected black applicants. The police department was able to show that those who scored high on the test actually performed more successfully on the job. For that reason, the Supreme Court ruled that the test, even though it had an adverse impact on black applicants, was lawful because it predicted future successful performance.

PRIMA FACIE EVIDENCE: *McDonnell Douglas Corp v Green*   This case resulted in a Supreme Court ruling that defined the four elements needed to prove a prima facie case of discrimination in Title VII cases:

◆ The complainant must be a member of a protected class.

◆ The complainant must have applied and been qualified for a position for which the employer was seeking applicants.

◆ Despite the qualifications, the applicant must have been rejected.

◆ After the rejection, the employer must have continued to seek applicants with the same qualifications.

Continues

HOSTILE WORK ENVIRONMENT: *Harris v Forklift Systems*   The Supreme Court heard this case to establish the standard to be used by lower courts for determining what constitutes a hostile work environment: The Court ruled that a hostile work environment exists when severe discriminatory behavior creates a hostile or abusive environment that discriminates against a member of a protected class. This determination can be made only by looking at all the circumstances:

◆ The frequency of the actions

◆ How severe the actions are

◆ Whether the behavior is humiliating or physically threatening

◆ Whether the behavior interferes with the employee's ability to do the job

Another relevant factor in this determination is the effect of the behavior on the employee's psychological well-being.

Now that you are familiar with some of the concepts related to equal employment opportunity, let's look at what specific laws require.

Laws Enforced by the EEOC

As discussed previously, the EEOC is mandated by Congress to enforce equal employment legislation. The first of these laws, Title VII, introduced the concept of protected classes and unlawful employment practices.

Amendments to Title VII

Over the years, Congress has amended the provisions of Title VII to clarify issues that arose from court rulings as well as to make changes to the responsibilities it delegated to the EEOC. These amendments include the following:

> **Pregnancy Discrimination Act of 1978 (PDA)**   The PDA was enacted in 1978 to specifically address the rights of women who are pregnant. It requires employers to treat pregnancy in the same way they treat any other short-term disability, including providing the same benefits to pregnant women as are provided to any employee with a short-term disability.

> **Civil Rights Act of 1991 (CRA)**   Congress made important changes to Title VII in 1991 when it enacted the CRA. It sets maximum compensatory and punitive damage awards for victims of intentional discrimination based on a sliding scale tied to the size of the organization. In addition, the CRA allows for jury trials in civil suits when damages are being sought by

either party. The CRA also provides guidance when discrimination occurs based on an employment practice that results in disparate impact on a protected class.

Equal Pay Act of 1963

The Equal Pay Act (EPA) was designed to ensure "equal pay for equal work" and was the first anti-discrimination act passed by Congress, preceding even Title VII. The EPA sets standards for determining whether or not jobs require equal work by looking at similarities in the working conditions, level of skill, amount of effort required to perform the job, and the level of responsibility that is required. In creating the law, Congress recognized that performance can be a major factor in determining level of pay and so included allowable exceptions to the EPA, such as merit systems, piecework payment systems, or a payment system that is based on seniority as long as the system is not designed to discriminate on the basis of sex.

The EPA is actually an amendment to the Fair Labor Standards Act, the federal law that determines the minimum wage and governs employee exemption status. This law will be discussed more fully later in this chapter.

Age Discrimination in Employment Act of 1967

The Age Discrimination in Employment Act (ADEA) added age to the list of protected classes initially described by Title VII. The ADEA prohibits discrimination against employees aged 40 years of age or older in any of the terms and conditions of employment, including forcing employees to retire at a particular age. The ADEA makes provision for exceptions such as a BFOQ that is reasonably necessary to the operation of the business. For example, many airlines require pilots to retire at age 60 based on the idea that individuals over age 60 are less able to perform duties that are necessary to ensure passenger safety.

These exceptions also allow state and local governments to place age limitations on the hiring of firefighters or police officers. In addition, employers can require executives who are age 65 or older and have been in an executive position for two or more years to retire when they are eligible for retirement benefits of at least $44,000 per year. Finally, the ADEA does not prevent employers from discharging or disciplining employees over age 40 for just cause.

Americans with Disabilities Act of 1990

The Americans with Disabilities Act (ADA) added disabled persons to the list of protected classes first introduced by Title VII. The ADA provides that persons who are otherwise qualified for a job cannot be denied a position or discriminated against in any term or condition of employment based on an actual or perceived disability. The ADA defines a disability as "a physical or mental impairment that substantially limits one or more of the major life activities" of an individual.

reasonable accommodation
A reasonable accommodation is an accommodation to the work environment or job duties that allows a disabled individual to successfully perform the essential functions of a job.

The ADA requires employers who are subject to its requirements to make *reasonable accommodation* to enable disabled applicants or employees to perform the essential functions of a job (I'll talk about essential job functions and how they should be identified in Chapter 3, "Building a Staffing Plan") for which they are otherwise qualified, recognizing that there might be times when the cost of accommodating a person with a disability places an undue hardship on an employer. Employers must engage in an interactive process with employees who request an accommodation to determine whether such an accommodation will allow the employee to perform the essential functions of the job. This process can result in one of three findings:

◆ A reasonable accommodation is available and will allow the employee to successfully perform the essential functions of the job.

◆ A reasonable accommodation is available, but the implementation cost would cause the employer to suffer an undue hardship.

◆ There is no reasonable accommodation available that will allow the essential functions of the job to be performed.

The factors to be considered in determining whether a specific accommodation constitutes an undue hardship on the employer include the size of the employer, the cost of the accommodation, and the employer's financial resources, among other considerations.

Family and Medical Leave Act of 1993

The Family and Medical Leave Act (FMLA) provides up to 12 weeks of unpaid leave to employees under certain conditions. FMLA leave must be provided by employers with 50 or more employees at one or more worksites within a 75-mile radius. To be eligible for leave, employees must have worked a minimum of 1,250 hours for the employer during the preceding 12 months.

FMLA provides a list of situations that qualify an employee to take an unpaid leave:

◆ Fathers and mothers are both eligible to take FMLA leave for the birth or care of an infant.

◆ Fathers and mothers are both eligible to take FMLA leave for the placement of an adopted or foster child with the family.

◆ When an employee's spouse, son, daughter, or parent has a serious illness, the employee is eligible to take leave to care for the family member.

◆ Employees with serious health conditions that prevent them from performing their job duties are eligible for FMLA leave.

FMLA leaves can be continuous, reduced schedule, or intermittent. A continuous FMLA leave occurs when the employee is unable to be at work for an extended period of time. An employee who needs to come in late or leave early for a period of time is eligible for a reduced FMLA leave schedule. An intermittent

FMLA leave is one in which the employee needs to be absent from work for multiple periods of time of varying lengths due to a single illness or injury.

Employees who find themselves in one of the situations described previously are eligible for three benefits provided by FMLA:

◆ Unpaid leave of 12 weeks within a 12-month period

◆ Maintenance of their health care benefits while on leave

◆ Reinstatement to their previous position or one that is equivalent to it when they return to work.

Uniformed Services Employment/Reemployment Rights Act of 1994

The Uniformed Services Employment/Reemployment Rights Act (USERRA) protects the rights of those who serve in military reserve units when they are called to active duty. Some of the requirements placed on employers by USERRA include the provision of a leave of absence for up to five years while employees are on active duty. During that time, employees must continue to accrue seniority and receive benefits, including pension plan accruals, and continue health care coverage similar to Consolidated Omnibus Budget Reconciliation Act (COBRA) rights, as if they were continuously employed. When employees return to work, they must be returned to the job they would have earned had they remained at the company.

Federal Contractors and Subcontractors

Private employers who receive money from the federal government are subject to the requirements of EOs and laws enacted by Congress that apply to government agencies and their contractors. As described earlier in this chapter, an EO is, at the federal level, a proclamation by the president of the United States that, when published in the Federal Register, becomes law after 30 days. After passage of Title VII, a number of EOs were created to extend equal employment opportunities to employees of the federal government and to ensure that private employers with government contracts complied with the requirements of Title VII.

Private employers who receive federal contracts of $10,000 or more within any 12-month period are required to take affirmative steps to provide equal employment opportunities to all applicants and employees. In addition, private employers with 50 or more employees who receive federal contracts of $50,000 or more are required to develop a written affirmative action plan that is filed with the Department of Labor (DOL). These EOs are enforced by an agency of the DOL known as the Office of Federal Contract Compliance Programs (OFCCP). The mission of the OFCCP is to enforce EOs and federal laws that prohibit discrimination on the basis of race, color, religion, sex, national origin, disability, or status as a veteran.

OFCCP establishes the requirements for Affirmative Action Plans and requires that they be completed and reviewed annually to ensure that equal opportunities are provided for all applicants and employees. OFCCP also conducts compliance audits and investigates complaints of discrimination. The following laws are enforced by the OFCCP:

EO 11246   In 1965, President Lyndon Johnson issued the first EO related to equal employment opportunity. EO 11246 required affirmative steps to be taken in advertising, recruiting, employing, training, promoting, compensating, and terminating employees. This EO was designed to provide equal opportunities on the basis of race, creed, color, or national origin.

EO 11375   In 1967, gender was added to the list of those protected by EO 11246.

EO 11478   In 1969, handicapped individuals and those over age 40 were added to the list of protected groups identified by EO 11246

Section 503 of the Rehabilitation Act of 1973   The Rehabilitation Act applies to federal agencies and contractors who have federal contracts of $10,000 or more during a 12-month period. This Act extended equal opportunities to individuals with physical or mental handicaps, and designated the OFCCP as the enforcement agency for it.

Much of the ADA, which came into being almost 20 years later, was based on requirements first introduced by the Rehabilitation Act.

Vietnam Era Veterans' Readjustment Assistance Act of 1974   The Vietnam Era Veterans' Readjustment Assistance Act (VEVRA) requires federal contractors to advertise most openings with a state employment agency. The state agencies must give priority to Vietnam vets when filling the positions. VEVRA provides additional protection for some disabled vets.

Equal Employment Reporting Requirements

Both the EEOC and the OFCCP require some employers to file annual reports demonstrating that their employment practices provide equal opportunities to all qualified applicants and employees. These reports are the EEO-1 report and the Affirmative Action Plan (AAP).

EEO-1 Reports   The EEOC requires private employers with 100 or more employees to file the EEO-1 report by September 30 of each year. In some cases, employers with fewer than 100 employees might be required to file if, for example, they are owned or controlled by another company and the total combined work force of the two companies is 100 or more employees. In addition, all federal contractors with 50 employees and contracts of $50,000 or more must file the report.

The EEO-1 report collects information about the gender and race of employees in various job categories.

Affirmative Action Plans   In addition to the EEO-1 report, federal contractors must complete an AAP within 120 days of receiving the contract. The OFCCP determines what must be included in an AAP. Currently, the information required includes an analysis of the job groups in the organization, an analysis of the percentage of minorities and women in the job groups, and an analysis of the demographics of the labor pool from which employees are recruited for each job group. If the analysis indicates that some protected groups are underrepresented in the job group based on the demographics of availability in the labor pool, placement goals are set to better reflect the availability of that protected class in the labor pool.

It's important to keep in mind that none of the laws related to equal opportunity require employers to select employees who are not qualified for a position. The purpose of these laws is to ensure that all qualified candidates receive equal consideration and opportunity to obtain positions for which they are qualified and to advance as their qualifications increase.

Immigration

After the attacks on the World Trade Center in New York City and the Pentagon in Washington, D.C. on September 11, 2001, many changes have been made to immigration policy in the United States. One of these changes was a reorganization of the federal agencies responsible for controlling immigration. As a result, the Immigration and Naturalization Service became the U.S. Citizenship and Immigration Service (USCIS), part of the Department of Homeland Security. Despite this, few changes occurred in the areas of immigration with which HR practitioners need to be familiar: work visas and employment eligibility.

The visa most commonly seen by employers is the H-1B visa, which allows workers with special skills to work in the United States for three years, with an extension to allow for an additional three years. In 1990, Congress revised the numbers and types of work visas that can be awarded to immigrants when it enacted the Immigration Act. The Act limited the number of H-1B immigrants to 65,000 per year and required that workers with this visa be paid the prevailing wage for their job category to ensure that U.S. citizens did not lose their jobs to lower-paid immigrant workers.

HR practitioners must also be aware of the requirement for employers to ensure that all new employees are eligible to work in the United States. This is done by completing an I-9 form for each new hire and verifying employment authorization by viewing documents that provide proof of identity and employment eligibility, such as an American passport (which proves both), or a state driver's license (to prove identity) and social security card (to prove employment eligibility). The I-9 form includes lists of the documents that have been approved by the USCIS for this purpose. Employers may not specify which documents they will accept from the lists, but are required to accept any valid documents that are specified for this purpose. These requirements are based on the Immigration Reform and Control Act (IRCA) of 1986, which was designed to control illegal immigration into the United States. The law also prohibits employment practices that discriminate against applicants on the basis of their national origin or citizenship status.

Compensation and Benefits

The history of federal legislation regulating compensation issues begins in 1931, when Congress passed the Davis Bacon Act. This law required that federal contractors with construction contracts pay their workers at least the prevailing wage for that type of work in the local area in which they are building projects for the federal government. The compensation law with the most impact on HR practitioners is the Fair Labor Standards Act (FLSA), which Congress enacted in 1938. The FLSA defines employees who might be exempt from its provisions, sets the minimum wage, defines the circumstances that require overtime payments, and establishes recordkeeping requirements for employers. The FLSA also established requirements for child labor by defining jobs considered too dangerous for children (such as working in a mine) and establishing minimum age requirements for most jobs.

Exemption Status

nonexempt job
A nonexempt job does not qualify for exemption from FLSA requirements, such as the payment of overtime and minimum wage.

Exemption status is the term used to describe whether a job must comply with FLSA requirements or not and is an area that is very often misunderstood and misused by some employers who believe that if they classify a position as exempt, they will save money because they won't have to pay overtime to the employees in that job. Employees in administrative positions also often misunderstand the purpose of exemption, seeking to have their positions classified as exempt as a status symbol. Misclassifying positions can result in costly fines for employers, so it is important that HR professionals understand the concept and its implications for the organization.

Any job that is not determined to be exempt from FLSA regulations is known as a *nonexempt job*, meaning that employees in that job must be paid in accordance with minimum wage, overtime, and other FLSA requirements.

exempt job
An exempt job meets one of the four tests for exemption from the Fair Labor Standards Act requirements: executive, professional, administrative, or outside sales.

An *exempt job* is one that meets criteria established by the FLSA. All jobs that are classified as exempt must be salaried positions; employees who are required to account for their time and paid based on the number of hours they work must be classified as nonexempt and subject to FLSA regulations. The most common exemptions fall into one of four categories: executive, administrative, professional, and outside sales; and the DOL provides exemption tests to assist employers in identifying jobs that meet the criteria for each of these categories. There are two tests for each category: the short test and the long test. The difference is that the short test requires a higher salary, whereas positions with lower salaries might still be considered exempt if the job duties meet certain criteria.

Let's look at the exemption tests for these categories now.

Executive Exemption Test

To meet the criteria for an executive exemption, the primary duties of the job must be related to the management of the organization and include responsibility for the supervision of two or more full-time employees. If the position is paid more than $250 per week, it may be exempt under the short test. If the position is paid between $155 and $250 per week, it may still be exempt if it also has the authority to hire, fire, promote, and evaluate employees; regularly exercises discretion when making decisions; and does not spend more than 20 percent of the time on duties other than management.

Administrative Exemption Test

A job with primary duties consists of office work that is related to management policy or general business operations can meet the criteria for administrative exemption if it pays more than $250 per week. Positions earning between $155 and $250 per week can be considered exempt if they also regularly require the use of discretion and independent judgment; assist a proprietor, owner, or administrator on a regular basis; need only general supervision to perform work with specialized knowledge requirements, training, or experience; and do not spend more than 20 percent of the time on duties unrelated to those listed previously.

Professional Exemption Test

The professional exemption applies to positions that meet one of four criteria:

- Requires a prolonged course of specialized, intellectual instruction
- Requires theoretical and practical application of highly-specialized computer system analysis, programming, or software engineering.
- Involves teaching in a school system or other educational institution
- Involves original creative work in a recognized artistic field

To meet the short test for professional exemption, a job involving one of the first three criteria must also be paid at least $250 per week, and consistently use discretion and judgment in performing the duties of the position.

To meet the short test for professional exemption, a job involving the fourth criterion must also be paid at least $250 per week and involve invention, imagination, or talent in the performance of the duties.

Jobs that are paid between $170 and $250 per week can also qualify for professional exemption if they also require the consistent use of discretion and judgment, are predominantly intellectual in nature and produce unique results, and do not require more than 20 percent of time to be spent on duties that are nonessential and not related to the duties described in the preceding list.

NOTE Some computer-related jobs that qualify for professional exemption and are paid at least $27.63 per hour can be considered exempt even when paid on an hourly basis.

Outside Sales Exemption Test

An outside sales job is identified by the DOL as one whose only duties require selling the company's product or service, and is regularly performed away from the employer's place of business. To qualify for exemption, less than 20 percent of the weekly duties of the job must be nonessential or unrelated to sales duties.

In addition to these exemption tests, the DOL has identified a number of specific jobs that are exempt from one or more of its requirements, and provides a complete list of these current exempted positions at www.dol.gov/elaws/esa/flsa/screen75.asp. These positions include such jobs as newspaper delivery jobs, which are exempt from minimum wage, overtime and child labor requirements; livestock auction jobs, which are exempt from overtime payments; and switchboard operator jobs, which are exempt from minimum wage and overtime requirements.

NOTE On April 20, 2004, the DOL published sweeping changes to the rules governing exemption status which are scheduled to go into effect on or around August 23, 2004. There is ongoing debate in Congress about these changes, and it is possible that they will be overturned before they go into effect. To be sure you are following the correct rules for exempting employees, check the DOL Wage and Hour Division website at www.dol.gov/esa/regs/compliance/whd/fairplay/main/htm.

Minimum Wage

The federal minimum wage was originally set at 25 cents per hour in 1938. Over the years, as the cost of living has risen, Congress has increased the minimum wage. As of 2004, it is currently set at $5.15 per hour. It is important to keep in mind, however, that many states have established their own minimum wage requirements. Employers in states with a higher minimum wage must pay the wage set by the state.

Compensable Time and Overtime

compensable time
Compensable time is time for which an employer is required to pay nonexempt employees.

One might think that it is fairly easy to determine the hours for which employees must be compensated, and it is usually easy to tell when they are performing their job duties during regular business hours. The FLSA addresses time that is not quite so clear-cut by defining *compensable time* for nonexempt employees. According to the FLSA, compensable hours for nonexempt employees include time for work that is "suffered or permitted" by the employer. Compensable time includes the time that employees continue to work after the end of their work day, for example, to finish an assignment before they leave for the day. The FLSA includes time spent by employees to prepare the work area or to clean it up at the end of the day. The FLSA defines other time that might be considered compensable for nonexempt employees, including waiting time, on-call time, rest and meal periods, and training time:

Waiting time   In some cases, the time an employee spends waiting for an assignment can be considered compensable time. The FLSA defines this as "engaged to wait," meaning that the employer has asked a worker to wait for an assignment. For example, if an accounting manager needs to submit financial statements for a board meeting the next day, she might ask her assistant to stay late and make copies so they are ready first thing in the morning. If the assistant reads the newspaper while waiting for the documents that need to be copied, he must be paid for that time.

In other cases, an employee might be "waiting to be engaged." In this circumstance, the employer does not need to pay the employee. For example, the 15 minutes an employee spends at her desk reading the newspaper while waiting for her carpool to arrive at the end of the day is not considered compensable time by the FLSA.

On-call time   Some jobs require employees to be available, either at the worksite or able to return to the worksite within a specified period of time. This time is known as on-call time. If the employer's requirements are so restrictive that employees cannot use the time for their own purposes, this period of time is considered compensable time.

Rest and meal periods   Rest and meal periods are not required by the FLSA, but can be required by state or local governments. When employers provide them, they are subject to FLSA requirements. If employers provide short breaks lasting fewer than 20 minutes, the time is considered compensable. Meal periods of 30 minutes or longer are not considered compensable under FLSA requirements.

Training time   When employers provide training opportunities for nonexempt workers, they must pay workers for the time unless all four of the following conditions are met:

◆ The training must be voluntary.

◆ It must take place outside normal work hours.

◆ It must not be directly related to the workers' current jobs.

◆ The workers must not perform any other work during the event.

Recordkeeping Requirements

The FLSA requires employers to maintain detailed records about their employees, the time records of the hours worked by nonexempt employees, and information about payments made. Table 2.1 describes the information that must be maintained for this purpose.

Table 2.1   Employee Records Required by the FLSA

Who	Information	Purpose
All employees	Payroll records	Name
		Date of birth
		Gender
		Occupation
		Deductions from pay
		Pay period
		Date of payment
Exempt Employees	Payroll calculations	Basis for salary calculations
Nonexempt employees	Payroll calculations	Basis for wage payment
		Regular pay rate
		Work schedule
		Work week and start time
		Straight time earnings
		Overtime earnings
		Total wages for pay period
Employees under age 19	Proof of age	Certificate of age
All employees	Hiring and promotion	Collective bargaining agreements
		Individual employment contracts
		Sale and purchase records
		Job announcements
		Job advertisements
		Job orders sent to unions or agencies

Pension Plans

In addition to the FLSA, compensation and benefit programs are regulated by the Employee Retirement Income Security Act of 1974 (ERISA). ERISA requires employers to set aside funds for employee pension plans so that the money is available for employees when they retire. ERISA also requires employers to provide documentation and explanations of other benefits to employees on a regular basis, and establishes rules for the beneficiary designations by employees.

Health Care Continuation Rights   Congress amended ERISA in 1986 with the Consolidated Omnibus Budget Reconciliation Act of 1986 (COBRA). While there is no federal law requiring employers to provide health care benefits, COBRA applies if coverage is provided by an employer with 20 or more employees. The law requires employers to continue health care benefits for employees or their dependents when certain qualifying events occur, such as a resignation, layoff, divorce or employee death.

Health Insurance Portability and Accountability Act (HIPAA)   In 1997, Congress amended ERISA again to prevent insurance companies from discriminating against employees based on the status of their health. HIPAA also placed limits on the way insurance companies were able to limit coverage for individuals with pre-existing conditions.

Safety and Health

The federal workplace safety law most often encountered in HR practice is the Occupational Safety and Health Act (OSH Act). Congress passed this legislation in 1970 to reduce the number of fatalities and injuries suffered by employees in the course of performing their jobs. The OSH Act created the Occupational Safety and Health Administration (OSHA), which is responsible for establishing safety and health standards in the workplace. According to the OSHA website, in the 30-plus years since it was created, workplace fatalities were cut in half, and workplace injuries were reduced by 40 percent.

The general duty standard of the OSH Act makes both employers and their employees responsible for safe working conditions. The Act requires all employers to provide workplaces "free from recognized hazards that are causing or are likely to cause death or serious physical harm" to employees. For their part, employees are required to conduct themselves at work in accordance with OSHA safety and health standards.

Congress delegated the responsibility for establishing specific safe working standards to OSHA, requiring that, whenever possible, the agency work with employers and industry groups to formulate effective standards. The purpose of these additional safety and health standards is to reduce the hazards inherent in many job functions. Some of these standards have broad applications across many industries, such as the development of emergency action plans and communication procedures for disseminating information about hazardous substances that might be encountered in the workplace. Other standards, such as the blood-borne pathogen or personal protective equipment standard, have more limited application in a single industry or job category.

The OSH Act also authorized OSHA to collect information about workplace fatalities, injuries, and illnesses from employers. OSHA provides three forms for this purpose:

- OSHA Form 300, Log of Work-Related Injuries and Illnesses
- OSHA Form 301, Injury and Illness Incident Report
- OSHA Form 300A, Summary of Work-Related Injuries and Illnesses

OSHA exempts some employers from these reporting requirements—generally, those who operate in industries with few incidents of fatalities or injuries, as well as employers with 10 or fewer employees.

Additional information about specific safety standards and industries that are exempt from the reporting requirements is available at www.osha.gov.

Employee and Labor Relations

Federal laws governing employee and labor relations generally fall into the categories of equal employment opportunity and labor-management relations. Laws relating to equal employment opportunity were covered previously, so in this section I'll discuss briefly the laws that apply to labor-management relations. In addition to federal law, a number of common law doctrines have been applied by the courts to employment relationships, and I'll talk about those here as well.

Labor-Management Relations Law

The history of federal laws that affected employment relationships in the United States began in 1890 with passage of the Sherman Anti-Trust Act. Although its original intent was to limit the capability of large businesses to monopolize the marketplace, it was used in 1894 to end a labor union strike against a railroad company. After that, the pendulum has swung back and forth several times, with passage of some laws providing protection for unions and employees, followed by other laws designed to return power to business owners.

Although there are many laws related to this topic, I will talk about the three that are most relevant to the topics in this book: the National Labor Relations Act (NLRA) which was passed in 1935; the Labor-Management Relations Act (LMRA), passed in 1947; and the Worker Adjustment and Retraining Notification Act (WARN), passed in 1988.

National Labor Relations Act (1935)

The NLRA was one of the laws introduced by President Franklin Delano Roosevelt as part of his "New Deal" to end the Great Depression. When it was introduced, it became known as "labor's bill of rights" because it granted employees the right to organize and form unions to bargain collectively with business owners for improved working conditions, wages, and benefits. The NLRA guarantees employees the right to work together for mutual aid or protection whether or not they form a union. Employers cannot restrict the right of employees to gather and discuss working conditions, pay, or other issues that affect the workplace.

The NLRA also identified five *unfair labor practices (ULPs)* that can be committed by employers. A ULP is any action that restrains employees from exercising their rights to organize and bargain collectively. Employers are prohibited from taking the following actions with regard to employee efforts to organize:

unfair labor practice (ULP)
A ULP is any action that prevents or interferes with the rights of employees to organize or bargain collectively.

◆ Employers cannot interfere with, restrain, or coerce employees from unionizing or working together to solve workplace problems.

◆ The NLRA prohibits employers from forming and controlling employee organizations that are designed to address workplace issues such as working conditions, pay, and benefits.

◆ Employers cannot take adverse actions against employees who participate in efforts to organize the workplace, such as assigning them to unpleasant tasks or terminating them.

◆ The NLRA requires employers to bargain in good faith with unions.

◆ Employers cannot make agreements with unions to stop doing business with other nonunion employers. This is known as a "hot cargo" agreement.

Labor-Management Relations Act (1947)

The LMRA was passed in 1947 to balance what many business owners viewed as abuses by the unions. This Act established ULPs for unions, placed limits on the ability of unions to force employees to join unions, and set some limits on strike and boycott activities. As the NLRA had for employers, the LMRA prohibited union actions that restrict employees from exercising their rights.

◆ Unions cannot either restrain employees from voicing their opposition to the union nor coerce them into joining the union.

◆ The LMRA prohibits union actions that restrain or coerce employers, such as refusing to bargain with the person chosen by the employer, take any adverse action against a supervisor based on the way the contract is interpreted, or require an employer to accept terms that the union negotiated with other employers.

- Unions cannot require employers to terminate employees who work against unionization efforts, or require that employers hire only union members.

- The LMRA requires unions to bargain in good faith with employers.

- It is a ULP for a union to participate in strike or boycott activities that are prohibited by the LMRA.

- Unions cannot charge excessive membership fees, but must keep them in line with the wages earned by members and industry standards.

- The LMRA prohibits unions from requiring employers to hire more employees than are necessary to do a job. This practice, known as "featherbedding," sometimes occurred when new technology reduced the number of employees needed to perform a task. Prior to the LMRA, unions wanted employers to continue to pay members who used to do the task, even if it was no longer necessary.

Worker Adjustment and Retraining Notification Act (1988)

The WARN Act seeks to provide employees with sufficient notice of a mass layoff or plant closing so that they can obtain additional training or find other employment before their jobs end. Employers who have 100 or more employees are required to comply with the notice requirements. WARN defines a mass layoff as one in which either 500 employees or 33 percent of the workforce and at least 50 employees are to be laid off. As defined by the Act, a plant closing occurs when 50 or more full-time employees lose their jobs due to the temporary or permanent closure of a single facility. Determining whether or not WARN notice is required can become difficult if an employer decides to stagger the workforce reduction over a period of time. If the total number of employees affected reaches the limits within a 90-day period, WARN notice must be given.

There are three exceptions to the notice requirement contained in the law: the faltering company exception, the unforeseeable business circumstance exception, and the natural disaster exception:

Faltering company exception   This exception applies to situations in which the company is actively seeking to avoid a plant closure by obtaining additional funding. If the company is reasonably certain that the funding will be obtained in a sufficient amount to avoid the closure, and if disclosing the closure has a negative impact on the company's capability to obtain the funding, the notice need not be given.

Unforeseeable business circumstance exception   This exception applies to both mass layoffs and plant closures, and can be used when there is a sudden negative change in business operations that could not have been predicted, such as the loss of a major customer without notice.

Natural disaster exception   This exception can be used in the event of a tornado, hurricane, earthquake, or other natural disaster that leads to either a mass layoff or a plant closure.

Common Law Doctrines

There are several common law doctrines that are often applied to employment relationships, including employment-at-will, constructive discharge, and defamation:

Employment-at-will   The basic concept of employment-at-will is that both parties in an employment relationship are free to leave it at any time and for any reason, whether the reason is a good or bad one, or even if there is no reason at all. This means that employees who are terminated (unless the termination is for a reason prohibited by a legal statute) have no legal recourse against the employer who ended the relationship. Over the years, courts in some states have eroded this concept, and there are today several recognized exceptions to it:

Implied Contract Exception   An *implied contract* can be created by the conduct of an employer. A common example of this is the application of a progressive discipline policy (I'll talk more about this in Chapter 6, "Building the Employee Relations Program"). If all employees who exhibit a particular behavior consistently receive the same consequences, the employer might have created an implied contract that any employee behaving in the same way will receive a similar consequence.

> **implied contract**
> An implied contract is conduct by an employer that can create a contract, such as the consistent use of a progressive discipline policy.

Express Contract Exception   An *express contract* can be a verbal or written statement by an employer or company representative such as a manager or supervisor. How often has a manager who is extremely pleased with an employee who completes a difficult assignment made a statement such as, "You have a job here as long as you want one!" In some cases, statements such as this have led courts to invalidate an at-will employment relationship.

> **express contract**
> An express contract is a verbal or written statement by an employer or company representative, such as "You have a job here for life" that might create an employment contract.

Public Policy Exception   The public policy exception to employment-at-will restricts an employer's ability to terminate a worker for refusing to commit an act that is against the law, such as perjury, on the employer's behalf.

Constructive Discharge   When an employer sets out to force an employee to quit by making the work environment extremely hostile and unpleasant, a court can determine that a case of *constructive discharge* occurred.

> **constructive discharge**
> Constructive discharge is conduct by an employer that makes the work environment so hostile and unpleasant that an employee quits.

Defamation   If an employer makes statements about a former employee that makes it difficult for that person to find other employment or damages that person's reputation in the community, the employer can be accused of defamation.

State and Local Legislation

In addition to the federal laws detailed in this chapter, all states and some local governments have additional laws that regulate employment relationships within their jurisdictions.

One area of employment law that is almost exclusively delegated to the states is that of workers' compensation. Up until the early part of the twentieth century, there was no legal protection for workers who were injured, maimed, or killed as a result of workplace accidents. Workplaces were far more dangerous at that time, and injuries or even deaths were not uncommon. Injured workers or the families of workers who died as a result of workplace accidents had to retain attorneys and file civil lawsuits in order to receive compensation for their medical bills, lost wages, and loss of their ability to earn a future living. Because workers were, for the most part, at an economic disadvantage to business owners during this period, very few could actually afford to pursue a civil action; and of those who did, only a small number could ever collect damages. As a result, the states began to develop workers' compensation insurance programs to ensure that workers were fairly compensated for injuries suffered at work. The requirements of these programs vary widely between the states.

Because state laws and regulations vary widely between the states, it is not possible to cover all that information in this book. To assist you in locating information for states in which your organization operates, Table 2.2 provides the names and website addresses for state employment agencies in each jurisdiction.

Table 2.2   State Employment Agencies

Jurisdiction	Employment Agency	Web Address
Alabama	Department of Industrial Relations	www.dir.state.al.us
Alaska	Department of Labor and Workforce Development	www.labor.state.ak.us
Arizona	State Labor Department	www.ica.state.az.us
Arkansas	Department of Labor	www.state.ar.us/labor
California	Department of Industrial Relations	www.dir.ca.gov
Colorado	Labor Standards Office	www.coworkforce.com
Connecticut	Labor Department	www.ctdol.state.ct.us
Delaware	Department of Labor	www.delawareworks.com
District of Columbia	Department of Employment Services	http://does.ci.washington.dc.us

Table 2.2   State Employment Agencies *(continued)*

Jurisdiction	Employment Agency	Web Address
Florida	Agency for Workforce Innovation	www.floridajobs.org/
Georgia	Department of Labor	www.dol.state.ga.us
Guam	Department of Labor	www.labor.gov.gu
Hawaii	Department of Labor and Industrial Relations	www.dlir.state.hi.us
Idaho	Department of Labor	www.labor.state.id.us
Illinois	Department of Labor	www.state.il.us/agency/idol
Indiana	Department of Labor	www.state.in.us/labor
Iowa	Division of Labor Services	www.iowaworkforce.org/labor
Kansas	Department of Human Resources	http://www2.hr.state.ks.us
Kentucky	Kentucky Labor Cabinet	www.kylabor.net
Louisiana	Department of Labor	www.ldol.state.la.us
Maine	Department of Labor	www.state.me.us/labor
Maryland	Department of Labor, Division of Workforce Development	www.dllr.state.md.us
Massachu-setts	Department of Labor and Workforce Development	www.detma.org/
Michigan	Department of Labor and Economic Growth	www.michigan.gov/bwuc
Minnesota	Department of Labor and Industry	www.doli.state.mn.us
Mississippi	Employment Security Commission	www.mesc.state.ms.us
Missouri	Department of Labor & Industrial Relations	www.dolir.state.mo.us
Montana	Department of Labor and Industry	http://dli.state.mt.us
Nebraska	Department of Labor	www.dol.state.ne.us/
Nevada	Office of the Nevada Labor Commissioner	www.LaborCommissioner.com
New Hampshire	Department of Labor	www.labor.state.nh.us

Table 2.2   State Employment Agencies *(continued)*

Jurisdiction	Employment Agency	Web Address
New Jersey	Department of Labor	www.state.nj.us/labor/index.html
New Mexico	Department of Labor	http://www3.state.nm.us/dol/dol_home.html
New York	Department of Labor	www.labor.state.ny.us
North Carolina	Department of Labor	www.nclabor.com
North Dakota	Department of Labor	www.state.nd.us/labor/
Ohio	Division of Labor and Worker Safety	www.state.oh.us/ohio/agency.htm
Oklahoma	Department of Labor	www.state.ok.us/~okdol
Oregon	Bureau of Labor and Industries	www.boli.state.or.us
Pennsylvania	Department of Labor and Industry	www.dli.state.pa.us
Puerto Rico	Department of Labor and Human Resources	www.osha.gov/oshdir/stateprogs/Puerto_Rico.html
Rhode Island	Department of Labor and Training	www.det.state.ri.us
South Carolina	Department of Labor, Licensing and Regulations	www.llr.state.sc.us
South Dakota	Department of Labor	www.state.sd.us/dol/dol.htm
Tennessee	Department of Labor	www.state.tn.us/labor-wfd/
Texas	Texas Workforce Commission	www.twc.state.tx.us
Utah	Utah Labor Commission	www.labor.state.ut.us
Vermont	Department of Labor & Industry	www.state.vt.us/labind
Virgin Islands	Department of Labor	www.usvi.org/labor
Virginia	Department of Labor & Industry	www.dli.state.va.us
Washington	Department of Labor & Industries	www.lni.wa.gov
West Virginia	Division of Labor	www.state.wv.us/labor

Table 2.2   State Employment Agencies *(continued)*

Jurisdiction	Employment Agency	Web Address
Wisconsin	Department of Workforce Development	`www.dwd.state.wi.us`
Wyoming	Department of Employment	`http://wydoe.state.wy.us/`

Summary of Federal Employment Laws

This chapter presents a number of federal laws with which HR practitioners need to be familiar. This is by no means a comprehensive list, but it does cover the basic information needed to build an HR department. Table 2.3 provides a summary of these laws and tells you which employers are subject to their requirements.

Keep in mind that the state or states in which your organization operates might have additional laws with different requirements. If that is the case, your organization must comply with the most stringent requirement.

Table 2.3   Summary of Federal Employment Laws

Federal Law	Full Title	Covered Activities	Employers Covered
ADA	Americans with Disabilities Act	Prohibits discrimination against disabled persons	15+ employees
ADEA	Age Discrimination in Employment Act	Prohibits discrimination against those 40+ years of age	20+ employees
CRA	Civil Rights Act of 1991	Sets maximum damage awards, allows jury trials in discrimination cases, codifies disparate impact	15+ employees
EEOA	Equal Employment Opportunity Act	Increases EEOC enforcement powers	15+ employees
EO 11246	Executive Orders 11246, 11375, and 12478	Identifies protected classes for federal contractors: race, creed, color, national origin, gender, and disabled persons	Federal contracts of $10,000+
EPA	Equal Pay Act	Requires equal pay for equal work, regardless of gender	Employers engaged in interstate commerce

Table 2.3   Summary of Federal Employment Laws *(continued)*

Federal Law	Full Title	Covered Activities	Employers Covered
FLSA	Fair Labor Standards Act	Sets the minimum wage, establishes exemption status, requires overtime, requires records	Employers engaged in interstate commerce
FMLA	Family and Medical Leave Act	Provides up to 12 weeks of unpaid leave for serious family illnesses	50+ employees within 75-mile radius
IRCA	Immigration Reform and Control Act	Requires employees to be legally authorized to work in the U.S.	4+ employees
LMRA	Labor-Management Relations Act	Prohibits closed shops, requires majority consent for union shops, allows state "right-to-work" laws	1+ employees
NLRA	National Labor Relations Act	Allows employees to organize and bargain collectively; identifies unfair labor practices	1+ employees
OSH Act	Occupational Safety and Health Act	Establishes and enforces workplace safety standards	1+ employees
PDA	Pregnancy Discrimination Act	Requires employers to treat pregnancy the same as any other short term disability	15+ employees
RA	Rehabilitation Act	Prohibits discrimination based on physical or mental disabilities	Federal contracts of $10,000+
Title VII	Title VII of the Civil Rights Act	Prohibits discrimination on the basis of race, color, religion, national origin or sex	15+ employees
USERRA	Uniformed Services Employment/ Reemployment Rights Act	Protects the rights of employees called to active duty	1+ employees

Table 2.3   Summary of Federal Employment Laws *(continued)*

Federal Law	Full Title	Covered Activities	Employers Covered
VEVRA	Vietnam Era Veterans' Readjustment Assistance Act	Contractors must list openings with state employment agencies and give priority to Vietnam vets	Federal contracts of $25,000+
WARN	Worker Adjustment and Retraining Notification Act	Requires 60-day notice of mass layoffs and plant closings	100+ employees

Terms to Know

bona fide occupational qualification (BFOQ)	implied contract
compensable time	nonexempt job
constructive discharge	prima facie evidence
disparate impact	protected classes
disparate treatment	quid pro quo harassment
executive order	reasonable accommodation
exempt job	tangible employment action (TEA)
express contract	unfair labor practices (ULPs)
hostile work environment	unlawful employment practices

Review Questions

1. What is a protected class?

2. What are common law doctrines?

3. Define a BFOQ.

4. Describe the difference between disparate impact and disparate treatment.

5. True or False: An employer must hire a disabled individual who applies for a job, even if that person is not the best qualified for the position.

6. What requirements must be met before an employee qualifies to take a FMLA leave?

7. True or False: All employers with more than 100 employees must have an affirmative action plan.

8. What four elements did the Supreme Court identify as necessary to prove a prima facie case of discrimination in the *McDonnell Douglas Corp v Green* case?

9. An employer requires the office receptionist to attend a special training on Saturday morning to learn to operate a new telephone system. The employer does not have to pay the receptionist for the time spent at the training. True or False?

10. An employer suspects that an employee is talking to coworkers about forming a union. The employer decides to change her work assignment so that she is isolated from her coworkers. Is this an unfair labor practice?

Chapter 3

Building a Staffing Plan

Establishing a human resource management (HRM) program begins with a staffing plan. Staffing is the HRM function that covers all the actions and processes necessary to attract, hire, retain, and manage qualified employees—whether they are being promoted, demoted, transferred, or terminated—as well as those that bring new employees into the organization.

A staffing plan outlines how an organization does this—it's a guideline used by HR practitioners to ensure that employees possess the skills needed to successfully carry out the work of producing the goods or services the organization offers to its customers.

This chapters examines the elements that are necessary to effectively staff an organization with the right people at the right time.

tegic Foundation

ier you practice HR in a public, private for-profit, or nonprofit organiza-
nore than ever you need to be certain that the costs of operating the orga-
on are kept to a minimum.

the public sector, lower operating costs enable government entities to pro-
ervices for their citizens without increasing taxes. In the for-profit sector,
costs ensure a return on the investment made by the owners of the business,
ier they are shareholders, entrepreneurs, or partners. In nonprofit organizations, raising money is a time-consuming task. Donors want to be sure that their
contributions are used on direct services and are reluctant to contribute to organizations in which overhead expenses exceed 10 to 15 percent of the total budget.
Since the costs related to employment (salaries, wages, benefits, and so on) often
represent the single-most expensive operating expense in an organization, it's
important to be certain that the employees you bring into the organization are the
ones who have the necessary knowledge, skills, and abilities to do the work. For
HR practitioners, the key to doing this is knowing the future plans of the organization. This information is available in the strategic plan. In this chapter, we will
examine what you need to do to be sure that the staffing strategies you select are
tied to the strategic goals of your organization.

Speaking the Language of Business Strategy

As will be discussed in Chapter 10, "Strategic Human Resource Management,"
business strategy is the guiding force behind human resource programs. Each
chapter in this book begins with a discussion of the strategic foundation for the
topic of the chapter, and ends with a discussion of the metrics used to evaluate
program success. To facilitate an understanding of these discussions, here are
some definitions of terms that will appear throughout the book.

Strategic Plan

A strategic plan is developed by organization leaders based on information
gathered from external sources (such as predictions of changes in the industry,
economic indicators such as inflation and unemployment rates, shareholder
expectations, and competition in the product market) and internal sources (such
as whether the workforce consists of highly skilled employees or those who are
poorly trained, whether machinery and equipment is state-of-the-art or inefficient, or the status of inventions or patents). Based on this information, leaders
develop a plan to increase shareholder or owner value, whether by reducing
expenses, increasing sales, introducing improved product lines, or some other

means. The strategic plan outlines where the organization intends to go. Knowing this information allows HR practitioners to develop HR plans and programs that contribute to the ability of the organization to successfully implement the plan and achieve organizational goals.

The strategic foundation section of each chapter provides a broad description of the impact the topic of the chapter can have on the organization strategy.

Metrics

In the current business environment, it is more important than ever to demonstrate the positive impact of HR programs and policies on the bottom line. Metrics are the means used to measure business performance in all business functions. For HR, metrics use the language of business to communicate how HR programs contribute to business success and convey that HR understands the importance of bottom-line results to operations.

The metrics section of each chapter describes some typical measures that you can apply to demonstrate how HR contributes to business results in a given area.

Identify Job Needs

To identify which jobs will be needed in your organization, you need to know where your organization is going; that is, what goals the senior management team has set for it. Based on these organization goals, the managers of individual operating units (such as finance or sales) can establish the goals and objectives they need to achieve in order for the organization goals to be reached. It is at this level that the work of building the *staffing plan* begins.

In Chapter 10, I'll talk about the importance of building partnerships with managers in departments across an organization. This is important for many reasons, one of which is that it provides a means by which HR can stay abreast of changes in job and skill requirements in different areas of the organization. With this knowledge, HR is able to proactively develop sources for candidates who have the skills needed to fulfill requirements in the future.

staffing plan
An HRM guideline that outlines the process of the way an organization recruits, hires, retains, promotes, and terminates employees.

Budget forecasts are also factors in identifying future job needs. Many organizations conduct an annual budget planning process, in which operating unit managers develop budgets for the following year. During this process, HR has an opportunity to work with managers in identifying what jobs will be needed during the following year.

It's important for any organization to be sure that the employees it hires are the ones it needs to achieve its goals. HR practitioners play a key role in making this happen by working with managers to develop staffing plans that identify the knowledge and skills the organization needs, by forecasting when employees will be needed, and by implementing recruiting processes that deliver qualified employees at the appropriate time. The following describes the overall process:

Step 1: Determine which positions need to be filled   A staffing plan begins with a list of the jobs the organization plans to fill during the next year. This information might be provided by line managers, or HRM might work with them to determine how many employees are needed. When HRM knows which jobs are needed, a job analysis (discussed in the next section) can be conducted to determine which duties and responsibilities will be assigned to the job, and which qualifications will be needed for an individual to be successful in it. With that information, a recruiting strategy is developed, the sources where candidates will most likely be found are identified, and recruiting methods are selected.

Step 2: Develop the hiring process   After the recruiting decisions have been made, the focus turns to the hiring process. In this part of the staffing plan, HRM identifies the hiring procedures that will be used, including how candidates will be screened, who will interview them, and who will select the best applicant.

Step 3: Build the employee retention plan   After new employees are on board, the process turns to activities designed to retain them in the organization, including development of replacement and succession plans so that employees are made aware of opportunities for career advancement within the organization.

Step 4: Design an exit process   Finally, the staffing plan describes the process to be used when employees leave the organization, whether the decision is made voluntarily as the result of a retirement or resignation, or of an involuntary termination such as a layoff, termination for cause, or other reason.

Whether or not these steps are part of a formal process in your organization, they are being done in some way—even if the HR department is not involved or even if there is no HR department. Someone in the organization is identifying what jobs are needed, determining the skills that candidates must have to successfully perform in the position, deciding how and where to recruit, and so on. Without a formal staffing plan, though, the actions in each step may not be well thought out. In that case, the end result is often an employee whose skills may not be those that are needed for the position or who does not fit well into the culture of the organization.

Recruiting Strategy

After staffing needs for the organization have been identified and clearly described, HR practitioners have the information they need to find qualified candidates to fill the available positions. Before you begin placing job advertisements, though, it's important to gather information about how you will present the company to prospective employees, determine the best way to fill the positions, and decide where to look for candidates with different qualifications.

Employment Branding

In recent years, HR has borrowed the "brand" concept from the marketing function and added it to the staffing toolkit for attracting qualified candidates. But what exactly is an *employment brand*? To explain it, let's begin with another marketing concept: the unique selling proposition (USP). In marketing, the USP defines what sets a product or service apart from its competition. So, in the context of HR, the employment brand explains what it's like to work in an organization and what makes working there unique from working somewhere else.

Why is this important? Employers often must compete with other organizations for a limited number of qualified candidates. A positive employment brand is a way for the employer to attract candidates to its organization instead of going to work for a competitor. Unless it is very new, your organization very likely already has a reputation, positive or negative, based on the experiences of employees who currently work there or who have worked there in the past. An effective employment brand is consistent with those experiences, so when new employees join the organization the reality of working there fits the expectations created during the recruiting process. Identifying what this reputation is, taking steps to improve elements of it that are less than favorable in attracting candidates, and utilizing it as a brand can make it easier to attract the kinds of candidates who will move your organization forward.

employment brand
An employment brand is used to describe the unique characteristics about an organization and what makes it a good place to work. It helps HRM to focus its recruiting strategy.

Operational Responsibilities

With an understanding of the strategic plan, HR practitioners are able to perform the daily activities designed to place the right people in the right positions for organizational success.

job analysis
A job analysis gathers information about various aspects of a job, including reporting relationships, interactions with others, exemption status of the position, qualifications, work environment, and KSAs needed to perform the job successfully.

Job Analysis

After the organization has determined how many employees will be needed to achieve its goals, it's important to identify which tasks, duties, and responsibilities these employees will perform. To do this, a *job analysis* is conducted.

When conducting a job analysis, be sure to concentrate on the *job requirements,* not the *abilities of the person* in the job. It can be difficult to differentiate, particularly when a single person has been in the job for a long time. The best way to do this is to begin by clearly identifying the purpose of the job and how it will contribute to the organization's goals.

NOTE

The analysis begins with an information-gathering process designed to obtain information about various aspects of the job. To provide the most comprehensive description, you should answer the following questions:

- What types of interactions will this job have with other jobs in the work group, the company, customers, vendors, or others?
- At what level will the position interact with these individuals?
- To which position will this job report?
- Is the position exempt from requirements of the Fair Labor Standards Act (FLSA)?
- What are the *essential functions* of the job? A list of essential job functions is necessary for compliance with the Americans with Disabilities Act (ADA) discussed in Chapter 2, "The Impact of Employment Law on HR Practice." What is the level of complexity of these functions, and how often are they performed? Do they require operation of any type of equipment? If so, what level of skill is required? The ADA definition of essential functions includes the following considerations:
  - The position exists to perform the function; without it, there is no need for the job.
  - There are a limited number of other employees who can perform the function or among whom the function can be distributed or shared.
  - The function is highly specialized, and the person hired to fill the job will possess expertise or special ability to perform the function.

essential functions
Essential job functions are those tasks, duties, and responsibilities that form the basis for the job's existence.

- What are the nonessential functions of the job? How complex are these tasks and how often are they performed? Do these functions require the operation of any equipment? If so, what type of equipment (computer, power tools, telephone, and so on) and level of skill is necessary?
- What is the environment in which the job will be performed? Is it an office or production line? Is it very noisy, hot or cold, or hazardous in some way?
- What physical requirements are necessary for successfully completing the essential job functions? Does the job require sitting or standing for extended periods of time? What level of mental capacity is needed to complete the work?
- What qualifications are required to successfully complete the essential job functions? This includes the *knowledge, skills, and abilities (KSAs)* that are necessary to successfully perform in the position as well as other more general competencies that employees will need.

◆ How urgent is the need for the KSAs? Will the organization need to hire a new employee who already has the KSAs, or will there be time to train someone internally to acquire the skills needed to do this job?

There are several methods for collecting information during a job analysis. Some of the most common methods include the following:

Questionnaires   The HR practitioner can provide a questionnaire designed to elicit information about job requirements. This can be completed by a supervisor, manager, or incumbent of a position. Questionnaires provide a means for collecting the information listed previously by asking questions for each aspect of the job.

Interviews   Interviews may be conducted with an employee who has been doing the job, a supervisor or manager, or coworkers with whom the job will interact. The purpose of the interview is to determine which tasks, duties, and responsibilities are to be performed by the job, along with the qualifications needed for successful performance. Questions asked by the interviewer are designed to obtain the information listed previously in this section. They are more time-consuming than questionnaires, but have the advantage of providing an opportunity for the interviewer to ask followup questions to clarify the information provided.

Task inventory   A task inventory is a comprehensive list of tasks that could be performed in a particular job category (for example, administrative support positions) and ranks each task as to its importance to a specific job. Table 3.1 provides a sample of a task inventory.

This brief example illustrates how some tasks in the inventory (such as the ability to communicate at a basic level) could be found in all jobs within the category; whereas others (such as explaining technical information to customers) might be found in only a few. In addition, a task inventory can provide information about the level of experience that is needed in the position. For example, a receptionist may need to have an advanced level of verbal communication skills, but need only an entry-level ability to explain technical information to customers.

Observation   This method requires someone (usually an HR practitioner or compensation specialist) to spend time in the normal work area and observe an incumbent performing the job. The observer makes notes about the tasks that are done and the interactions that occur; and then determines which skills, knowledge, and abilities are necessary to perform the tasks.

The result of the job analysis is raw information about various aspects of the job that must then be compiled into a single document used to explain the job to

knowledge, skills, and abilities (KSAs)
KSAs are the qualifications that are needed by an individual in order to perform successfully in the position.

the employee, coworkers, supervisors, and others within the organization. This document, known as a job description, lists the tasks, duties, and responsibilities of the position, contains information about reporting relationships, and describes how the job interacts with others.

Table 3.1   Sample Task Inventory

Task	1	2	3	4	5	Entry	Int	Adv
	Task Importance					Training Level Required		
Communicate verbally at a basic level								
Communicate verbally at a high level								
Communicate in writing at a basic level								
Communicate in writing at a high level								
Explain technical information to customers								
Provide excellent customer service								

Job Descriptions

job description

A job description is a written document that is produced as the result of a job analysis. It contains information that identifies the job, its essential functions, and the job specifications or competencies that enable an individual to be successful in the position.

A *job description* is a basic HR document used for a variety of purposes in an organization. It is the means by which management communicates to employees what they are expected to accomplish. It contains the information needed to conduct a successful search for qualified candidates and is used to determine the appropriate level of pay for the position. It is also the basis for the performance management process. Finally, a properly written job description that details the essential job functions, along with the related physical and mental qualifications needed for successful performance, is key to complying with requirements of the ADA.

There are many formats for job descriptions; a search of the Internet will produce many different styles and types that can be adapted to your organization. The format selected by an employer must include some basic elements; however, it is also important that the format fits the needs of the individual organization.

The following illustration shows one possible job description format and the elements it should contain:

JOB DESCRIPTION		
Job Title: Receptionist	**Department:**	Administration
Reports to: Office Manager	**Exemption Status:**	Nonexempt
Salary Grade: 2	**Date Published:**	January 12, 2004

Position Summary:
Under general supervision, the receptionist answers the telephone, greets visitors, and logs them onto the security system; and prepares sales packets as directed by members of the sales team.

Supervisory Responsibilities:
Performs duties under only general supervision; determines process and actions to be taken on routine assignments.

	% Time:
Essential Functions: Using the Nortel T24 KIM Call Director, answers an average of 45 incoming calls per hour within three rings and directs callers to the appropriate person, department, or voice mailbox.	95%

	% Time:
Nonessential Functions: May be required to drive to the post office for mail pickup from time to time.	5%

Equipment Operated:	**Education, Licenses, or Certificates Required:**
Nortel T24 KIM Call Director, PC, copy machine, postage machine	Must have a high school diploma or equivalent. Must have a valid driver's license.

Communication Skills Required:
Must be able to verbally communicate effectively with employees at all levels in the organization, as well as with customers, vendors, callers, and visitors. Basic written communication skills are also necessary.

Experience Required:
1–2 years of experience in an office environment performing entry-level clerical work.

Skills Required:
Basic knowledge of Microsoft Office, including Outlook and Word.

Physical Requirements:
This job requires the ability to sit for approximately 2–3 hours at a time, to listen and talk on the telephone about 95 percent of the time, and to occasionally lift packages weighing 25 pounds.

Mental Requirements:
Requires cognitive skills that allow movement from one task to another, to attend to detail, to process information, and to interpret it as needed.

Work Environment Conditions:
Indoor office environment with controlled temperatures and sealed windows on 44th floor of high rise building.

Approved by:	Title:	Date:

The elements in a job description fall into one of three categories: identifying information, job functions, and job specifications. Let's take a look at what is included in each of these areas.

Identifying Information

As shown in the previous illustration, the information at the top of the job description is fairly self-explanatory. In this section, you want to provide information that identifies the job, where it is located within the company, and whether it is exempt or nonexempt from FLSA requirements (as discussed in Chapter 2). This section also includes the title of the person who will be supervising this job. In some (but not all) companies, the salary grade or range is included here. (We'll talk about these topics in Chapter 4, "Building a Compensation Plan.")

The job title should be reflective of the purpose of the job as well as its level within the organization. Titles should be meaningful as well. Don't use the word *director*, for example, unless the position is in fact one of authority. Similarly, a *manager* is someone who, in part, supervises others.

Real World Scenario

Titles Gone Awry

During the dot-com boom, employers created some pretty wild titles to attract employees with skills that were in high demand. This led to title inflation, in which someone performing duties at an entry or intermediate level was given a manager or director title. I found my personal all-time favorite silly job title on an Internet job board: "Director of First Impressions." I had no idea what this could possibly mean. Was it an interior designer? Or a public relations expert? Not exactly … it turned out that this was an entry-level receptionist position!

Other information to include here is the date the job description was written. Jobs change over time, so you want to be sure that the description is reviewed periodically and updated to include tasks or requirements that may be added after the description is written.

Finally, this section ends with a summary of the purpose for the position. This is a short paragraph of two to three sentences that describes the purpose of the position, delineates its overall level of responsibility, and summarizes the results of the job analysis. Although the summary appears at the beginning of the job description, it is often written as the last step in the process to sum up the details recorded in the document, for example.

Under general supervision, the receptionist answers the telephone, greets visitors and logs them onto the security system, and prepares sales packets as directed by members of the sales team.

Job Functions

The heart of a job description is the information it contains about the tasks, duties, and responsibilities forming the basis for the job's existence. There are two levels of job functions, those that are essential to the job as defined by the ADA, and those that are non-essential or could, without great inconvenience to the employer, be moved into another job. This is necessary so that, if a candidate or employee requests a reasonable accommodation in order to perform the job, the employer can demonstrate that the essential functions were designated as such prior to the request for accommodation, document the reasons that they are deemed essential to the job, and serve as the basis for determining whether or not a requested accommodation is, in fact reasonable for the employer to implement.

This section of the sample job description in the previous illustration begins with information about the supervisory responsibilities of the position. If the position has responsibility for supervising others in the organization, the titles and numbers of positions are included here. Positions, such as this receptionist, who do not supervise others, have a level of responsibility to manage their own time and work products, and this information can be included here. For example:

Performs duties under only general supervision; determines methods and procedures on routine assignments.

Following the description of supervisory responsibility are the sections of the job description that list each job function. Each of these statements (whether they are essential or non-essential functions) should use an action verb to describe what is to be done, include the desired result of the task and identify equipment or other specific information about the task. Using our receptionist position as an example again, one task could be described as follows:

Using the Nortel T24 KIM Call Director, answers an average of 45 incoming calls per hour within three rings and directs callers to the appropriate person, department or voice mailbox.

Job function statements written in this way inform employees about not only what is to be done, but also about the results that are expected. They also provide an idea of how much time will be spent on the function during the course of a day. To the extent that it is possible, each function should be accompanied by an estimate of the percentage of time that will be spent on it. This is not always easy to determine, particularly for functions that are done only infrequently. It is important information to have because it is used to justify the exemption status of the position.

Job Specifications

Job specifications are the KSAs that are needed by an individual to be successful in the job. These requirements include education, previous experience, skills, and the necessary physical and mental abilities. The need to describe specific physical and mental requirements is based on ADA requirements that reasonable accommodation be made for disabled employees. To determine whether or not an accommodation is reasonable, the employer must first define what is needed to do the job. The previous illustration shows some examples of how these requirements can be described in an office environment.

job specifications

A job specifications section of a job description describes the KSAs needed by an individual in order to perform successfully in the job.

Some organizations are moving away from job specifications toward what are known as *job competencies*. They are more broadly defined than are job specifications because they are intended to describe characteristics that will allow an individual to be successful in a variety of positions. Organizations that are using competencies do so because they believe it allows them to respond more rapidly to changes in business circumstances. Competencies generally fall into one of four areas:

- ◆ Technical skills, such as those needed to use software or operate machinery and equipment

- ◆ Knowledge, learned information and intangible attributes such as time management and the ability to solve problems

- ◆ Interpersonal skills such as teamwork and customer service

- ◆ Behavioral characteristics such as reliability, trustworthiness, and approachability

job competencies

Job competencies are broadly defined characteristics that allow an individual to be successful in a job.

In addition to job competencies, a number of organizations have identified core competencies based on corporate values that employees at all levels throughout the organization are expected to exhibit at work. These core competencies are often included on a job description along with the job competencies or specifications.

Sourcing Candidates

Today, there are many possible ways to fill jobs in an organization. Not only can full-time employees be hired, but depending on the type of work that needs to be done, it may be possible to hire temporary workers, part-time workers, or independent contractors. It is also possible to outsource an entire function to a different company specializing in that type of work. Keeping in mind that employers want to keep operating costs to a minimum, HR practitioners can provide their expertise in this area to help hiring managers determine the most cost-effective way to get a specific job done. Let's examine some of the ways in which this can be done.

Hiring employees

Hiring employees who work directly for the organization has been the traditional way of getting work done in organizations, which can mean hiring a full-time or part-time employee—depending on how much work needs to be done.

Some employers have found job sharing to be a satisfactory solution to staffing needs. In job sharing, two part-time employees are hired to fill a single position. This provides flexibility for the employer in that it is possible to hire people with different skills or strengths to do the same job, adding value to the work that is produced.

Another way of filling jobs, particularly those of a short duration, is to provide internships for college students or recent graduates. This is a low-cost solution for employers: It provides students with the opportunity to obtain experience in their chosen professions and gives employers an opportunity to see the student in action on the job. For the student, this arrangement can lead to an employment offer after graduation. For the employer, it is an effective recruiting tool, reducing the level of uncertainty in the future hiring process.

Alternative Staffing Methods

Alternative staffing methods provide employers with options for getting work done that are often less costly than hiring employees. There are several methods to choose from: using temporary employees, independent contractors, professional employer organizations, and outsourcing. Let's take a look at how these alternatives can be beneficial for the employer.

Temporary Employees Most people are familiar with "temps," temporary employees who are employed by an agency and sent to work in various companies for short periods of time. Employers find this useful when special projects must be completed, deadlines must be met, or regular employees are on leave for extended periods of time. Although the work gets done, the employer does create an ongoing responsibility to provide work for the employee and is not responsible for unemployment benefits or other costs.

Independent Contractors Independent contractors are individuals who are self-employed and perform work for several businesses or organizations. Some employers believe that hiring someone as an independent contractor is an easy way to avoid paying Social Security and other taxes, and to save money by doing so. The determination about whether someone is classified as an employee or an independent contractor is actually subject to guidelines established by federal and state governments to determine

alternative staffing methods
Alternative staffing methods, which are used to staff an organization without hiring regular full-time employees, include temporary employees, part-time employees, independent contractors, PEOs, and outsourcing.

whether or not an employment relationship exists. These guidelines fall into three categories: behavioral control, financial control, and the type of relationship that exists between the parties.

Professional Employer Organizations   Professional employer organizations (PEOs) are organizations that act as the employer of record for several businesses. Many PEOs provide a full range of human resource services, including payroll and benefit administration. The employees are hired by the PEO, which then leases them back to the business for a fee. For smaller organizations, a PEO can provide a solution that allows it to offer benefit packages that are competitive with those of larger organizations at a reasonable cost.

cost-benefit analysis

A cost-benefit analysis collects all available information about the costs of an HRM proposal, identifies benefits such as cost savings and reduced turnover, and projects whether the proposal will be cost-effective.

Outsourcing   Outsourcing is gaining in popularity among all types of organizations, both public and private. It allows an organization to have an entire function performed by a provider specializing in that particular function; for example, benefits administration. Because the service provider specializes in the function, it can often do the work more cost-effectively, freeing the business assets to be used for purposes that produce income.

Hire or Outsource? Making the Decision

Deciding whether to hire employees or to use an alternative staffing method requires an analysis of how much each method will cost and what benefits will be realized from each of them. This is known as a *cost-benefit analysis*, and utilizing this process helps you to decide which alternative is in the best interest of the organization. Table 3.2 gives you an idea of how to begin an analysis.

Table 3.2   Cost-Benefit Analysis

Costs	Hire Employee	Independent Contractor	Outsource
Purpose of Analysis			
Direct			
Salary			
Benefits			
Taxes			
Workers comp			
Telephone			
Computer			
Indirect			
Office space			

Table 3.2   Cost-Benefit Analysis *(continued)*

Costs	Hire Employee	Independent Contractor	Outsource
Insurance			
Total			
Benefits	**Hire Employee**	**Independent Contractor**	**Outsource**
Tangible			
Intangible			
Total			
Impact on Net Profit	**Hire Employee**	**Independent Contractor**	**Outsource**
Immediate			
Long-term			
Total			

A cost-benefit analysis begins with a clear definition of what the analysis will accomplish; in this case, it could be something like this: "The purpose of this analysis is to determine the most cost-effective method of administering the employee benefit program." The next step is to analyze what it currently costs the organization to have the function completed. For example, if a function is currently performed by an employee, you would provide the direct costs (salary, benefits, taxes, and so on) and the indirect costs (office space, insurance, and so on), and then record the total current costs. The same thing is done for the benefits, both immediate and long-term. It is often difficult to put a dollar value on benefits (such as "employee satisfaction"), but it is important to attempt this whenever possible. If not, the benefit can be stated as follows: "Employees can concentrate on their work and spend less time dealing with health insurance problems when the benefit administrator is available onsite." Finally, you calculate the impact of these costs and benefits on the bottom line.

After you calculate the total cost for the current method, a similar analysis is conducted for whatever other methods are being contemplated. When the analysis is complete, the result is a quantifiable recommendation for the action that is in the best long-term interest of the organization.

Recruiting Methods

In the not-too-distant past, the most common means of finding candidates was to advertise an opening in the newspaper. Today, there are many methods to find the qualified candidates you need to staff your organization. The method you choose depends largely on the type of position you are trying to fill, the availability of qualified candidates in the labor market, and whether you want or need to increase the level of diversity in your organization.

Labor Markets

The term "labor market" is used in several different contexts. In its broadest sense, it refers to anyone who is seeking a job in any field anywhere in the world. In a recruiting context, it is more often defined as the group of people with the KSAs needed to fill a particular position. In this sense, a single employer might seek candidates from many labor markets at any given time. For example, qualified candidates to fill a receptionist position might be readily available in the local geographic area in which the employer is located, known as the local labor market.

For positions requiring a very high level of training and skill, such as a systems architect, an employer might need to extend a search for candidates with the necessary skills to a national or even an international labor market. The labor market, then, is defined as the group of possible employees who possess the KSAs required for a particular job.

Increasing Workforce Diversity

As discussed in Chapter 2, some organizations are required (based on government contracts) to maintain an ethnically diverse workforce. Organizations with 100 or more employees, whether or not they have government contracts, are required to file annual reports about the level of diversity within their organizations. In still other organizations, there is a belief that ethnic diversity is a good business practice. For any of these reasons, organizations might choose recruiting methods and practices designed to increase the diversity of the workforce in their organizations.

Common Recruiting Methods

As mentioned earlier, there are a variety of recruiting methods available to employers today. The methods selected for any given position will be those that reach the greatest number of candidates with the experience, training, and skills needed in that position. Following are some of the more common methods:

> **Media sources**   These sources include advertisements in newspapers, in magazines, on radio, and on television. For entry-level and unskilled jobs, newspaper advertisements can reach a large number of qualified candidates from which employers can select the best-qualified candidate. Professional journals reach candidates who stay current in their fields of practice. Radio and television ads, although expensive, can provide candidates when employers need to fill a large number of jobs quickly.

Internet job boards   For many white-collar job seekers, these job boards provide access to a large number of positions throughout the country. For employers who want to reach a wide audience, this can be a cost-effective way to do so. The drawback of job boards is that they often result in a large number of applicants without any of the qualifications for the job being advertised. This large pool makes the process of finding those candidates who are qualified very time-consuming.

State employment offices   Each state has an agency that provides some type of job search assistance to those who are unemployed. Employers are usually able to list open jobs with these agencies for little or no cost.

Company websites   Most corporate, government, and nonprofit websites have an "employment" or "careers" page on which current openings are listed. In some cases, interested candidates can complete applications on line.

Colleges and universities   Employers who are seeking candidates for management training programs or entry-level professional positions can often recruit graduating seniors through the employment offices of colleges and universities.

Job fairs   A job fair allows HR practitioners to see a large number of candidates at a single time. In many cases, managers and employees from outside the HR department attend the fair with HR representatives to provide interested candidates with information about specific openings.

Alumni employees   There are times when highly qualified, high-performing employees leave an organization for personal reasons or to accept higher level positions. In many cases, these alumni employees are excellent recruiting sources, either to bring them back or to get referrals for other candidates they recommend.

Previous applicants   Sometimes the recruiting process produces several highly qualified candidates for an opening. Many HR practitioners maintain contact with the qualified candidates who were not selected to have them on tap when other openings become available.

Vendors, customers, and suppliers   The organizations with whom employers do business often have access to and are willing to refer candidates with the KSAs needed for a specific position with which they interact on a regular basis.

Labor unions   Employers who work under collective bargaining agreements with a union can often obtain qualified candidates through the union hiring hall.

Employment agencies   There are two basic types of employment agencies: those who work on a contingency basis, and those who perform retained searches. Agencies that perform contingency searches submit candidates to employers for consideration; if an employer hires the candidate, a fee is paid to the agency. A retained search firm, on the other hand, is paid a fee to conduct a search, and whether or not a candidate is hired, the employer must pay the fee in full.

Walk-in candidates   In some situations—such as retail stores, construction businesses, and restaurants among others—job candidates routinely approach the business manager to ask whether there are any openings or to apply to a "Help Wanted" sign in the window or ad in the paper.

Hiring Procedures

Based on the job analysis, you now have a list of the qualifications that are needed by candidates to perform successfully in the position and within the organization. If the recruiting strategy you selected was successful, you also have a pile of resumes or applications for the position you advertised. It's time now to move on to the next step: hiring the candidate whose qualifications will best meet the needs of the organization.

A streamlined process for hiring new employees demonstrates that the employer is organized and appreciative of the time applicants spend in the process. It can become a key element of your employment brand as the first (and sometimes only) time candidates interact with the organization. Let's face it—any time a candidate who is not selected for a position leaves the process feeling fairly treated, that good impression will be communicated to others. You never know when that good impression will lead an outstanding candidate to the organization—one who has the potential to become a star employee.

There are several components of an effective hiring procedure:

- Employment documents
- Screening interviews
- Pre-employment testing
- In-depth interviews
- Candidate evaluation
- Background/reference checks
- Applicant communications

Let's take a closer look at each of these components and how they contribute to selecting the best candidate for the job opening.

Collecting Employment Documents

A key component of any hiring process is the documentation that allows HR practitioners and hiring managers to evaluate candidate qualifications. The two main documents used for this purpose are the resume and the employment application.

A *resume* is a document that candidates prepare to present their work history and qualifications for a position. Because there are many appropriate formats for presenting a work history, it can be difficult to compare information about different candidates. In addition, the latest advice given to job seekers is to make their resumes into marketing documents designed to attract the employer's attention. Resumes prepared in this way present the applicant in a favorable light, but may not include all the information an employer wants to review prior to making a hiring decision.

Employment application forms also come in different formats, but they have one key advantage over resumes: The employer selects a single format to be used, which makes the process of evaluating candidate qualifications easier on HR practitioners and line managers. Another advantage of application forms is that they ask for and provide space to complete information that is generally not included on resumes, such as supervisor names and pay rates. Finally, application forms can and should include a statement that is signed by applicants attesting to the truth and accuracy of everything included on the application, and notifying them that false statements could be grounds for dismissal. This statement can be important if it is discovered during a reference or background check, or even at a later time after the applicant has been hired, that the application contains false information. In many organizations, employees are dismissed immediately if it is found that they lied on their application forms.

When purchasing or creating an application form for use in your hiring process, be sure that it complies with employment laws in your state. Information that may be legally requested by employers in one state may place an employer at risk for a claim of discriminatory hiring practices in another.

NOTE

Whether your organization chooses to use resumes or application forms, these documents (along with cover letters that may be submitted by applicants) form the basis for the initial determination of whether or not individuals possess the qualifications needed for the position. A great deal of information can be gleaned from this review. Some questions you want to answer as you review the documents include:

- Does the candidate have the KSAs needed to do the job?
- Do the previous jobs held by the candidate indicate a steady career progression?
- Are there unexplained gaps in the employment history?
- Is the document free from misspelled words, typographical errors, and poor grammar? How will this affect performance in the job?
- If an application form, has all the requested information been provided? Did the applicant sign the document?

Answering these and other similar questions as you review the application documents and jotting down questions you have about the candidates who meet the job qualifications become the basis for questions that will be asked during the screening interview—the next step in the selection process.

Screening Interviews

The goal of the *screening interview* is to gain a better understanding of the information provided by the candidate in the resume or application. This is the point in the process in which the HR practitioner asks the candidate to explain information that may be unclear and to provide additional information that is needed to better understand the candidate's qualifications. These initial interviews may be conducted in person or over the telephone, depending on the needs of the organization, the time available to conduct them, and the geographic location of the candidates.

An interview assessment form is a useful tool for keeping track of results of the screening process and helps to decide which of the candidates will move on to the next step in the process. The following illustration provides a sample format to use in assessing candidates at this stage and during the in-depth interviews later in the process.

CANDIDATE ASSESSMENT INFORMATION					
Position Title:	**Candidate Name:**				
Hiring Manager:	**Interview Date:**				
Factors	**Rating**				
	Not a fit				Excellent fit
Knowledge, skills, and abilities required by the job.	1	2	3	4	5
Communicates at an appropriate level for the job.	1	2	3	4	5
Work history suitable for the position.	1	2	3	4	5
Educational background suitable for the position.	1	2	3	4	5
Candidate's personality fits well with culture.	1	2	3	4	5
	1	2	3	4	5
	1	2	3	4	5
Overall assessment:	1	2	3	4	5
Hire recommendation: Yes No					
Comments:					
Interviewer Name: Interviewer Signature: Date:					

When developing a similar tool for use in your selection process, the factors in the sample should be replaced as appropriate with factors specific to your organization and individualized for different positions as needed.

Pre-employment Testing

Pre-employment testing is a tool used by some organizations for purposes of evaluating a candidate's suitability for a position. There are several different types of tests that can be used to gather different kinds of information about candidates.

Aptitude test   Aptitude tests are designed to measure a candidate's knowledge and capability to apply that knowledge to specific tasks.

Cognitive ability test   Cognitive ability tests are used to measure an individual's ability to analyze problems, solve them, and to draw conclusions about situations. They also measure the capacity for learning, thinking, and remembering information.

Personality test   Personality tests are designed to determine whether candidates have characteristics associated with success in a particular type of work. For example, a shy, introverted candidate may not be a good fit for a job that involves cold calling potential customers.

Integrity test   Integrity tests determine how honest candidates are in different situations.

Psychomotor assessment test   Psychomotor assessment tests measure coordination and manual dexterity.

Physical assessment test   Physical assessment tests determine whether candidates are capable of performing specific physical tasks within a certain period of time; they are common for jobs that require regular physical work, such as firefighters.

As you recall from the court cases described in Chapter 2, employers must use factors that are related to job performance during the selection process. In 1978, the Equal Employment Opportunity Commission (EEOC), the federal Civil Service Commission, the Office of Federal Contract Compliance Programs (OFCCP), and the federal Department of Justice collaborated to develop guidelines designed to provide compliance assistance for employers in this regard. These guidelines, known as the Uniform Guidelines on Employee Selection Procedures, apply to employers who are subject to the requirements of Title VII, EO 11246 (as amended) and other federal equal opportunity legislation. These guidelines set out the criteria to be followed in testing candidates, requiring that selection tools be both reliable and valid predictors of future job performance. A reliable selection tool is one that produces results that are consistent over time. In other words, equally qualified candidates who take the test many months apart will attain similar scores when they take the test. A valid selection tool is one that accurately measures what it is supposed to measure. For example, a valid test for candidates for a truck driver position is a driving test. The complete text of the guidelines is available on the EEOC website at www.uniformguidelines.com/uniformguidelines.html.

In-depth Interviews

At this point in the process, the number of qualified candidates has been narrowed down to those with the best qualifications for the job. HR now presents the hiring manager with these candidates for evaluation, along with the candidate assessment forms, test results, and any other information gathered during the screening process. The HR role at this point is to provide expertise and support to the hiring manager making the selection. If candidates will be interviewed by more than one person, information about the job, qualifications being sought, type of interview to be conducted, and process to be used to evaluate candidates should be shared with everyone on the interview team.

Creating an Interview Team

In many companies, candidates meet with several interviewers before a final selection is made. When this is the case, it's important that all the interviewers have access to information about the job that is being filled, the qualifications that are needed, and what the manager is looking for in the successful candidate. In addition, the interviewers should receive training about how to ask legally appropriate questions, interview styles that will be appropriate, biases that can creep into the candidate evaluation process, and the method to be used for compiling the evaluations of the candidates.

When selecting an interview team, the hiring manager should choose individuals who add value to the selection process. Depending on the level of the position being filled, this added value could be obtained by including individuals from the workgroup the new employee will be joining, coworkers from other work teams or departments with whom the employee will work on a regular basis, or managers of other departments who will have regular interactions with the new hire.

After the interview team has been selected, a pre-interview strategy meeting should be conducted. The purpose of this meeting is to ensure that all interviewers begin the process with the same information about the job to be filled, the qualifications considered essential for success in the position, and other information the hiring manager will consider when making the final selection.

This meeting is an appropriate time to reinforce appropriate interviewing techniques with team members and to provide training or other support for inexperienced interviewers. All interviewers should be reminded of the legal constraints on the types of questions that may be asked of candidates. Table 3.3

provides examples of inappropriate questions and ways to obtain job-related information about the same topics in a legally appropriate manner.

Table 3.3   Illegal and Legal Interview Questions *(continued)*

Sample Illegal Questions	Sample Legal Questions
What clubs or social organizations do you belong to?	Do you belong to any professional or trade associations or other organizations you think are relevant to this job?
Do you go to church?	
Age	
How old are you?	Are you over the age of 18?
When did you graduate from high school?	Can you, after employment, provide proof of age?
Arrest Record	
Have you ever been arrested?	Have you ever been convicted of _____ _____? (Name a crime that is plausibly related to the job in question.)
Disabilities	
Do you have any disabilities?	After reviewing the job description, are you able to perform all the essential functions of the job?
Have you had any recent or past illnesses or operations? If yes, list them and give dates of occurrence.	Can you demonstrate how you would perform the following job-related functions?
How is your family's health?	Any job offer will be made contingent upon a medical exam. Are you willing to undergo one if we offer you a job?
When did you lose your vision/arm/ hearing? How did it happen?	
Marital/Family Status	
What is your marital status?	Are you willing to relocate?*
With whom do you live?	This job requires frequent travel. Are you willing and able to travel when needed?*
What was your maiden name?	Is there anything that will prevent you from meeting work schedules?*
Do you plan to have a family? When? How many children will you have?	
What are your child-care arrangements?	

Table 3.3   Illegal and Legal Interview Questions *(continued)*

Sample Illegal Questions	Sample Legal Questions
Military	
Were you honorably discharged?	In what branch of the armed services did you serve?
What type of discharge did you receive?	What type of training or education did you receive in the military?
Origin/Citizenship	
Are you a U.S. citizen?	Are you authorized to work in the United States?
Where were you/your parents born?	What language(s) do you read/speak/write fluently? (Acceptable if related to essential functions.)
What is your race?	
What language did you speak in your home when you were growing up?	
Personal	
How tall are you?	This job requires the ability to lift a 50-pound weight and carry it 100 yards. Are you able to do that?
How much do you weigh?	This job will require work on the week-ends. Are you able to do so?
Would working on weekends conflict with your religious beliefs?	
* acceptable when asked of every candidate	

Keep in mind that laws in your state may vary from federal laws with regard to the appropriateness of some questions, and be sure to incorporate those requirements when asking questions that could be construed as discriminatory.

Asking Inappropriate Questions During an Interview

During an interview for a position as an executive assistant, the interviewer, a senior corporate executive, asked an applicant a series of personal questions:

Are you married?

Do you have any children?

Continues

> Are you planning to have any more children?
>
> Those questions made the candidate, a young woman with excellent qualifications for the position, very uncomfortable because she knew that what he asked was not related to the job requirements. As with many job seekers, she had to decide whether to answer the questions, to point out that the questions were inappropriate, or to refuse to provide the information—none of which were attractive options to her.
>
> She chose to answer the questions and provide the information that she was married and had two young children. She decided to ask the executive why he was asking for that information. When she did, he told her that he didn't think she had any business working and that she should be staying home with her children.
>
> The candidate was not offered the position. Although she simply chose to continue her job search elsewhere, this presented a clear case of gender discrimination at this company. Should she have chosen to do so, she could have filed a complaint with the EEOC or her state equal employment opportunity agency.

Preparing for the Interview

Prior to beginning the interview process, all interviewers should develop a strategy for conducting the interviews. This is done by reviewing the information available about each candidate, including cover letters, resumes, application forms, test results, and any other available information. During this review, the interviewers should make notes about areas that they want to explore in more depth with the candidate; for example, if there are gaps in employment, an interviewer would probably ask what the candidate was doing during that time. The interviewer will also decide what type of interview to conduct during this time. The following is a list of some of the more common interview types. Many effective interviewers ask several types of questions during an interview to obtain different types of information.

Behavioral interview   A *behavioral interview* asks questions that are designed to get candidates to pinpoint a situation that occurred in a prior position, describe the actions they took to handle it, and discuss the results that were achieved.

Directive interview   The interviewer controls a *directive interview* by asking a predetermined set of questions. In this type of interview, the same questions are asked of all candidates. This interview style allows candidate responses to be compared and evaluated easily because the same information is gathered.

Nondirective interview   In a *nondirective interview*, the interviewer asks broad questions and allows the candidate to choose how to answer them. Although this interview type produces in-depth information about each candidate's qualifications, it is more difficult to compare and evaluate candidates because the information gathered may vary greatly.

Patterned interview   Before conducting a *patterned interview*, the interviewer establishes broad areas that will be explored with each candidate. Although the same areas will be covered with each candidate, the specific questions may vary greatly between them.

Panel interview   In a *panel interview*, several interviewers interview candidates at the same time. This type of interview is an excellent way to train inexperienced interviewers. In addition, it ensures that all interviewers hear the same information and it provides an opportunity for them to follow up on questions asked by other members of the panel.

Stress interview   *Stress interviews* are most often conducted for jobs that involve duties or tasks involving a high level of stress on a regular basis, such as an air traffic controller or law enforcement officer. These interviews are designed to see how well candidates can "think on their feet" and respond rapidly to questions.

In addition to the type of interview that is conducted, interviewers should include both open-ended and close-ended questions during the course of the interviews. A *close-ended question* is one that is answered with a simple yes or no, or a fact. Two examples of a close-ended question are:

What was your salary when you left your last job?

Did you conduct screening interviews in your last job?

An *open-ended question* is one that invites the candidate to provide information. Good examples of open-ended question include two that are usually dreaded by applicants:

Tell me about yourself—what should I know about you?

What are your weaknesses?

This type of question places no restrictions on the information that candidates provide or how they present it. It also provides insight into the way candidates think about issues and view themselves.

Common Interview Biases

Although most people like to think that they are free from biases that affect their decision-making ability, there are a number of biases that can affect the interview process. Discussing these biases with the hiring manager and interview team before the interview process begins can help interviewers to understand when bias may be affecting the way the interviewer views the candidates. Let's take a look at some of the more common biases.

Central tendency bias   The *central tendency* bias is at work when the interviewer consistently ranks all candidates as equally qualified and cannot select one who is the best.

Contrast bias   The *contrast bias* occurs when interviewers base their evaluation of all candidates on how they compare to one who is particularly weak or particularly strong.

Cultural noise bias   The *cultural noise bias* occurs when candidates tell an interviewer what they think the interviewer wants to hear, and the interviewer accepts the information without asking more questions to determine whether the statements are accurate.

First impression bias   The *first impression bias* occurs when interviewers judge a candidate on an initial reaction. For example, a candidate who is late for the interview may be judged to be unreliable regardless of their qualifications and performance in the interview.

Halo/horn effect bias   The *halo/horn effect bias* occurs when a candidate has a single quality, good (halo) or bad (horn) that overshadows all other information the interviewer gathers during the interview. The interviewer in this case will give less weight to information that contradicts this one quality.

Nonverbal bias   A *nonverbal bias* becomes apparent if an interviewer judges a candidate based on body language; for example, if the candidate frowns while answering a question.

Recency bias   The *recency bias* is at work when the interviewer consistently thinks that the candidate most recently interviewed is the one most qualified.

Similar-to-me bias   The *similar-to-me bias* occurs when a candidate has something in common with the interviewer; for example, if they were born in the same town or both play soccer.

Stereotyping bias   The *stereotyping bias* occurs when the interviewer makes judgments about a candidate because the candidate belongs to a particular group. For example, an interviewer might believe that a woman cannot travel because she might have young children at home

Post-interview evaluation

After all candidates have been interviewed, the hiring manager must make a decision about which of them will be the best fit for the job that needs to be done. This process is simpler, of course, when only one interviewer is involved in the process. When an interview team is used, each interviewer needs to provide an

Real World Scenario

How Not to Conduct an Interview

During the dot-com boom, most of the companies in the Silicon Valley in California were desperate to find qualified employees. Often, people were hired without a clear idea of what they were going to be doing, no goals were set, and little communication occurred because hiring managers were too busy to provide basic information needed by new employees.

One organization I joined provided me with a case study in "how not to hire employees." A typical hiring scenario went something like this. One of the recruiters sourced potential candidates from Internet job boards, contacted them, and did a hard sell on the company—talking about how great a place it was to work and what a fabulous product was being developed. Interviews were set up, and when the candidates arrived they were given an interview schedule. (So far, so good.) Unfortunately, this was the first time the candidate learned that they would be meeting with four interviewers and that the interview was scheduled to last for at least four hours.

The interviewers, who were from different departments in the company, were given no information regarding the position or qualifications that were needed. In many cases, they had little interaction with the department into which the candidate was being hired. Few of them were experienced at interviewing and were given no training prior to meeting with candidates. They were given a copy of the candidate's resume, sometimes only a few minutes before they were to conduct the interview. In one case, the first person to interview a candidate began the interview by saying, "I have no idea why I'm even talking to you."

evaluation to the hiring manager. A candidate assessment information form, similar to the one illustrated previously, helps interviewers to provide their evaluations in a way that can be easily reviewed.

After a candidate has been selected, the HR practitioner conducts a background check to ensure that information provided by the candidate is accurate. This can be done either prior to making an offer to the candidate or by making the offer contingent upon successful completion of the reference check. There are three types of background checks generally conducted prior to employment: reference checks, criminal checks, and in some cases, polygraph tests. Let's examine each of these areas in more detail.

Reference checks   One of the best ways for employers to protect themselves from dishonest or even dangerous employees is to check the references provided by potential new hires. A reference check verifies the legitimacy of the information provided by the applicant on an employment application or resume.

Criminal checks   A criminal check is another way to screen potential employees to be certain that they are who they say they are and to protect other employees, customers, vendors, and others who visit the workplace. If, for example, the owner of a carpet-cleaning business finds that a potential new hire has been convicted of sexual assault and served time in prison for the crime, the owner might decide that this person would not be an appropriate hire for a position in which female customers, employees, or visitors might be placed at risk.

Polygraph tests   The Employee Polygraph Protection Act of 1988 prohibits the use of polygraph tests by private employers except under very limited circumstances. For example, candidates for positions as security guards, armored car personnel, or those with access to pharmaceutical products might be required to pass a polygraph test prior to employment. Applicants for positions in organizations with federal contracts or subcontracts with defense, national security, or federal law enforcement might also be required to pass a polygraph.

Employment Offers

Finally, the result of the recruiting process is the hiring of a new employee. It's important that the offer process be consistent with the employment brand and set the stage for welcoming the new employee to the organization. The initial offer may be made verbally, in person, or on the telephone. Once this verbal offer is accepted, a written offer containing the position title, the starting pay (expressed as an hourly wage or monthly salary), and the start date should be prepared immediately to solidify the agreement. For some positions at high levels in the organization, offers are made in the form of employment contracts, which are generally prepared by attorneys who specialize in employment law. In most cases, however, offers of employment are made in the form of offer letters.

As you might recall from Chapter 2, the common-law doctrine of employment-at-will states that either party may leave an employment relationship at any time, for any reason, with or without notice. This concept is important when writing offer letters because it is easy to unintentionally create an express contract if the letter is not worded properly. For this reason, it is a good idea to have a generic offer letter drafted by an attorney who specializes in employment law. This letter can be revised as needed for different positions. Any time the letter is revised to change the terms or conditions of employment to accommodate special circumstances for individual employees, it should be reviewed by an attorney to make sure the organization is not unnecessarily exposed to a legal claim.

If the organization is an at-will employer, the offer letter should contain a statement to that effect, along with a statement that all the terms and conditions of employment are contained in the letter. The statement should specify that any changes to the terms and conditions must be made in writing and signed by the CEO or someone designated by the CEO.

Depending on the position and on the organization, it might be appropriate for potential employees to sign a non-disclosure agreement (NDA) or an intellectual property agreement (IPA). These documents are prepared by attorneys and designed to protect the organization from the release, intentional or unintentional, of confidential information to anyone who doesn't have authority to see it. Information that is considered confidential includes such things as customer lists, inventions, software code, proprietary manufacturing processes, trade secrets, or financial information. NDAs and IPAs describe how long the information must be kept confidential, and often include a non-solicitation clause to prevent former employees from soliciting their co-workers to take jobs at a new company when they leave.

Finally, the offer letter should contain a statement of acceptance by the employee, and a place for the employee to sign, date, and return the offer letter. It's also important to include a statement to the effect that the offer must be accepted in writing and returned by a specific date or it will be automatically withdrawn.

Applicant Communications

Anyone who has ever looked for a job and gone through an interview process knows how frustrating it is during each step of the process. Often you find yourself wondering what is happening at the company, what kind of impression you made on the interviewers, and ultimately whether you will be selected for the position. Although it is not possible for an HR practitioner to provide as much feedback as candidates want to have, it is very appropriate to keep candidates who are still under consideration advised of the status of the decision-making process. Equally important is to let candidates who are no longer being considered know this so they can move their focus to other jobs in their search.

What benefits does an employer gain by including a process for communicating with applicants during a selection process? To begin with, applicants begin to form their impressions of what it would be like to work in the organization during the selection process. Treating all applicants with dignity and respect communicates a favorable impression of the organization to them. This favorable impression reinforces the positive employment brand that employers create to attract the best candidates to their organizations.

There are several points during the selection process that are appropriate for communicating with applicants:

- A simple acknowledgment that their resume or application form was received, and that they will be contacted if their qualifications meet the needs of the open position.
- When all candidate screening interviews are complete.

◆ Applicants who are called in to meet with hiring managers should be given an idea of how long the decision-making process will take.

◆ Finally, when the selection has been made, it is appropriate to contact the applicants who were not selected to thank them for their time and let them know another candidate was selected.

Candidates who are treated with respect will leave the process with a good impression of the organization, and you just never know when that will pay off for the business.

Employee Exit Procedures

There was a time when employees spent an entire career at a single company. Those days, as we all know, are gone and are not likely to return. An employee exit procedure can help to make the transition process go more smoothly for the organization, the team members who remain with the company, and the employee who is leaving the organization.

When employees resign, it is important that they provide a written and signed resignation notice to their direct supervisor. The supervisor informs the HR department, which sets the exit processes in motion.

One of the first decisions to be made is whether it is appropriate to make a counteroffer to the employee. There are many reasons that an organization might want to do this; for example, if the employee is one who consistently performs at a high level and brings value to the organization, it is appropriate to find out the reasons for the resignation. Perhaps there has been a misunderstanding with a supervisor, or maybe a company policy is making it difficult for the employee to maintain an acceptable balance between work and family commitments. When the reasons for the resignation are clear, the company can decide whether to change the circumstances that led to the resignation. Counteroffers should be made with caution, though: most of the time, an employee who resigns and is enticed to remain with the organization will leave within six months.

If it is determined that a counter offer is not to be considered, the next decision to make is whether the employee should continue to work through the notice period that is given. There is no right answer to this question because there are so many factors that must be considered. If the decision is made for the employee to leave on the day notice is given, the employer should pay the employee through the notice period that was provided. Depending on the state in which the organization is located, this may not be a legal requirement. It may be necessary based on past practices, or the organization may have established a pattern of doing so.

As soon as HR is aware of the resignation, notice of the employee's last day should be given to the finance, facilities, and IT departments. Each of these departments should review its records to determine whether there are any outstanding issues that must be resolved before the employee leaves. For example, if the employee has an unpaid payroll advance, loan, or other financial obligation to the company, arrangements must be made with the employee to repay the debt. Employers may not necessarily decide to just deduct the amount that is due from the final paycheck because this is prohibited in some states. If an employee agrees to have the funds withheld from the final paycheck, this agreement should be made in writing so that it is clear the employee was aware of and agreed to this arrangement. If the employee does not agree to have the funds withheld, the employer should prepare a promissory note, including a repayment schedule; if the employee defaults on the payments, the employer will need to seek recourse in small claims court.

In some states, employees must receive their final paychecks on their last day; in other states, the checks may be mailed within a defined period of time. In either case, HR should arrange for the final paycheck and review the amount to be paid with the employee to resolve any issues or questions before the employee leaves.

On the employee's last day, HR, IT, and/or the facilities department make arrangements with the employee to turn in any property that belongs to the organization, such as keys, equipment, uniforms, pagers, cell phones, laptop computers, credit cards, company vehicles, or other items. The IT and facilities departments also take steps to cancel access to the company network, voice mail and e-mail. Care should be given to make an appropriate announcement to the employee's coworkers and others with whom the employee was in contact on a regular basis. The work transition should be as smooth as possible while respecting the employee's privacy. This is particularly important when the employee is leaving involuntarily.

An important step in the exit process is the exit interview. (We'll talk more about exit interviews in Chapter 7, "Building the Communication Plan.") During this interview, employees are informed about benefit issues such as COBRA continuation or transferring their vested pension or 401(k) funds to private accounts. They should also be asked to verify a current mailing address for any future communications, such as W-2 forms or benefit change notices.

Administrative Responsibilities

All of the activities that take place in the staffing function generate mounds of paperwork, from applications to test results and new hire documents. This paperwork must be maintained to comply with various federal and state laws; the federal laws described in Chapter 2 that are related to records generated by the staffing process include Title VII, the ADA, the ADEA, the FLSA, the NLRA, and the Uniform Guidelines on Employee Selection Procedures. In Chapter 6, "Building the Employee Relations Program," I'll talk about where various records should be kept and who should have access to them; for now, Table 3.4 provides a list of key documents that are collected as a result of staffing activities.

Table 3.4   Staffing Record Retention Requirements

Record or Document	Retention Period	Covered Employers
Job announcements, advertisements, job orders sent to agencies or unions	2 years	15+ employees
Name, address, social security number, gender, date of birth, occupation, job classification	5 years	All employers
Records of all employment actions: employment applications, resumes, hire, re-hire, layoffs, recalls, terminations, promotions, demotions, transfers, compensation, selection for training programs	1 year	15+ employees
Apprentice selection records	1 year	15+ employees
Pre-employment records for temp positions	1 year	20+ employees
Temporary employee records	90 days	20+ employees
Employment test results	1 year	20+ employees
Physical examination results	1 year	20+ employees
Written training agreements, job and selection criteria, records of minority and female applicants	1 year	All employers
I-9 signed by employee and employer	3 years from hire date or 1 year after termination, whichever is longer	4+ employees
Individual employment contracts	3 years	All employers
Certificate of Age	Until termination	All employers
Applicant race and sex	2 years	15+ employees
Employee race and sex	2 years	15+ employees
Veteran status	2 years	15+ employees
Disability status	2 years	15+ employees
W-4 form	2 years	All employers

Metrics

As mentioned at the beginning of this chapter, it is important for HR practitioners to provide metrics that demonstrate the effectiveness of HRM programs. Several standard metrics provide useful information of staffing effectiveness, including replacement cost, cost-per-hire, time to fill, time to start, and yield ratios.

The costs to replace employees include those that are easily measured, such as those related to advertising and posting jobs, recruiter fees or salaries, time spent in interviewing candidates, expenses for temporary employees who fill in during the search process, training, and loss of productivity.

Cost-per-hire is calculated by collecting data for all relevant costs, such as those related to the sourcing and interviewing process, testing expenses, recruiter salaries or fees, travel expenses and relocation costs. The total costs are then divided by the number of employees hired to obtain the average cost-per-hire.

The time to fill a position is determined by counting the number of days between the date approval for filling the position was received and the date an offer was accepted. The time to start metric counts the days between approval and the new employee's first day on the job. Depending on your organization's needs, one or both of these measures may be appropriate.

Finally, yield ratios are used to measure the effectiveness of the recruiting process itself. This is useful in determining if the dollars spent on different recruiting methods are producing a sufficient number of qualified applicants. Some of the most common yield ratios include the number of qualified applicants divided by the number of total applicants, the number of offers made divided by the number of qualified applicants, and the number of offers accepted divided by the number of offers made.

Terms to Know

alternative staffing methods	cost-benefit analysis
employment brand	essential functions
job analysis	job competencies
job description	job specifications
knowledge, skills, and abilities (KSAs)	staffing plan

Review Questions

1. What arguments can you use to convince management of the necessity for a staffing plan?

2. What information can you obtain with a turnover analysis?

3. Describe the importance of job descriptions and how they are used in organizations.

4. What is an essential job function and why is it important?

5. What are job competencies?

6. What are the methods used to obtain information during a job analysis?

7. Why should physical and mental requirements be included on a job description?

8. How can an employer benefit from developing an employment brand?

9. What are alternative staffing methods?

10. What is the difference between an open-ended and a close-ended question? When is each appropriate?

Chapter 4

Building the Compensation Plan

In This Chapter

- Compensation strategy
- Elements of compensation plans
- Elements of benefit plans
- Methods for determining job worth
- Administration of compensation and benefit programs
- Metrics to evaluate the effectiveness of compensation plans

Although some employees think of compensation as simply the cash compensation they receive in the form of salaries or wages, cash is only part of the story. Compensation includes direct compensation, the cash employees receive in their paychecks, and indirect compensation, which includes a wide variety of benefits. This chapter provides you with an overview of these elements, how organizations use them to incent and retain employees, and how the appropriate level of compensation for various jobs is determined.

In this chapter, you'll learn about the various elements of compensation used by organizations to attract candidates and retain employees. We'll also look at how an organization's compensation strategies can further its strategic goals.

Compensation Strategy

As we discussed in Chapter 1, "The Human Resource Profession," a strategy is simply a plan for achieving goals. As with other HRM strategies, the compensation strategy must contribute to and support the ability of the organization to meet its goals by attracting and retaining qualified employees.

NOTE — To simplify things for discussion purposes, I'll be using only the term "HR practitioner" throughout this chapter. In reality, many large organizations employ compensation specialists to develop and manage this function. In smaller organizations, the compensation function may be managed by HR generalists, with or without the assistance of consultants.

Development of a compensation strategy begins with a clear understanding of the organization's goals and objectives. (This topic is covered in detail in Chapter 10, "Strategic Human Resource Management.") Based on this information, it is possible to devise a compensation strategy that includes the following elements:

◆ Compensation philosophy

◆ Financial constraints

◆ Total reward program

◆ Structure for administering pay

Determining the appropriate amount of compensation for different jobs is one of the most important responsibilities of a human resource management (HRM) program. Many factors must be considered when determining what is appropriate—getting it wrong can have serious implications for an organization, impacting the morale of the employee population as well as the organization's ability to hire and retain qualified employees. Qualified and motivated employees play a major role in an organization's ability to produce its goods and services and earn a profit, so attracting and retaining them is crucial for success. Decisions made about compensation and benefit issues affect other functional areas of the total HRM plan as well. There is significant interaction between the performance management plan and compensation in many organizations, particularly when salary increases are based on an employee's level of performance.

Compensation Philosophy

An effective compensation philosophy reflects an organization's structure and culture. Although there are probably as many compensation philosophies as there are organizations, for the most part they fall into one of two categories: those based on entitlement and those that reward performance.

Real World Scenario

The Importance of Compensation Strategy

By Marilyn Evans, CCP

- ◆ Focuses employees on the achievement of both individual and corporate objectives

- ◆ Focuses employees on developing and maintaining skills that drive results and ensure corporate bench strength

- ◆ Attracts and retains key talent

- ◆ Facilitates organizational change, evolution, and innovation

- ◆ Drives desired behaviors

- ◆ Manages and rewards performance

- ◆ Supports integrated strategies in other HR functions such as staffing, career development, and safety

- ◆ Manages fixed and variable compensation costs

An *entitlement philosophy* rewards employees based on their length of service. This philosophy can be found in union environments in which wage increases are based on seniority; and in public organizations such as federal, state, and local governments. For many years, this philosophy was prevalent in businesses throughout the United States, but it has been replaced by many organizations in recent years with a philosophy that ties performance to pay.

A *performance-based philosophy* is one that rewards employees based on the level of contribution they make toward the achievement of individual, business unit, or organizational goals. Depending on the mix of direct and indirect components included in the plan, performance-based compensation can be used to shape employee performance and guide employees to produce results that the organization has identified. This compensation philosophy has been adopted by an increasing number of organizations, driven largely by the need to operate more efficiently in a global business environment.

entitlement philosophy
An entitlement philosophy is one in which salary and promotion decisions are based on length of service; this philosophy is exemplified by a union environment.

performance-based philosophy
A performance-based philosophy is one in which salary increases and promotions are awarded to those employees who contribute to the achievement of organization goals.

Many factors are considered when making the decision about which of these approaches best meets the needs of a particular organization. Some of these factors can be revealed by answers to the following questions:

♦ What is the culture of the organization? Is it very hierarchical? Are there many layers? Is there a rigid chain of command or is it a team-based culture with few layers of management? How open are the communications? How much input do employees have in making decisions about the work they do? It is critical that the compensation philosophy reflect, and be in alignment with, this culture.

♦ What are the goals of the compensation plan? Does the organization want to reward the highest-performing individuals with higher incentives, thus encouraging employees to produce better results? If so, how will the performance be measured?

♦ How does the organization rank the value of different jobs internally to ensure that the compensation program is viewed as equitable by employees?

♦ Does the organization have a clear understanding of what it must do to ensure that its compensation and benefit programs comply with the applicable federal, state, and local statutes?

♦ Finally, what steps will be taken to ensure that the compensation plan is easily understood by employees and cost-effective to be administered?

The insights provided by the answers to these and similar questions form the basis of the compensation philosophy. The philosophy statement provides a guideline for HR practitioners to follow in developing the rest of the compensation strategy.

Financial Constraints

A key consideration for development of an organization's compensation strategy is an analysis of its ability to pay. Based on the answers to the questions in the previous section, the leaders of an organization may want to attract employees with the highest levels of skill by paying higher base salaries than other businesses competing for the same employees. Doing this requires that the organization have the necessary financial resources. If the resources are not available, alternative methods of paying employees must be developed. For example, the organization can tie part of the total compensation package to performance goals with the use of incentive pay. In this way, the employees who make the greatest contribution to achieving goals receive the largest rewards.

Another factor that must be considered here is the labor market. If there are only a limited number of individuals who possess the skills needed by the organization and there is a high demand for the same skills in other organizations, competition for individuals with those skills increases the cost of hiring them. There are three ways in which organizations can look at labor markets in terms of pay: leading the market, meeting the market, or lagging the market. An organization that wants to *lead the market* provides higher compensation than its competitors do for the same skills. An organization that wants to *meet the market* pays the same as its competitors. In some cases, it may be possible for the organization to attract the employees it needs with sufficient skill levels by *lagging the market*, or paying less than the competition.

When financial resources are tight, organizations may find it necessary to lead the market for those skills critical to its success, while they meet or lag the market for skills that are less critical to its success or more available in the labor market. Under these circumstances, the value of other aspects of a total rewards program can be emphasized to attract and retain employees.

Total Rewards

Each organization selects components for its compensation package that it believes will achieve the results it desires. In very small organizations, this may be accomplished with the use of only the *total compensation* component of a reward program: the cash compensation that is paid to employees. Very large organizations, on the other hand, may find it beneficial to develop different compensation packages for different job categories. The most common examples of this are sales teams and executives. Because it is easy to track how many sales are produced by each salesperson, the direct relationship between sales made and compensation earned is clear, so establishing incentive pay for increased sales is a proven method of motivating the sales team. Executive compensation packages are often tied to company performance, such as increased stock prices, net profits, or other quantifiable measures; and they can include a wide variety of special benefits, known as *perquisites*, (also known as executive perks) that are not made available to the general employee population. Some examples of perquisites include first-class travel arrangements for business trips, the use of a company jet, additional vacation time, or club memberships.

A *total rewards* program includes all the methods (cash, equity, and benefits) used by employers to pay employees for the work they provide for the organization. An effective total rewards package includes a variety of components that attract and retain employees who have skills needed by the organization. Because

total compensation
Total compensation includes all types of direct cash compensation employees receive.

total rewards
Total rewards include monetary compensation (direct and indirect) and nonmonetary compensation.

people have different needs, based on their individual circumstances, the components included in the package should be sufficiently varied to address the different requirements of people at different stages in their lives. For example, employees with young children may be looking for benefits that help them raise their children, such as day care or time off to attend school activities. On the other hand, employees with older children may be attracted by benefits that help them pay for college.

To fully define a compensation strategy, it is important to know what elements are available for inclusion in a total rewards package. These elements fall into two basic categories: monetary compensation and nonmonetary compensation. The full package offered by an organization, which is known as a total rewards program, includes elements from both categories. Let's now take a look at what is included in each of these categories.

direct compensation
Direct compensation includes salaries or wages, incentive awards, bonus payments, sales commissions, and other monetary compensation paid directly to employees.

Monetary compensation   The term monetary compensation is used to describe compensation for which the organization expends funds. It includes payments made directly to employees as well as benefits the company pays on behalf of its employees. There are two forms of monetary compensation: direct and indirect. *Direct compensation* refers to salaries or wages, incentive awards, bonus payments, and sales commissions. *Indirect compensation* refers to benefits provided by organizations, such as medical and dental insurance, workers' compensation, mandated benefits such as Social Security and Medicare, and retirement plans, among others. Another term that is sometimes used when referring to monetary compensation is *remuneration*.

indirect compensation
Indirect compensation is a type of monetary compensation that consists of benefits paid by the organization on behalf of employees, such as medical insurance, workers' compensation, or mandated benefits.

Nonmonetary compensation   Nonmonetary compensation includes aspects of working in a particular organization that are unique and beneficial for employees and can be an important factor in attracting and retaining them. Many facets of the work environment can be included in this category, such as a location that is within walking distance of public transportation or free parking for employees. Other, less-common benefits that improve employee work-life balance can be placed in this category as well, such as telecommuting or flex time arrangements. Because many of these nonmonetary benefits are related to the organization's culture, Chapter 6, "Building the Employee Relations Program," will discuss them in greater detail.

Now that you have an idea of the basic categories for compensation elements, let's take a look at some specific examples of direct and indirect compensation. The following illustration shows the total direct compensation formula:

> *Annual Base Salary*
> *+ Variable Pay (e.g., bonus, incentives, and commissions)*
> **= Total Cash Compensation**
>
> + Equity (e.g., stock options)
> **= Total Direct Compensation**
>
> + Employee Stock Purchase Plans
> + Health & Welfare Benefits
> + Retirement Programs (e.g., 401K)
> **= Total Remuneration**

Courtesy of Marilyn Evans, CCP

Direct Compensation

Most employees are very familiar with some types of direct compensation because they receive paychecks on a regular basis. Direct pay can be made in various forms, which are described in the following sections.

Base pay　The form of compensation with which virtually all employees are familiar is base pay, which is the basic form of compensation employees receive in exchange for the work they do for the employer. The amount of base pay that specific jobs are worth is based on external factors such as the labor market, and on internal factors such as how much value the employer places on the job in relation to other jobs in the organization.

Variable pay　It is becoming increasingly common for employers to provide at least some compensation that is tied to specific performance goals. This is known is *variable pay*. Variable pay includes sales commissions, bonuses (one-time payments that are unrelated to base pay), and incentives. Incentives, which come in many forms, are designed to reinforce behavior or activities that the employer wants to encourage.

Equity　Sharing equity with employees provides benefits to them as well as to employers because it provides them with a feeling of ownership in the company. This is important because, in many cases, employees who are also owners have a greater interest in seeing the company meet its goals and succeed in the marketplace. As a result, employees are more likely to view their individual interests from the point of view of what is best for the employer and not solely from their interests as individuals.

variable pay
Variable pay is tied to specific performance goals and includes sales commissions, bonuses, and incentives.

All equity plans provide methods of conveying ownership in the company to individuals. This ownership can be done through by incorporating a stock option plan, by awarding stock to employees directly, or by establishing a plan that allows employees to purchase stock at preferred rates.

Direct compensation, then, consists of elements that provide employees with some form of cash compensation. Indirect compensation, on the other hand, includes benefits that the company pays on behalf of its employees. Let's examine now some of the different kinds of indirect compensation that are provided by employers.

 Real World Scenario

Using Direct Compensation to Reward Performance

By Marilyn Evans, CCP

Variable compensation (incentives/bonuses/commissions) is defined as a lump sum payment in addition to annual base salary for performance against objectives over a specific period of time. Payments are typically calculated as either a percent of annual base salary or a percent of generated revenue, profits, sales, etc.; and can be paid out annually, quarterly, or monthly. Typical variable compensation plan objectives include:

◆ Recognize and reward performance that has a direct impact on company business.

◆ Reinforce behavior and results that consistently support the company's strategy and objectives.

◆ Increase productivity, sales, profit, market share, etc.

◆ Reinforce the link between individual, team/unit, and/or corporate performance.

Equity plans exist to share company ownership with employees and might have the following objectives:

◆ Align employee and shareholder interests.

◆ Create employee long-term capital accumulation vehicle.

◆ Provide an incentive for a longer-term business focus.

◆ Directly link company and employee success.

◆ Foster employee ownership culture.

◆ Retain key employee talent and skills.

Indirect Compensation

There are many forms of indirect compensation, but the most common are known as employee health and welfare benefits. These benefits include various forms of insurance and retirement options that employers provide as part of a total rewards package. Some of the benefits employers provide are mandated by federal or state laws or regulations, and include such things as Social Security, unemployment insurance, workers' compensation, and COBRA health continuation rights. (These benefits were discussed in Chapter 2, "Legal Requirements and Record Retention.") All other benefits are provided voluntarily, which means that individual employers can select benefits that will attract and retain individuals who are most likely to have the skills they need to achieve their goals. For the most part, health and welfare benefits fall into five categories: health care, insurance, work-life balance, time off, and retirement. Table 4.1 displays some of the more common benefits in each of these categories, along with some common benefits that don't fall into one of these categories.

Table 4.1   Types of Benefits

Category	Benefit	Mandated or Voluntary
Health care	COBRA benefit continuation	Mandated
	Dental insurance	Voluntary
	HIPAA portability rights	Mandated
	Medical insurance	Voluntary
	Mental health benefits	Voluntary
	Prescription drug coverage	Voluntary
	Vision care	Voluntary
	Wellness programs	Voluntary
Insurance	Life insurance	Voluntary
	Long-term disability insurance	Voluntary
	Prepaid legal insurance	Voluntary
	Short-term disability insurance	Voluntary
	Unemployment insurance	Mandated
	Workers' compensation	Mandated
Work-life balance	Adoption benefits	Voluntary
	Dependent care assistance	Voluntary

Table 4.1 Types of Benefits *(continued)*

Category	Benefit	Mandated or Voluntary
	Employee assistance plans	Voluntary
	Flextime	Voluntary
	Gym memberships	Voluntary
	Job sharing	Voluntary
	Onsite child care facilities	Voluntary
	Telecommuting	Voluntary
Time off	Bereavement leave	Voluntary
	Family and Medical Leave Act	Mandated
	Meal periods	Voluntary*
	Paid holidays	Voluntary
	Paid rest breaks	Voluntary*
	Paid sick leave	Voluntary
	Paid vacation leave	Voluntary
Retirement	401(k) plans	Voluntary
	Early retirement programs	Voluntary
	Individual Retirement Accounts (IRAs)	Voluntary
	Pension plans	Voluntary
	Social Security	Mandated
	Medicare	Mandated
Other benefits	Credit union membership	Voluntary
	Educational assistance	Voluntary
	Onsite cafeteria	Voluntary
	Onsite fitness facilities	Voluntary

*These benefits are voluntary according to the federal Fair Labor Standards Act, but may be mandated by state laws. Be sure to check with your state employment agency or your employment attorney to find out what is required for your organization

Framework for Administering Compensation

The final element of a compensation strategy is the framework that allows the plan to be administered fairly, equitably, and in the way in which organization leaders designed it. Generally, compensation administration includes the following elements:

- Job descriptions
- Job evaluation
- Pay grades
- Pay ranges
- Wage and salary guidelines
- Communication plan

The work of administering compensation is a function of the operational role of the HR department and is discussed in the following section.

Operational Responsibilities

Developing a strategy that is tied to organization goals is only the first step in building a compensation program—the next step is to administer it. Chapter 3, "Building a Staffing Plan," contains a detailed discussion for the first element of a compensation administration program: the development of job descriptions. I'll just say here that those descriptions provide the basis for the next element of the program: job evaluation. The information gathered as a result of the evaluation of the jobs in an organization is the basis for the third element of the program: creation of the pay grades and ranges.

In the fourth element of the compensation administration program, wage and salary guidelines are established to ensure that compensation decisions throughout an organization are made based on the same criteria; for example, the guidelines may provide parameters for line managers to use when calculating a salary increase for an employee who is promoted. This helps to ensure that employees in similar jobs with similar levels of skill and experience are paid equitably, even when they have different managers and work in different business units.

Finally, it is crucial to the success of the compensation strategy that all employees who are affected by it, and that would be all employees in the organization, clearly understand how it works. Let's take a closer look now at these elements of compensation administration.

Job Evaluation

The *goal* of job evaluation is a simple one: to determine the value of each job to the organization. The *process* of job evaluation is not so simple. Very often, the determination must be made to some degree based on subjective judgments of the HR practitioners conducting the evaluation. Job evaluation can also become a political process when line managers insist that jobs in their departments are worth more to the organization than similar jobs in other departments. To the extent that it is possible, the job evaluation process seeks to eliminate the subjectivity of the process and reduce the politics involved by providing quantitative justification for the results. A key element in doing this is to keep in mind that the process is designed to evaluate the *job*, not the *person in the job*. Job worth is based on two factors:

Internal equity   The value of the job to the organization relative to other jobs

External equity   The value of the job in the marketplace

Internal Equity

The starting point for determining *internal equity* is the job description, which contains a list of the specific duties of the position; the knowledge, skills, and abilities (KSAs) that are necessary to perform the duties; and an assessment of the difficulty level of the job. With this information, HR practitioners can determine the worth of jobs to the organization. The three methods most commonly used to determine internal equity are described in the following sections.

internal equity
Internal equity places a value on the worth of each job to the company. This value is based on the content of the job, its level of responsibility, and how much impact the decisions in the job have on organization results.

Job ranking   Job ranking is the simplest method for determining internal job worth. It involves placing the jobs in order from the one with the highest value to the organization to the one with the lowest value. The ranking method is most useful in smaller organizations because it is easier to make this evaluation when only a few jobs are involved; the more jobs involved, the more difficult it becomes to do this in a meaningful way. Even though this method is effective in determining the relative value of jobs to each other, it does not provide information about how much more valuable one job is than another as is possible with other evaluation methods. This is probably the most subjective method of job evaluation.

Job classification   The classification method places jobs in salary grades by matching the duties in the job description to a broad description, or criterion, for each salary grade. The criterion used to make this determination varies; some commonly used in different organizations include such things as the level of education and experience required to do the job, the use of independent judgment in performing tasks, the level of complexity of the job, the responsibility or scope of the position, and the impact that errors made in the position could have on the organization. As an example, an organization may decide to measure the value of its jobs based on the impact of errors that could be made by an incumbent. The criteria could be as follows:

Level 1: Minimal organizational impact

Level 2: Impact limited to work group

Level 3: Impact affects business unit or function

Level 4: Moderate, organization-wide impact

Level 5: Severe, organization-wide impact

In most cases, the descriptions would, of course, be more detailed and designed to meet the specific needs of a particular organization.

Because the classification method ties the value measurement to a salary grade, there is often a great deal of political pressure from business unit managers to place jobs in a higher classification than may be warranted for reasons unrelated to the true value of the job. This pressure also makes the classification method somewhat subjective.

Point method   One of the most commonly used methods of job evaluation is known as the point method. This method relies on the use of compensable factors, various aspects of work that are common to a group of jobs. These factors are identified, and degrees of difficulty are defined based on the value they contribute to the organization. Some factors can be used for all jobs in the organization, such as education, experience, skills required, level of responsibility, and working conditions. Other factors will be unique to specific groups of jobs, depending on the particular needs of the organization. The factors are then weighted, with the greatest weight placed on factors that are considered the most important within the job group. Next, points are assigned to each degree of difficulty for each of the factors. The jobs are evaluated, and a point total is calculated. After all the jobs have been evaluated, and point totals have been calculated, they are grouped together based on the total number of points and placed in salary grades.

One major advantage of the point method is that it separates decisions about the value of jobs to the organization from wage and salary decisions. This makes it less subjective than either the ranking or classification methods.

External Equity

External equity is used to compare the jobs in an organization to the same or similar jobs in other organizations to find out how much they are worth in the labor market. This is determined by comparing the job description for each job with the descriptions for jobs in other organizations to make sure they have the same or similar duties, and then determining how much those jobs are worth, on average, to the other organizations. This is done by conducting a salary survey, which is a method of collecting salary data about jobs from organizations in similar industries or within defined geographical areas to find out how much specific jobs are worth in the labor market.

There are a number of consulting firms that conduct salary surveys. These surveys can be purchased, or they may be available free or at a discount if your organization participates in the survey. Depending on the type of job you are evaluating, surveys may be available for your local geographic area or industry; or for specific professions, such as engineering, marketing, or sales.

There are many jobs that are found in all organizations and industries. These positions include accountants, administrative assistants, and (of course) human resource professionals, among others. These jobs are known as benchmark positions because they are so common and it is easy to find survey data for them. Collecting salary data about benchmark positions is the first step in the job evaluation process.

A mistake commonly made by those unfamiliar with salary surveys is comparing salary data based on a job title without referring to the job description in the survey. Comparing jobs based only on their titles can be a problem because titles mean different things in different organizations. In a very large organization, for example, an HR Director performs duties and has responsibilities that are very different from an HR Director in a small organization. Using the survey description to determine the appropriate level for comparison results in survey data that is more relevant to the evaluation process.

external equity
External equity compares jobs in the organization to other similar jobs in other organizations to make sure that the organization's wages and salaries are sufficient to attract the qualified employees it needs.

Creating Pay Grades and Ranges

The information gathered in the job evaluation process provides the basis for developing pay grades and ranges.

Pay Grades

After jobs have been evaluated based on the method selected by the organization, and salary data has been collected for benchmark positions, pay grades can be developed. Pay grades group together jobs that the organization has determined to be of relatively equal value. For example, an accounts payable coordinator and a marketing coordinator may be placed in the same pay grade based on the results of the job evaluation. Even if the type of work performed by each position is very different, the services provided by both jobs can be viewed as equally important to the organization.

Determining the number of grades to use depends on several factors, including the size of the organization and how much difference there is between the lowest-paid job and the highest-paid job.

Pay Ranges

After the organization has established pay grades based on the results of the job evaluation, a pay range for each grade can be calculated. The range should be broad enough to allow for salary growth as employees become more proficient at their jobs. The salary data gathered from surveys provides the information needed to establish the midpoint of the range. Earlier in this chapter, we talked about the concept of leading, matching, or lagging the labor market. The decision made about which of these philosophies will be followed during the development of the compensation strategy determines the midpoint of the range. Let's illustrate how this can work for a retail sales position.

Real World Scenario

Setting the Midpoint of the Salary Range

Survey data indicates that retail sales clerks in Kansas City earn $11.25 per hour. An upscale department store is opening a new store in town and wants to attract the most qualified sales personnel for this store, so it decides to lead the market by paying its sales staff 30 percent above the market. As a result, the midpoint of the range is $14.50, which is what the department store will pay to fully qualified sales representatives.

Another retail store in the same area attracts customers with low prices, so the owners want to keep costs as low as possible. They don't mind high turnover because there are always plenty of applicants for open positions. This store decided that it wants to lag the market by 15 percent, so it sets the midpoint of the range for its sales staff at $9.57 per hour.

After the midpoint of the range is set, the low and high ends are calculated. In the preceding example of the retail sales staff, the upscale store has decided that it wants a range of 35 percent so that employees who perform well can be rewarded with salary increases. The low end of the range will be 17.5 percent lower than the midpoint, or $12.00 per hour; the high end of the range will be 17.5 percent above the midpoint, or $17.00 per hour.

Traditionally, salary ranges have been narrowly defined as a reflection of the hierarchical organization structures. So after a certain point, an employee would need to be promoted to a job in the next salary grade to receive a pay increase. In addition, the range structure provides employees with a clear picture of possible career growth opportunities. In recent years, due to the flattening of organizations and emphasis on teams and workgroups, a new way of looking at salary ranges, broadbanding, has become popular. As its name implies, a broad-band salary range is wider than a traditional salary range and better supports rapidly changing business conditions. With broadbanding, an organization might have very few ranges (as few as perhaps four or five for the entire organization). When it is necessary to change direction in response to new market opportunities, the thinking is that a broadband salary structure allows employees to be redirected without the need for a new job evaluation to be done for the change in duties.

Wage and Salary Guidelines

After the salary structure of pay grades and ranges is determined, guidelines need to be established to ensure that wage and salary decisions are made equitably throughout the organization. While job evaluation focuses on the value of the *job* to the organization, wage and salary guidelines focus on the value of *individual contributions* to the job. There are several concepts important to establishing wage and salary guidelines.

Compa-ratios   A compa-ratio is a simple calculation used to determine where an individual's salary falls in the range. This is useful information for managers to have when they are conducting performance appraisals and when determining the appropriate amount of a salary increase. Compa-ratios are expressed as a percentage of the midpoint of the salary range and are calculated by dividing the individual's pay by the midpoint of the range.

Using the preceding example of the sales representative, we can calculate the compa-ratio for two employees: Employee A will be paid $13.75 per hour and Employee B will be paid $15.25.

Employee A: $13.75 ÷ $14.50 = .95

Employee B: $15.25 ÷ $14.50 = 1.06

A compa-ratio of 1.0 represents an employee who is fully qualified for the job. Employees who have less experience or whose skills are not fully developed are generally paid less than the mid-point of the range. Those who are experienced and have demonstrated a high level of proficiency on the job will be paid above the midpoint, and the compa-ratio will be greater than 1.0.

red-circle rate
A red-circle rate occurs when a job incumbent makes more than the maximum of the salary range.

Red-circle rates   There are times when employees will be placed in a salary range even if the amount of pay they are earning exceeds the high point of the range. This is known as a *red-circle rate*, which can occur for many different reasons, including situations in which jobs are eliminated due to a layoff and employees are moved into lower-paying jobs. When this occurs, the pay for employees is frozen until the range is increased or until they are promoted into positions in a higher salary range.

Green-circle rates   *Green-circle rates* occur when employees are being paid less than the low end of the salary range. This can occur for several reasons. Two of the most common are that the ranges are periodically adjusted for changes in the labor market and a less-experienced employee who was at the low end of the range is now below the range. Another circumstance in which this sometimes occurs is when an employee is hired as a trainee and must learn the skills needed for the job. In either case, adjustments can be made to bring affected employees into the range at a compa-ratio that is appropriate to their performance.

green-circle rates
A green-circle rate refers to a job incumbent whose salary falls below the minimum of the range for the salary grade.

Communication Plan

Finally, now that the organization has a compensation plan that is fair, equitable and designed to elicit the best performance from its employees, employees need to be made aware of how decisions about their pay are to be made. When the organization is open and honest about the way in which pay decisions are made, employees are more likely to believe that they are being treated fairly. In Chapter 7, "Building the Communication Plan," we'll talk about some strategies for developing communication plans that accomplish this goal.

 *Real World Scenario*

A Company's Total Rewards Strategy and Philosophy Guides How Employees Are Compensated

By Marilyn Evans, CCP

A company's statement of its philosophy and strategy for rewarding employees addresses four key questions:

Compensation Plan Objectives   What do we want our plan to achieve? Such as

◆ Employees who consistently perform in a manner that supports company objectives and shareholder interests

◆ Competitive total compensation opportunities that attract and retain talent

◆ A direct link between business results and individual performance and rewards

◆ A competitive salary structure to guide logical and cost-effective pay decisions

Target Market Position   How much do we want, or can we afford, to pay? This states the target market position of the company's total rewards program within the appropriate competitive labor market(s), for example, "Our total compensation (base salary, incentives and stock) is above the market average (or 50th percent) for the software products/services industry."

Continues

Plan Components   What combination of cash, equity, and benefits shall we use to deliver compensation to our employees?

Guiding Principles   How will we administer pay? For example:

◆ Balance performance measures between company and individual measures commensurate with position role and responsibilities

◆ Reward positions with direct impact on company success with team and/or corporate-based incentives (e.g., executives)

◆ Opportunities to increase compensation will be a function of BOTH external market rates and internal position responsibilities

◆ Increases to employee base salaries will reflect individual performance and external market rates

Administrative Responsibilities

The administrative responsibilities of the compensation function involve HR practitioners in determining budget processes, coordinating with the payroll function, maintaining records from the performance appraisal process, and administering the organization's benefit programs.

In many industries, compensation and benefit costs represent the bulk of an organization's operating expenses. With the costs of medical insurance plans rising exponentially each year, establishing a control mechanism to hold the line on costs is essential. This control mechanism, the budget, requires the managers of individual business units to project what they think it will cost to operate their units during the next year. HRM participates in this process by providing data for salary projections based on surveys conducted during the job evaluation process. HRM also projects the cost of the company's benefit package for the next year and analyzes the information to determine whether changes to the benefit package are needed to control costs.

Another crucial administrative function for compensation is ensuring that information about changes to employee pay is communicated to the payroll department. This coordination of information is necessary to ensure that employees receive the pay that is due to them. As part of this function, HRM maintains records about pay decisions, which include information about how the pay decisions were made as well as documents about individual pay changes. For companies that base their pay decisions on the result of a performance appraisal process, maintaining records includes making sure that copies of employee appraisals are maintained in employee personnel files.

One of the most time-consuming responsibilities in this area is benefits administration. Whether this task is performed internally or is outsourced to a company specializing in this area, HRM is the place employees turn to when they have problems with benefit providers. This task may require multiple phone calls, e-mails, or letters before a resolution is reached, so benefit administration can take up a large part of an HR practitioner's time. If this function is done internally, it's a good idea to have a benefit broker who represents the organization's interests with the providers to facilitate the process.

The administration of compensation and benefit programs is one of the most highly visible functions in any organization because it impacts every employee. If a wage increase or bonus is not processed correctly, or if the employee's 401(k) contribution is not correct, it is usually noticed right away. This is one area of HRM that can serve to build credibility for HR practitioners when performed accurately. It is also one of the easiest ways to lose credibility, particularly when errors affect top executives. So, although it can be tedious work, it is crucial to the livelihoods of employees and their families.

Metrics

Compensation is one of the areas of HRM that lends itself to immediate feedback on whether or not it is working—when the HR team conducts a search for candidates to fill a job opening and it does not produce qualified candidates, one of the factors that must be considered is whether the amount of pay being offered is sufficient to attract candidates with the skills the employer is seeking.

Another indicator of the viability of the compensation system is how well it is being administered by managers. One means of measuring this is to calculate compa-ratios for employees in the same job categories to determine whether the level of skill and experience the organization seeks to attract is being compensated in line with the compensation strategy.

In addition, the results of annual performance appraisals can be presented in a chart or graph and compared to targets set by management to determine whether the process is being uniformly and fairly implemented by management.

Terms to Know

direct compensation	entitlement philosophy
external equity	green-circle rates
indirect compensation	internal equity
performance-based philosophy	red-circle rate
total compensation	total rewards
variable pay	

Review Questions

1. What is the purpose of a compensation strategy?

2. What is a performance-based compensation philosophy?

3. What is a total rewards program?

4. What is indirect compensation?

5. How are job descriptions used in the compensation function?

6. Why are wage and salary guidelines important to the compensation plan?

7. How is job worth determined?

8. What is the point method?

9. What are the limitations of the ranking method?

10. Why is the midpoint of the salary range important?

Chapter 5

Building a Safe and Secure Workplace

Employer concern for the work environment developed for the most part only after legislation establishing workplace safety standards was enacted in 1970. The Occupational Safety and Health Act (OSH Act) affects virtually every business in the United States. Congress intended it to reduce the occurrence of workplace injuries, illnesses, and deaths and created the Occupational Safety and Health Administration (OSHA) to develop and enforce standards to accomplish this goal.

This chapter describes some of the issues employers face in providing a hazard-free workplace, how employers benefit from workplace safety, and OSHA requirements.

Strategic Foundation

Although most people agree that a healthful, safe, and secure work environment benefits employees, some business owners question how this environment contributes to the achievement of corporate goals. They argue that the cost of improving health and safety adds no value to the bottom line; instead, it has the opposite effect of making it more difficult to compete in world markets by increasing product costs. The answer to this argument is that occupational health, safety, and security programs make significant contributions to the achievement of corporate goals by reducing costs related to absenteeism and workers' compensation, building good will in the community, protecting assets, and improving productivity.

While it can be difficult to measure how much money individual employers save, the implementation of safety and health standards reduces accidents and illnesses, which reduces the amount of production time lost. This increases productivity, which means that it costs less to produce products or services for customers. Cost savings are also realized when fewer claims for workers' compensation insurance premiums are filed. Fewer injuries and illnesses lead to improved productivity and employee morale. Finally, the cost of penalties and fines is substantial: in 2003, OSHA levied fines totaling more than $82,000,000 against employers who did not comply with established standards.

Employee relations is another area in which a safe and secure workplace adds value for employers. When employees feel safe at work, they are likely to be more productive and engaged. Because safety concerns are a major motivating factor in unionization attempts, businesses that provide a safe working environment may find they are less likely to be targeted for unionization. Employers who are known for demonstrating concern for employee welfare by providing a secure environment will find that it helps them attract qualified employees, particularly if the industry is one in which work hazards are prevalent. Employees who have a choice will more often choose to work for the employer with a good safety record than for one who demonstrates a lack of concern for employee safety.

Effective security measures protect business assets, whether physical assets such as buildings and equipment, financial assets, or human assets. This reduces losses that could otherwise occur as a result of pilferage, theft, or destruction of property.

Operational Responsibilities

Depending on the size and nature of the organization, responsibility for health, safety, and security functions can be assigned to individuals along with other unrelated duties, assigned to a single individual who focuses on the function, or (in very large organizations) have entire departments devoted to them. In this chapter, I'll provide you with an overview of the key elements of these programs and how they are implemented in an organization.

Workplace Health Issues

The connection between illness and the work environment became known as long ago as the ancient Greek and Roman civilizations when the effects of lead and mercury poisoning on mine workers were first identified. For many centuries, mines were the chief source of workplace illness. Over the years, as medical knowledge increased, miners and their illnesses presented a challenge to doctors interested in reducing or eliminating them. During the sixteenth century, two physicians, Georgius Agricola and Philippus Aureolis, studied and wrote about the effects of mining, describing illnesses that still affect miners today.

When the Industrial Age began in the eighteenth century, mines were no longer the only source of occupational illnesses, and side effects from other industrial processes began to affect the health of workers. In 1784, the cause of a disease known as cotton mill fever among textile workers (also known as brown lung, or byssinosis) was identified as resulting from breathing cotton fibers generated during the manufacturing process. During this time the connection between cancer and an occupation was first made when it became clear that there was an increased occurrence of some forms of cancer in chimney sweeps. As industrialization increased during the nineteenth century, other illnesses were identified and connected to manufacturing processes.

As Chapter 2, "The Impact of Employment Law on HR Practice," described, the first comprehensive law designed to protect American workers was enacted in 1970. The Occupational Safety and Health Act (OSH Act) created two federal agencies to identify hazards, develop standards for preventing illness and injury, and enforce the use of these standards in American workplaces. Working in collaboration, OSHA and the National Institute for Occupational Safety and Health (NIOSH) have identified three categories of health hazards—chemical, physical, and biological—and established standards designed to protect workers from them. In addition to these hazards, substance abuse and job-related stress are factors that can have a negative impact on the health of employees. The following sections describe how these issues affect the health of employees in the workplace.

Chemical Hazards

Chemical hazards that pose a physical or health hazard to workers are most often found in manufacturing processes, but can also affect workers in other environments as well. Over the years, a number of hazardous chemicals have been identified, and OSHA has developed standards designed to eliminate or reduce their harmful effects. These standards protect workers who are exposed to asbestos, corrosives, pesticides, gas fumes, or solvents during the course of their work by requiring the use of appropriate preventative measures.

Exposure to chemical substances can result in a wide variety of effects, including burns, respiratory ailments, and (in some cases) cancer. For example, when a worker inhales asbestos fibers, the result can be a disease known as asbestosis, in which an individual suffers from shortness of breath, coughing, tightness in the chest, and chest pain. The symptoms may take years to appear and can eventually cause a rare form of cancer known as mesothelioma. To prevent this disease, workers who may be exposed to asbestos fibers should be provided with respiratory protection and work clothing that is either disposable or is laundered at the worksite to prevent the spread of contamination to family members.

For the most part, when people think of hazardous chemical exposures, they think of manufacturing and industrial work areas. Chemical risks, however, can occur in other work environments, such as office buildings. As an example, the carbonless copy paper often used for multi-part forms has been linked to irritations of the skin, eyes, and upper respiratory tract. These symptoms can be prevented or reduced with simple measures such as washing hands after handling the paper; limiting contact between hands, eyes, and mouths; and ensuring that the workplace has adequate ventilation, humidity, and temperature controls.

To aid employers in identifying possible chemical hazards in their workplaces, OSHA requires chemical manufacturers to provide a material safety data sheet (MSDS) for each chemical product they produce. The MSDS is to be included with the product when it is delivered to the end user to aid in identifying preventative measures. Employers are required to maintain copies of the MSDS sheets in areas where the chemicals are present, and in the event of an inspection by an OSHA investigator, must be able to produce the documents if requested. Even products as common as toner cartridges for copy machines include an MSDS that should be maintained in or around the office copy machine.

According to OSHA, the information to be included on an MSDS includes a description of the stability of the substance, identification of any materials or substances that it must not come into contact with, and what, if any, hazards will occur as it ages. These documents also provide information about the chemical composition of the substance, how it can be absorbed by the body (inhalation, ingestion, or through the skin), whether it is considered to be a carcinogen, and what protective equipment is needed to prevent workforce illnesses. Employers are required to communicate this information to employees who handle these substances during the course of their work, and the MSDS provides an effective means to ensure that the required information is provided.

Physical Hazards

Physical hazards include such things as electrical currents, excessive noise, too much or too little light, radiation, and vibrations. When exposure to any of these elements exceeds established standards, the results can, at a minimum, have long-lasting negative effects on worker health and productivity. At worst, over-exposure can be fatal. With the increased use of computers in the workplace, ergonomic injuries have become more prevalent in workers whose work requires them to spend the bulk of their time typing. An *ergonomic injury* is one that is related to the way the physical environment is designed; for example, the placement of the keyboard relative to the height of the employee's chair can affect the occurrence of a musculoskeletal disorder (MSD), such as carpal tunnel syndrome. Considering the physical requirements of jobs while designing workspaces can reduce the occurrence of MSDs.

ergonomic injury
An injury related to the physical design of the work place or task.

Biological Hazards

Biological hazards such as bacteria, molds, contaminated water, and dust are also known to cause illness to workers. Many of the illnesses resulting from these hazards have long-lasting effects and may even be fatal to workers. These illnesses, which are most often the result of mining and industrial operations, include byssinosis, silicosis, and pneumoconiosis. Byssinosis, also known as brown lung disease, affects textile workers who breathe the dust created during the processing of cotton, flax, and hemp. Silicosis is found in workers who are exposed to silica dust as a result of their work in mines or metal casting operations; it results in symptoms that include chronic coughing, shortness of breath, weight loss, and fever. Pneumoconiosis, which is better known as black lung disease, is found in coal miners and produces shortness of breath and a chronic cough.

The occurrence of these diseases has been reduced with the use of preventative measures that include the use of facemasks by workers and steps taken by employers to reduce dust levels in the workplace.

Substance Abuse

Employees who are substance abusers, whether they are abusing on the premises or simply come to work under the influence of drugs or alcohol, are often responsible for increased absenteeism and are more likely to be the cause of workplace accidents, injuries, or deaths in the workplace. At the extreme, abusers may become violent and disruptive to operations. Employees who are under the influence while at work can expose their employers to costly lawsuits when they endanger the lives of coworkers, vendors, and customers. Situations created by substance abusers can result in lower morale among employees who need to pick up the slack for a coworker who is frequently absent or unable to perform at an acceptable level. These issues add to employer health care and workers' compensation costs.

It is important to note that employees who are recovering substance abusers are protected by the Americans with Disabilities Act (ADA) as long as they are in recovery; if they "fall off the wagon" and begin using again, they are no longer protected by ADA requirements.

Unless employers receive funds from federal contracts, subcontracts, or grants, they are not required by law to provide a drug-free working environment. Many employers choose to do so, however, because it makes good business sense and reduces the costs associated with substance abuse. To assist employers in this effort, the federal Department of Labor (DOL) has outlined five elements that contribute to an effective program. In addition to the five elements recommended by the DOL, it is crucial that the program have the support of the senior management team; without this, it is difficult to make the program work. The five elements recommended by the DOL include:

- A drug-free workplace policy that states the employer's rationale for establishing the program, describes prohibited behaviors, and spells out what consequences will result if employees engage in these behaviors. Development of the policy should include input from employees to aid in obtaining buy-in when the policy is launched. The employer should ensure that the policy is clearly communicated to all employees when it is implemented and on at least an annual basis after that.

- A training program for managers and supervisors that provides them with all the information they will need to explain the program to their direct reports and to enforce the policy. The training should provide them with the information necessary to recognize the symptoms of drug abuse, discuss the importance of documenting poor performance as it is related to drug abuse, and provide the resources for referring employees who may be in need of assistance.

- An effective drug-free workplace program includes an element that educates employees about the policy and how the program operates.

- It is also important to include in the program some means for providing assistance to employees who are in need of help with substance abuse or other personal problems. One cost-effective method for doing this is by using an employee assistance program (EAP) that can provide a variety of services. (We'll talk about this in more detail later in this chapter.)

- The final element of the DOL's recommendations for a drug-free workplace program is the inclusion of a drug-testing process (described more fully later in this chapter).

Job-Related Stress

The fast pace of global business operations and the pressure to attain quarterly profit levels leaves most American workers frazzled at work. When personal and family pressures are added to the mix, stress is often the result. NIOSH identifies *job stress* as "harmful physical and emotional responses that occur when the requirements of the job do not match the capabilities, resources, or needs of the worker." That sounds like the job conditions most of the people I know must work within on a daily basis! Employees who are overloaded with deadlines and worried about the impact of a pending acquisition or merger on their job security often work excessive hours just to maintain their current positions. Doing this to the exclusion of other pursuits and "downtime" away from work can result in burned-out employees who cannot cope with the demands of their jobs.

Another cause of job-related stress is something that is within the control of managers: providing clear communication regarding job assignments and expected results. In addition, encouraging a dialogue with employees about assignments and providing them with as much control over their own work routines as is possible helps to reduce job-related stress. Managers should also be on the lookout for the physical, emotional, and mental symptoms of stress described in Table 5.1 in their workers. They should encourage employees who exhibit these symptoms to add balance to their lives by spending time away from work or engaging in some form of physical exercise—both of which are known to reduce stress.

job stress
Occurs when employees do not have the capabilities and/or resources to accomplish their job requirements and cannot control the circumstances in which they must operate.

Table 5.1   Symptoms of Stress

PHYSICAL	EMOTIONAL	MENTAL
Headaches	Mood swings	Forgetfulness
Indigestion	Irritability	Inability to concentrate
Fatigue	Depression	Disorganization
Intestinal problems	Hostility	Poor judgment

When employees exhibit these symptoms, managers can engage them in conversation about the work environment and suggest that they take advantage of the EAP if one is offered by the employer.

At the same time that workers today feel pressured to spend 60 to 80 hours per week at work, many recognize that this behavior is detrimental to their health and are looking for ways to balance their work lives with their personal lives. When employees can mentally disengage from work pressures on a regular basis, they are more focused and productive during the hours they spend at work.

Workplace Health Programs

In an effort to lessen medical costs, reduce turnover rates and absenteeism, and increase productivity, many employers establish programs designed to help employees maintain a healthy lifestyle and provide support for non-work-related issues. These programs generally fall into one of the three areas described below.

Health and Wellness Programs   Depending on the size and financial conditions of individual employers, these programs vary widely in the services they offer and the way they are delivered. Some wellness programs include educational programs for weight control, smoking reduction, and exercise. Some companies provide onsite gym facilities as part of their programs, and others subsidize individual gym memberships for employees.

Employee Assistance Program (EAP)   An EAP is a cost-effective benefit that provides a variety of counseling and support services for employees. Depending on the provider, these services can include legal and financial counseling, psychological counseling, alcohol and drug counseling, and crisis support. The EAP can be called in to provide support for employees in the event of an act of violence in the workplace or the death of an employee. These programs can be particularly useful during layoffs by providing counseling to both those who are being terminated and those who remain with the company. Some EAPs also provide some form of outplacement counseling after a layoff as well.

Drug Testing Programs   Drug testing can be a divisive workplace issue, so employers must give careful consideration to a number of issues prior to implementing a program in their organization. As with all other employment-related testing, drug tests should be related to the job functions being performed; for example, jobs that require the use of machinery, equipment, or vehicles as part of regular job duties. Employers should begin a drug-testing program by developing a substance abuse policy. The policy should consider issues such as state or local laws, the substances to test for, which employees are to be tested, the procedures to be used, what consequences will occur, and how the policy is communicated to employees.

First and foremost, the program must be applied fairly and consistently in the organization. Employers may choose to test employees in all jobs at all levels, or they may select employees in job groups that require, for example, the use of machinery or vehicles as part of their regular duties. If a single job group is subjected to testing, all employees in that group must be equally eligible for testing. If an employer decides to test all workers involved in the operation of production machinery, for example, all the employees in that group must be equally likely to be tested.

Prior to implementing a drug testing program, it's important to consider the consequences that employees will face if they test positive for drug abuse. Will the company have a zero-tolerance policy, so that a single instance results in termination? Or will there be some other consequence such as a suspension or required counseling? Whatever consequences are chosen, the employer must be willing to implement them fairly and consistently to avoid charges of discrimination.

Employers must also determine which drugs will be included in the test process. Most often, employers test for marijuana, cocaine, amphetamines, opiates, and PCP. The decision about which drugs are tested helps to determine the testing method to be used, whether it is based on a sample of blood or urine, or uses a hair follicle or fingernail sample.

Another issue to be considered is when testing will be conducted. Table 5.2 describes five options for conducting tests.

Table 5.2   Drug Test Timing Options

Option	When Used
Applicant	Applicants may be required to take and pass a drug test *only after a job offer* has been made. The offer may be contingent upon a successful result, but the test may not be required until the offer has been accepted.
Random	Tests may be conducted randomly, with employees selected arbitrarily, as long as all employees in the group are equally likely to be selected. Some states place restrictions on random testing based on privacy concerns.
Post-accident	Tests may be conducted after an accident occurs. It is a good idea to establish what types of accidents will require testing; for example, whether minor accidents (such as tripping and falling) will require a test, or only more serious accidents, such as those involving medical attention or hospitalization.
Reasonable suspicion	When supervisors notice employees behaving unusually or if they have physical symptoms associated with drug or alcohol use (such as dilated pupils or slurred speech), they may require employees to submit to a drug test. This type of testing requires that supervisors be trained to recognize symptoms and behaviors that are commonly associated with drug abuse.
Regular schedule	Tests may be conducted on a regular basis, although this allows employees who normally abuse substances to abstain for a period of time prior to the test or to purchase products designed to mask drug use for the test.

The increased use of drug testing programs has spawned a number of businesses that sell products and information designed to mask drug use and allow abusers to pass drug tests. These businesses offer products that can thwart blood, urine, and hair follicle testing, so employers must take steps to ensure that the drug testing facilities they use can detect and prevent the use of these products in their testing programs.

Workplace Safety Issues

As discussed in Chapter 2, "Legal Requirements," the OSH Act of 1970 established OSHA to work with unions, employers, and industry associations to develop standards for safe work environments. Subsequent to the establishment of OSHA, many state legislatures created similar agencies to address workplace safety issues specific to the businesses and environmental conditions in their states. Employers must be aware of and comply with safety standards established by either federal or state agencies; when the agencies have conflicting requirements, business owners must comply with the regulation that has the strictest requirement.

Many of the safety standards developed by OSHA deal with situations specific to a single industry or production process, whereas other safety standards have broad application across industries and businesses. Let's take a brief look at some of the more common standards that HR practitioners may encounter.

general duty standard
The OSHA standard requiring all employers to provide a safe and secure workplace for employees.

General Duty Standard   As mentioned in Chapter 2, the *general duty standard* applies to all organizations and requires employers to provide a safe work environment for their employees. Employees also have a responsibility under this standard to conduct themselves in a way that complies with all OSHA standards and rules pertaining to the jobs they perform for the organization.

Hazard Communication Standard (HCS)   The HCS standard requires employers to inform employees of the dangers of chemicals used in the workplace. This is the standard that requires chemical manufacturers to provide the MSDS sheets previously discussed.

Occupational Noise Exposure Standard   This standard sets allowable levels of workplace noise and identifies procedures for measuring noise and audiometric testing for employees who must work in noisy environments.

Personal Protective Equipment (PPE)   PPE standards require employers to provide appropriate garments and equipment for dealing with different types of hazards, such as compressed gas, radiation, explosive substances, and ammonia. The standard also requires employers to train workers in the proper use and maintenance of the equipment.

Lockout/Tagout   This standard is designed to reduce injuries and deaths by preventing machinery or equipment from starting unexpectedly during repairs and maintenance.

Blood-Borne Pathogens   A *blood-borne pathogen* is a microorganism in human blood that can cause disease. Although health care workers are most at risk of contracting illnesses transmitted by blood and other body fluids (such as Human Immunodeficiency Virus [HIV]), workers in other industries can be exposed to them as well. This standard requires employers to develop a written exposure control plan that advises employees of the steps they can take to prevent or reduce the effects of exposures.

Employers can often partner with their workers' compensation insurance carriers, who have a vested interest in ensuring safe work environments, to establish workplace safety programs that comply with federal and state requirements. These insurance carriers often employ workplace safety specialists who provide assistance for employers through onsite visits designed to assist employers in complying with OSHA regulations, and thus reduce workers' compensation costs. These specialists might offer suggestions with regard to noise issues, air quality, lifting, forklift handling, and other safety issues. Employers whose business processes involve the use of industrial chemicals will find assistance with the vendors who manufacture these substances, including onsite training; sometimes awarding certification to acknowledge employees who have developed expertise in handling toxic chemicals.

Real World Scenario

Survival Basics: Setting Up a Safety Program

By Phyllis A. Simmons

You've been given the responsibility for safety, probably in addition to your regular duties. You may be wondering "What does a safety person do?" or "Where do I start?" Don't panic. Here are three essential building blocks to help you get started:

1. Understand your responsibilities.

2. Learn the safety requirements for your organization.

3. Involve employees in the process by creating a safety committee.

Continues

Understanding Your Responsibilities

Understanding your role and responsibilities is the first step. Meet with the person who appointed you to obtain a clear understanding of your role and responsibilities as well as the expectations of managers and supervisors. This stage will help you identify how much time is needed, what you need to know, and how much support is available. Here are key questions to ask senior management:

- What are my responsibilities?

- Will I have any authority to enforce safety polices?

- What are the safety expectations of managers and supervisors?

- How will senior management support the program?

- What type of training will I receive?

What does a safety person do? The purpose of most safety managers is to oversee the overall safety program and OSHA compliance, and help prevent workplace injuries. You will usually be involved in tasks ranging from program development to setting up compliance systems. Most of your start-up time will be spent setting up systems and using your leadership skills to convince others that safety is important. The following list gives you an idea of some typical tasks of a person responsible for safety:

- Develop and update safety policies.

- Set up safety training programs for supervisors, employees, and new hires.

- Review employee accident reports and help investigate accidents.

- Maintain OSHA-required documentation.

- Serve as the safety committee facilitator.

- Provide recommendations to senior management to reduce workplace injury rates.

- Conduct safety inspections and audits with supervisors.

- Assist in managing the workers' compensation and return-to-work programs.

Here are crucial survival tips:

> **You Are Not Alone**   In many companies, the safety person manages the overall program, and the supervisors are responsible for implementing and enforcing safety policies in their departments. Accident investigation, conducting job specific safety training, and correcting hazards are usually the supervisors' responsibility.

Continues

Partner with Supervisors   It's important to meet with managers and supervisors before developing the program. To help reduce resistance to change and to create buy-in, ask senior management to meet with supervisors to ask for their ideas and explain the benefits of the safety program. By having this meeting, safety becomes a shared responsibly and it doesn't just fall on your shoulders. This critical step sets the tone for your entire program.

Assess and Build Safety Knowledge   Because your role carries legal responsibilities and involves the safety of others, it's important to assess your safety knowledge. Are you familiar with workplace hazards such as machine guarding, respiratory protection, and chemical safety? If you lack knowledge in a particular area, seek technical assistance from OSHA or other safety organizations. The American Society of Safety Engineers (ASSE) offers a wide variety of technical books and resources: http://www.asse.org.

Learning the Safety Requirements for Your Organization

After you understand your responsibilities, the next step is to find out the safety requirements for your state. OSHA requirements can vary from state to state. For example, monthly safety inspections are required in some states, but in others you can choose the frequency. Standards vary because some states have their own *State OSHA*. States that don't must follow Federal OSHA standards. Here are a few OSHA survival tips:

◆ To find out if your company falls under a State OSHA or Federal OSHA plan, visit the Federal OSHA website map at: http//: www.osha.gov or contact your local OSHA Consultation office. Many OSHA websites also have safety program and training information to help you get started.

◆ Important: Safety standards are constantly changing; therefore, you will need to have up-to-date information. Consider a regulatory update subscription service to keep track of new requirements or check the OSHA website.

◆ When Federal OSHA changes or adopts new safety standards, State OSHAs have a certain time frame to adopt similar or more stringent standards. You may need to change or update your program when this occurs. To make sure your policies stay current, plan to review them at least annually.

Setting up a Safety Committee

After you become familiar with required programs, it's time to set up key processes to ensure programs are effectively implemented. Processes might include recordkeeping, accident reporting, training, and workplace inspections. The most common system you will probably set up is a safety committee:

Where to Start   Even though safety committees are not required in every state, it's an effective way to ensure two-way communication between management and labor, and involve employees in the process. Before you schedule a committee meeting, take some time to design the overall structure and define the purpose and mission of the team. Ask yourself "What's the purpose of the team?" "Who should be on the team?" "What do we want to accomplish?"

Defining the Purpose   A safety committee is a multidisciplinary team designed to focus on injury prevention. Develop a statement of purpose to help create a common vision and direction for the team.

Continues

Here are typical examples of what committees do:

Develop or Approve Policies   Analyze the cause of employee injuries and make recommenda-tions; complete a special project such as a safety fair or design a safety recognition program; fulfill regulatory requirement as specified by OSHA; audit the company's safety program and submit rec-ommendations to management.

Plan the Overall Structure   Identify the facilitator(s), role of the members, meeting frequency and length; identify the person to record and post minutes; decide on the standard agenda topics for each meeting. In some states, OSHA has specific guidelines for safety committees—check the standards for your state.

Select Members   Try to have representatives from every department. A common pitfall is to have a committee composed of managers. It's important to have employee members to hear their safety concerns and suggestions. Decide on the length of service. It's good to rotate members at least annually.

Keep Meetings Active   Meetings are most productive when they are organized and focused and members are involved. Here are a few crucial meeting survival tips:

◆ Send out the meeting agenda ahead of time and highlight follow-up items to help members come prepared.

◆ Give members active roles so they are involved in the meeting. Ideas: Ask individual members to be responsible for safety suggestions, taking minutes, leading a talk, or following up on a safety idea that was implemented.

◆ Reserve 10 minutes of each meeting for best practice recognition. Ask managers and supervisors to share their accomplishments.

At the end of a committee project or at milestones, take time to recognize team accomplishments; for example, have a special luncheon and give out small gifts or safety awards. As you start building your program, keep this in mind: successful safety programs can be achieved only with the help of employees, supervisors, managers, and senior management. You will need to use your leadership skills to involve others in the process.

Workplace Security Issues

workplace security
Activities designed to protect business assets from loss.

Workplace security issues cover a wide range of circumstances, ranging from protecting physical assets from fires, natural disasters, and manmade damage to protecting employees and preventing the theft of intellectual property and financial assets. A workplace security program begins with a *risk assessment*. This process looks at the possible threats that could come from outside the organization as well as areas of internal weakness that make the organization vulnerable to a loss of some type. A risk assessment begins by answering the following questions about each threat or weakness that has been identified:

- How likely is it that the situation will occur?
- If the situation occurs, what would be the cost to the organization?
- How would the situation affect the organization's ability to continue operations?

Armed with this information, the organization can identify and implement measures necessary to reduce the likelihood that an emergency situation will occur. Let's take a look at some ways organizations protect themselves.

risk assessment
Identifies possible external threats and internal vulnerabilities, assesses the possible costs and impact on business operations, and develops plans to prevent or reduce the effects of an incident if it occurs.

Physical Assets

Physical assets include buildings, property, computers, vehicles, heavy machinery, and other equipment that is owned by organizations. The security function ensures that these assets are protected from fires, natural disasters, and vandalism. For some businesses, this can mean simply the installation of fire alarms, smoke detectors, and locks for the doors. For other organizations, it can include security guards and cameras, fences, key card entry and locking systems, or gates.

A controversial investigative tool that is sometimes used to protect company assets is the polygraph test. As discussed in Chapter 3, the use of polygraph tests in private industry is severely limited by the Employee Polygraph Protection Act of 1988 (EPPA). Under this act, however, employers are allowed to use polygraphs during an ongoing investigation into the loss or theft of property. Employers may require employees who had access to missing property to submit to a polygraph test. In that case, an individual licensed by the state in which the test is conducted must administer the test.

Human Assets

Many of the measures taken by employers to protect physical assets are utilized in protecting employees as well. Employees need to be protected from fires and natural disasters, and need to know what actions to take should an emergency occur. Security systems that protect employees may be as simple as restricting issuance of keys and changing locks when terminated employees do not return their keys, or when keys are lost or unaccounted for. They may also include some of the more sophisticated systems mentioned in the previous section.

Training programs that teach employees what to do in emergencies are often some of the best ways to protect them. These programs can provide information on how to react in the event of a release of hazardous substances in the workplace and how to protect themselves in situations such as working alone late at night or what to do in the event an act of violence is committed in the workplace.

workplace violence
Occurs when individuals who lack the ability to control their actions become overly stressed and react to a situation with physical violence.

Workplace violence most often occurs when an employee who has difficulty controlling his or her behavior becomes highly stressed and acts out. The stress may not be job-related (it may have to do with family or another personal situation), but the violence is usually set off by an incident in the workplace. Employers have an obligation under OSHA's General Duty Standard to take steps to prevent acts of violence in the workplace. They can do this by being aware of the symptoms of stress and working with individuals who exhibit them, referring them to the EAP for counseling if needed to reduce the level of stress.

Employers should also develop a plan for handling an act of violence if it occurs in the workplace and communicate the plan to employees so they know how to protect themselves if violence occurs. This plan of action should be included in the organization's emergency response plan and provide tools for employees to use to protect themselves and summon help when they feel threatened.

Intellectual Property

intellectual property (IP)
An intangible asset that includes inventions, customer lists, software code, and business processes unique to the operation of a business.

Intellectual property (IP) includes assets such as software product code, ideas, inventions, and business processes that are used to produce a company's products or services. This type of property can be difficult to protect from a loss of some type because it is usually not a physical "thing"; instead, it exists in the mind of an individual, is on paper, or is contained on a computer drive or disk. For this reason, it is sometimes difficult to prevent the loss of this type of information. One way for an organization to protect itself legally is with the use of an intellectual property agreement (IPA) or a nondisclosure agreement (NDA). These documents are completed by employees before they begin to work at an organization and are designed to let them know what type of information is considered confidential, how the use of that information is restricted, and how long the information is to remain confidential.

Financial Assets

Financial assets such as cash, product inventories, supply inventories, and accounts receivable need to be protected from embezzlement and theft. This function is very often the responsibility of the Chief Financial Officer (CFO) of an organization, who establishes what are known as internal financial controls to ensure the proper handling of these assets. Internal controls are designed to ensure that different pieces of a financial transaction are handled by different individuals. For example, the employee who records invoices from suppliers is not usually the same employee who signs checks. This prevents an employee from embezzling money by creating a phony vendor invoice, issuing and signing a check for the invoice, and then keeping the money.

Due to the widespread corporate malfeasance that came to light as a result of the financial scandals at Enron, Worldcom, Tyco, and Global Crossing, Congress enacted the Sarbanes-Oxley Act of 2002. Several provisions of this law are designed to protect financial assets from manipulation or theft by corporate officers. One of the most important provisions is the requirement that CEOs must now be accountable for the accuracy and fairness of financial reports that they prepare and distribute. In addition, restrictions were placed on auditing firms to ensure that they remain disinterested third parties. Sarbanes-Oxley also established criminal penalties for senior managers whose actions are fraudulent or obstruct justice.

Working with OSHA

Like it or not, OSHA is a fact of life for most businesses in the United States. Although some employers may find the safety standards costly and inefficient, OSHA does make an effort to work with them to reduce those costs by providing a forum for businesses and labor to collaborate on proposed health and safety standards. The agency also provides consultation services to work with individual businesses to solve safety and health problems without going through an OSHA inspection. The benefit of the consultation process is that it provides a means for the employer to find out whether or not its operations are in compliance with standards without the risk of incurring fines and penalties. The result of a consultation is a list of workplace hazards that must be corrected. The OSHA consultant works with the employer to establish a time frame for abating the hazards and follows up from time to time to ensure that the changes are being implemented. An employer who requests a consultation must be willing to make the changes identified during the process; if not, the consultation findings are referred to an enforcement officer for appropriate action and could result in the assessment of fines.

OSHA Inspections

In most cases, an OSHA inspection occurs as the result of a serious work-related injury or death, or of a complaint from an employee about dangerous working conditions. Inspections are conducted by a Compliance Safety and Health Officer (CSHO) and follow a prescribed format which includes these steps:

1. Presentation of CSHO credentials
2. Opening conference
3. Facility tour
4. Closing conference

At the beginning of an inspection, CSHOs present their official credentials and ask to speak with the employer's representative. It is important for the receptionist or whoever is likely to be approached by a CSHO first to know who to contact when this happens. At that time, the validity of the CSHO credentials can be verified by calling the local Federal or State OSHA office.

During the opening conference, the CSHO informs the employer of the reason for the inspection and explains the inspection process. At this time, the employer is asked if an employee representative is designated to participate in the inspection. The employee representative is often selected by the safety committee, or is designated by the union (if in a union environment). If there is no designated employee representative, the CSHO may select employees at random during the facility tour and ask questions about the safety conditions.

During the course of the inspection, the CSHO may want to review the employer's safety and health program; examine accident, injury, and illness reports and records; ensure that the employer is in compliance with appropriate OSHA standards; and suggest possible corrective actions for any unsafe working conditions that are identified during the inspection.

The closing conference usually includes both the employer and employee representatives, and it is during this time that the employer representative has an opportunity to provide records and documents to demonstrate compliance activities that have been occurred. The CSHO discusses the findings of the inspection and provides information about OSHA services and any additional steps that will occur as a result of the inspection.

Safety and Health Plans

OSHA requires employers to develop plans describing how safety, health, or emergency situations will be handled if they should occur. There are some common elements to all these plans, including a clear policy statement and the commitment of senior management to its implementation, a description of the ways in which employees are able to participate in creating the plan, and an identification of the employees responsible for specific tasks outlined in the plan. The plans must also define the process for employees to use when reporting workplace hazards and outline the training program that will be used to inform employees about safety and health requirements.

injury and illness prevention program (IIPP)
Also known as a safety and health management plan. Describes the work environment, known hazards and actions that have been taken to report and correct them, as well as methods used to facilitate communication about safety and health issues between employees and management.

Safety and Health Management Plan   In addition to the information included previously, a safety and health management plan (sometimes also referred to as an *injury and illness prevention program [IIPP]*) establishes a process for communication between employees and employer, identifies and assesses hazards that are known to exist in the organization, and describes the steps that have been taken to correct those hazards. The plan also includes a process that ensures an ongoing review of the work environment so that new hazards can be identified and corrected. A description of proper procedures that are to be used for maintenance of machinery and equipment is a key component of this plan as well. Finally, the plan defines the procedures to be followed to report and investigate any workplace accidents that do occur.

Emergency Response Plan (ERP)   The *emergency response plan* describes what employees should do in the event of emergency situations at work. This plan includes procedures for different types of emergencies (such as fires, floods, earthquakes or severe storms) as well as incidents involving workplace violence or terrorist attacks. The plan informs employees about the alarms that will notify them when an emergency situation occurs, describes how they are to exit the building, and defines a process to ensure that all employees are accounted for after an evacuation. For business processes involving the use machinery or equipment in operations, the ERP describes how critical plant operations will be shut down in the event of an emergency and identifies those who are responsible for these activities.

emergency response plan (ERP)
Describes what actions will be taken in the event of different emergencies or disasters that can occur at the workplace, including fires, floods, severe storms, and earthquakes; as well as incidents of workplace violence or terrorist attacks.

Administrative Responsibilities

There are several administrative tasks that are part of an occupational health and safety program. The most important of these is the *OSHA recordkeeping requirement* that applies to businesses with 11 or more employees. There are three forms that are required by this process, described as follows.

OSHA recordkeeping requirement
Most employers with 11 or more employees are required to maintain records of workplace illnesses and injuries during the year, and to post a summary of these incidents between February 1 and April 30 of the following year.

OSHA Form 300, Log of Work-Related Injuries and Illnesses   Employers use this form to keep track of all work-related injuries and illnesses that occur during the year.

OSHA Form 300A, Summary of Work-Related Injuries and Illnesses
Each year between February 1 and April 30, employers are required to post a summary of the injuries and illnesses that occurred during the previous year. This form allows the information to be posted without listing the names of the employees who were affected.

OSHA Form 301, Injury and Illness Incident Report   This form must be completed within seven days after the employer is notified that a work-related injury or illness has occurred. It includes information about the employee and the circumstances surrounding the incident, and is used when completing Form 300.

Exempt Employers   Some employers are exempt from OSHA's record-keeping requirements. In addition to employers with fewer than 11 employees, OSHA identifies industries with historically low incidents of workplace injury and illness and exempts them from maintaining records. This list includes businesses that operate in the retail, service, finance, insurance, and real estate industries. Businesses in one of these industries must complete the OSHA reports only if they are notified in writing by either the federal Bureau of Labor Statistics or by OSHA to do so.

OSHA requires that these forms be maintained for five years after the year in which the incidents were reported.

Metrics

As with all other aspects of an HRM program, practitioners must be able to demonstrate with meaningful measurements that health, safety, and security programs are adding value to the organization. Occupational health and safety is one area of HRM that lends itself to the collection and maintenance of statistics. It is important that whatever metrics you use to evaluate safety are relevant to the working conditions and concerns that occur in your organization. For example, a warehousing operation might require employees to lift heavy boxes and items on a frequent basis. If employees are not lifting in the correct way or are otherwise not following established safety procedures, the result could be an increase in the number of back injuries. When HRM becomes aware of this problem, either from an increase in the absentee rate or claims for workers' compensation, or when completing the annual OSHA Form 300A, it is possible to establish a baseline measure that reflects the current number of back injuries and implement training programs to retrain employees in proper lifting techniques. A statistic that is very useful for this purpose is OSHA's recordable case rate formula. The following illustration demonstrates how this formula is used:

$$\text{Back Injury Rate (BIR)} = \frac{\text{Number of back injuries} \times 200{,}000}{\text{Total hours worked by all employees during the period}}$$

Total number of employees: 350 FTE
Number of back injuries = 53

$$\text{BIR} = \frac{53 \times 200{,}000}{350 \times 2{,}000} = \frac{10{,}600{,}000}{700{,}000} = 15.15\%$$

Total number of employees: 375 FTE
Number of back injuries = 35

$$\text{BIR} = \frac{35 \times 200{,}000}{375 \times 2{,}000} = \frac{7{,}000{,}000}{750{,}000} = 9.3\%$$

This formula establishes a baseline for how much time is normally worked by 100 employees during one year. Assuming that they work an average of 40 hours per week and 50 weeks per year, 100 employees would work a total of 200,000 hours per year if no injuries occur. To calculate the back injury rate (BIR), the formula also assumes that employees in the organization work 40 hours per week and 50 weeks per year.

Another measurement that is easier to understand and communicate is the number of days worked without an accident. Some manufacturing organizations post the statistic on large billboards at the front of the factory as a reminder to employees as they come to work each day. This measurement can become a source of pride for employees, and can be used as part of a friendly competition between work teams. It has the benefit of being easy to calculate—whenever an accident occurs, the count starts over at 1 and continues until another accident occurs.

Terms to Know

emergency response plan	ergonomic injury
general duty standard	injury and illness prevention program
intellectual property (IP)	job stress
OSHA recordkeeping requirement	risk assessment
workplace security	workplace violence

Review Questions

1. How does a safe, healthful, and secure workplace benefit an employer?

2. What is the difference between OSHA and NIOSH, and why are they important to employers?

3. What is a chemical hazard?

4. What is a physical hazard?

5. What is a biological hazard?

6. Why should employers be concerned about substance abuse?

7. What steps can employers take to reduce the level of job-related stress for their workers?

8. What are the benefits of an employee assistance program?

9. What do employers need to consider prior to implementing a drug testing program?

10. Why should employers create safety and health plans?

Chapter 6

Building the Employee Relations Program

When employees think about human resources, what usually comes to mind are activities related to employee relations: the work environment, employee involvement, and disciplinary actions, among others. This chapter explores the impact of HRM on employee relations issues in organizations and the role played by HRM in creating an environment that encourages a high level of performance, thus increasing productivity for the organization: a win-win situation for both employees and employers.

Employee relations is pivotal to HRM because it focuses on relationships in the workplace: those between the organization and its employees, between managers and their team members, and between coworkers. Whatever characteristics are present in the employee relations program will be reflected in the way activities in other areas of HRM are implemented.

Strategic Foundation

employee relations (ER)
The functional area of HRM related to managing workplace relationships

Let's begin with a look at the connection between *employee relations* (ER) programs and the successful achievement of organizational goals. From an employer's point of view, employees are hired to produce the goods or services that are needed to satisfy customers and achieve business goals. To the extent that the work environment furthers this goal, ER programs are beneficial to organizations because the way an employer treats its employees can directly affect whether or not they are as productive as possible. Although it is often difficult to tie individual ER activities to specific organization goals, these activities are an essential element of an HRM program. From a strategic point of view, the organization culture embodies many elements of an ER program.

Organizational Culture

organizational culture
The atmosphere, values, and beliefs shared by individuals at all levels within an organization, following the example of senior management which sets the tone for other employees.

The organizational culture establishes standards of behavior, many of which are unwritten, for all employees. The tone for the culture begins with senior organization leaders, heavily influenced by the CEO and other members of the executive team. Whether the organization's leaders treat employees with dignity and respect, as replaceable cogs in a production wheel, or somewhere between those two extremes, their behavior is generally emulated by managers and supervisors at lower levels in the organization and, in turn, affects the way individual employees do their jobs. If, for example, CEOs who are workaholics spend 16 hours every day at their jobs, executives who report to them will do the same in order to impress their bosses. Managers who want to impress the executives will put in 16-hour days, and, as this work ethic trickles down through the organization, front-line employees who want to impress their direct supervisors and managers will do so as well. This makes the culture one in which, to be successful, employees at all levels spend at least as much time at work as their managers do. On the other hand, CEOs who maintain a balance between their work lives and outside activities create an atmosphere that encourages other employees to do the same. In these organizations, employees who want to "impress the boss" develop interests unrelated to their work and have more balance in their lives as a result.

Management Style and Philosophy

Senior managers also influence an organization's culture through their leadership and management styles. Over the years, many theories have been developed to explain exactly what leadership is and how it works (these theories are explained in Chapter 8, "Building Training and Development Programs"). To keep it simple for this discussion, effective leaders can create a vision and inspire people to follow it. There are many ways to do this: some business leaders rely on charisma to inspire their employees, for example, whereas others utilize a more directive and authoritarian approach. Leadership styles that encourage employees to contribute ideas and allow them to have some control over individual work activities generally foster cultures in which employees can be very productive.

Similar to leadership styles, management styles help to shape the organization culture. Some managers lead by building consensus among employees, encouraging them to take risks and be creative in doing their jobs. Other managers use a more directive approach and expect employees to do what they are told without questioning the reasons. There are times when this approach might be necessary, as in an emergency situation or on occasion with some employees who don't respond to other styles. For the most part, though, a directive management style creates an "us-versus-them" atmosphere in which employees are less motivated to perform at the highest level possible.

Culture is also affected by the management philosophy of the organization's leaders. We talked about how philosophy affects employee compensation in Chapter 4, "Building a Compensation Plan," and it affects the employee relations strategy as well. Just as an entitlement philosophy rewards employees for the length of time they spend in a job, it affects the culture as well because employees believe they only need to show up to be rewarded. Entitlement organizations tend to breed employees who "don't rock the boat"; employees in these organizations are often discouraged by coworkers from performing at a high level because it raises performance expectations across the board. Organizations with a performance-based philosophy, on the other hand, tend to encourage employees to be creative in performing their work, suggest new ways of doing things, and be more involved in the work they do.

Employee Involvement

The level of employee involvement in an organization is often related to the management style and philosophy of its leaders. When organizations encourage a high level of employee involvement—not only in individual work decisions, but in organization decisions as well—employees have a sense of control over their daily activities. The more involved employees are in decisions that affect them, the greater is the level of "buy-in" they have for implementing those decisions, and this involvement usually results in a higher level of productivity.

Some companies hold what are known as "all-hands" or "town-hall" meetings, in which the top executive and senior management team meet with all employees, either in person or via video or teleconferencing. In these meetings, any employee can ask questions about the direction of the organization, discuss decisions that have been made, or make suggestions for operating changes. This access to senior management encourages employees to feel that they are a part of making the organization successful, so they have a stake in performing their individual jobs at a high level.

Chain of Command

chain of command
The structure that identifies the level of authority, scope of responsibility, and accountability for different positions in an organization.

Another aspect of organization culture is known as the *chain of command*. This term, borrowed from the military, describes various levels of authority within the organization and identifies which employees are accountable for different functions and tasks. The extent to which an organization strictly adheres to a chain of command or requires communications to be made vertically (from employee to boss to the top boss) rather than horizontally (between employees who are working on different parts of the same project) has a major influence on the culture. This factor contributes to the level of openness in communications throughout the organization. The following illustration provides an example of a traditional organization structure and typical chain of command in a large organization.

Traditional Organization Reporting Structure

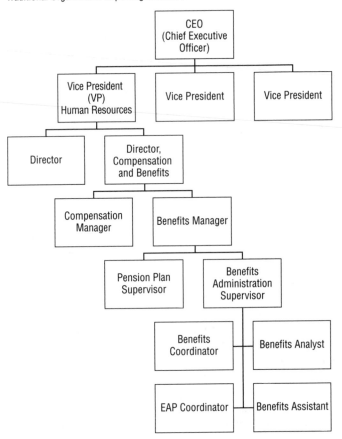

On the positive side, a chain-of-command structure helps to ensure that everyone is aware of activities within his or her area of responsibility. On the negative side, strict adherence to this structure can result in a highly bureaucratic organization in which employees insist on doing things for no better reason than to follow a rule that has been in place for decades without giving any thought to whether or not the rule is necessary or makes sense in the current business environment. This tendency can make it very difficult for organizations to respond rapidly to changing market conditions so that they lose business opportunities.

Effective organizations find ways to keep individuals at all levels in the loop on information that they need to do their jobs, and provide accountability. For example, in a strict chain-of-command hierarchy, an information request can pass through many layers on the way up and down the organization. At each level, the potential exists for delay. Based on the traditional organization structure previously illustrated, you can imagine how long it would take for a request for benefit information from the CEO to go to the benefits clerk and back up through the chain. It could easily take days if someone in the chain were out of town or otherwise unavailable.

To reduce the time involved, an organization that is committed to reducing bureaucracy can instead operate in a way that allows the CEO to e-mail the request to the benefits clerk directly, copying the VP of HR on the request. The clerk can respond to the CEO, copying the benefits supervisor and the VP of HR on the response. In this way, the CEO has the information in a timely fashion, the VP is aware of the question and the response, and the benefits supervisor is also aware of the communication. This second way of obtaining information shortens the time involved, provides the information to the person who needs it, and keeps those who need to know in the loop.

Diversity

A culture that celebrates *diversity* in its workforce is one in which all employees feel that they belong to the team. This again is a function of the views held by the organization's executive team. When executives demonstrate their commitment to developing a workforce that includes a diverse racial, ethnic, religious, gender, physical ability, and age makeup, the culture becomes one in which employees from all backgrounds are accepted and included in work activities. Not only is this equal opportunity the law, it is good business practice. It is human nature for people to feel more comfortable with others who are like them, so a diverse workforce is more likely to attract customers from diverse backgrounds and cultures. In this way, workforce diversity helps organizations to achieve their business goals.

diversity
An equal opportunity practice in which individuals from a wide variety of backgrounds and protected classes are included in an organization.

Retention Programs

retention program
Retention programs provide employees
with opportunities that encourage them
to remain with the organization.

Most employers spend a great deal of money to attract qualified employees to their organizations, so retaining them and the knowledge they acquire about the organization is important. The goal of a *retention program*, then, is to make sure that the organization is meeting the needs of qualified employees by providing them with challenges and opportunities that will make them want to stay with the organization. In order to accommodate the differing needs of employees, the program should include a variety of tools that will be attractive to different employee groups.

The first step in a retention program is to hire employees who have the knowledge, skills, and abilities (KSAs) for the position and who are also a good fit with the organization's culture. For example, an individual who was successful in a highly structured organization might not succeed in a similar position with an organization that operated more informally. In Chapter 3, "Building a Staffing Plan," I talked about developing an interview strategy to make sure that everyone involved in hiring employees acquires the skills to hire the right people. This is a key element of hiring the right people.

After the right people are hired, the retention program begins even before new employees begin their first day of work. Some companies provide welcome letters and benefit information as soon as an offer is accepted, so that new hires have time to read and discuss the information with their families before making these important decisions. On the first day of work, orientation programs welcome new employees and provide information that will be needed for success in their new jobs (discussed in more detail later in this chapter). As new employees become integrated into the organization, their direct supervisors or managers need to find out about their career goals and how the organization can assist them in achieving those goals. (We'll talk more about this in Chapter 9, "Building a Performance Management Plan.")

Based on research studies conducted over a period of years, a number of trends that encourage employees to stay with a particular organization have been identified. Some of these tools are listed here:

- Opportunities for advancement
- Public recognition by their peers
- Visibility with higher levels in the organization
- New challenges and responsibilities
- Opportunities for growth and career development
- Training opportunities
- Being appreciated for the work they do
- Availability of flexible work arrangements such as telecommuting or flextime
- Mentoring programs

The retention program should include a wide variety of tools for managers to use with different employees. For example, some employees are thrilled to have an opportunity to make a presentation to the senior management team, while others who are frightened to speak in public are terrified if they are offered the same opportunity. It's important for managers to find out what their employees are looking for in terms of development and growth so that an effective retention plan can be developed.

Unions and Labor Relations

We talked briefly about ways for organizations to create work environments in which employees are valued and treated with dignity and respect. Organizations do this because they recognize that in the long run, employees will be more productive in a supportive environment. Some organizations don't see the value in creating this type of environment, choosing instead to treat employees poorly—thinking it saves money. These organizations might apply policies inconsistently, establish burdensome work rules and procedures, require excessive overtime, or make employees work in unsafe conditions, among many other possibilities. Employees working in these organizations may come to believe that to be treated fairly they need to form a union to represent their interests. Unions are usually happy to oblige employees who want to unionize their workplaces, promising better compensation and improved working conditions or job security.

Many changes occur to the employment relationship when a union is involved. The focus moves from employee relations to *labor relations*, and it now involves a third party, the union, in the relationship. Unions bargain with the employer to develop a contract, known as a collective bargaining agreement (CBA). Each time the CBA is negotiated, the union and the employer agree on how different issues will be handled while the CBA is in effect. The goal of the union is to ensure job security for their members, so it becomes more difficult for employers to terminate workers who do not perform as well as they should. Salary increases, benefits, and working conditions are also negotiated with the union and become part of the CBA. In this environment, management loses some of its authority with workers. Most employers prefer to avoid unions by establishing fair and consistent policies designed to treat employees with dignity and respect, compensate them fairly, and establish methods for resolving workplace disputes.

As you can see from this discussion of the connection between ER programs and organization strategies, a program that creates a supportive environment for employees encourages them to be creative and generally results in a more productive workforce.

labor relations
Describes the relationship between employers and employees who are represented by unions.

Operational Responsibilities

The operational aspect of ER covers a wide spectrum of activities related to workplace relationships, from the initial introduction of employees to the organization, to conducting workplace investigations, to maintaining the balance between employee rights and employer rights. Let's begin this section with a discussion of the different roles played by line managers and HR practitioners in organizations.

Line managers are responsible for managing their workgroups, so it's important for them to build effective relationships within those groups. Most managers can build relationships when things are going well, but it becomes more difficult to address difficult or uncomfortable issues when problems occur, such as employees who are not performing up to established standards or are disrupting the group in other ways. Sometimes managers want HR practitioners to step in and be the "bad guy," but this is rarely a good idea. The appropriate role for HR to play in these situations is as a coach or facilitator, working with managers to develop the skills necessary to handle similar situations on their own. (We'll talk more about this later in this chapter when we discuss disciplinary actions.)

HRM is often identified as the place for employees to go when they are having problems in the organization. Whether the problems are petty (such as disagreements between coworkers) or serious (such as allegations of harassment or other misconduct), HR practitioners must be able to respond to each situation appropriately. That is the essence of operational ER responsibilities. Let's look now at some of the programs that are typically part of this function.

On-Boarding

After the excitement of making it through the selection process for a position in a new organization, new employees are usually brimming with good will and looking forward to a new challenge. All too often, this enthusiasm is dashed when they arrive for work on their first day and find the following situations:

- The receptionist doesn't know who they are.
- Nobody in the workgroup knows who they are.
- Their desk isn't ready.
- The phone hasn't been connected.
- The computer hasn't been set up.
- The manager is out of town on a business trip for a week and left no instructions, other than "read the annual report and get to know the organization."
- The orientation video is 10 years old and doesn't tell them much about what is going on with the organization.

It's enough to make new hires wonder whether or not they made the right decision in accepting a new job.

New employees confronted with this unfortunate reality often decide on the first day of work that they have made the wrong decision and either return to their old jobs (if that is an option) or continue their job search, leaving within a few months. This not only sends a terrible message to those employees, if it happens often enough it can become part of the employment brand that potential hires hear about when they consider joining an organization. This can make it more difficult for employers to attract qualified employees to their organizations and can increase hiring costs.

An effective *on-boarding* process, traditionally known as new hire orientation, begins before the employee comes to work on the first day. Making the transition from candidate to employee really begins with the employment offer, as was discussed in Chapter 3. Between the time the offer is accepted and the first day of work, a number of actions designed to make new employees feel welcome can be implemented. At a minimum, a place for employees to work, including all the equipment that will be needed to do the job, needs to be arranged; and appropriate personnel, such as the IT department and the receptionist, need to be informed. If the organization has a building security system, arrangements to add new hires to the system can also be made in advance to smooth their arrival on the first day.

on-boarding
The process of welcoming new employees to the organization, integrating them into operations, and ensuring that they have the support they need to be successful.

Although taking care of new hire paperwork is an essential part of on-boarding new employees, it is equally important to make sure that they are integrated into business operations and have the necessary information to begin contributing as quickly as possible. How this is done depends to a great extent on the organization culture. Traditional orientation processes often lasted from one hour to one day and involved filling out paperwork, making benefit selections, reading the employee handbook, and being introduced to new coworkers. On-boarding processes have been expanded to ensure that new hires have an ongoing support system that helps them adjust to their new work environment and integrates them into the company. Some programs last for several months and can include the following:

- The assignment of a buddy or mentor who is available to answer questions
- Formal training programs
- Personal messages from the CEO and other senior managers
- Lunch with their new work team

These are a few of an almost endless variety of activities that make new hires feel welcome, supply them with the tools they need to do their jobs, and provide ongoing support for them to ensure that they are successful.

workplace investigation
A workplace investigation is conducted when allegations or suspicions of misconduct come to the attention of the organization. These investigations occur when claims of sexual harassment are made, after an accident occurs in the workplace, or when management suspects that other misconduct has occurred.

Traditionally, new hire orientations were strictly the responsibility of the HRM department, and in many cases this is still true. Increasingly, though, many on-boarding activities are carried out by hiring managers who can better provide new employees with the specific information that they will need to become productive. In these situations, HRM is responsible for developing the process, training hiring managers to utilize it, and working with them to ensure the smooth integration of employees into the work group.

Conducting Workplace Investigations

When an employee comes to HR alleging that workplace harassment or other misconduct has occurred, it is essential that HR conduct an investigation into the allegation. *Workplace investigations* must be conducted in a timely manner, particularly if the allegation concerns sexual harassment. Letting a situation involving sexual harassment continue without an immediate investigation could result in additional liability for the employer if the allegations are found to be justified.

Real World Scenario

Recognizing and Preventing Sexual Harassment

After the enactment of Title VII in 1964, the federal courts identified sexual harassment as a form of prohibited sex discrimination. Court decisions subsequently have defined behavior that is considered sexual harassment, held employers liable for the harassing actions of their employees, and identified actions that employers can take to reduce their liability.

What Is Sexual Harassment?   As introduced in Chapter 2, "The Impact of Employment Law on HR Practice," there are two types of sexual harassment: quid pro quo and hostile work environment. The basis of sexual harassment is an unwelcome sexual advance or request for sexual favors, or other conduct (physical or verbal) that is sexually motivated. Quid pro quo harassment occurs when an individual in a position of authority makes acceding to these advances or requests a term or condition of employment, or considers the response to a request of this nature when making employment decisions. By definition, quid pro quo harassment involves an individual of higher rank within an organization, such as a supervisor or manager who has the authority to make employment decisions.

On the other hand, a hostile work environment can be created by a coworker, vendor, customer, or other visitor to the workplace. While the harasser in these circumstances may not be able to directly make or influence employment decisions, the conduct involved (verbal taunts, sexually explicit graffiti, magazines, or photographs for example) has a negative effect on the ability of the victim to perform work assignments or simply creates an atmosphere that is hostile, intimidating, or offensive.

Continues

When Are Employers Liable? Court decisions have held that employers are *always* liable for quid pro quo harassment by their supervisors and managers.

Employers have been held liable for the existence of hostile work environments when they *knew or should have known* about the behavior and failed to take actions necessary to correct it.

What Can Employers Do? The best way for employers to protect themselves from liability for sexual harassment claims is to make sure that harassment does not occur in the first place. Some steps that have been recognized by the EEOC and federal courts as good faith efforts to prevent harassment include the establishment of policies and procedures designed to prevent harassment and deal with allegations promptly, and a commitment to enforcing the policies and procedures when harassment occurs.

Sexual Harassment Policy An effective policy that is designed to prevent sexual harassment must begin with the support and commitment of the CEO. Without this support, those employees who have may have a tendency toward harassing others may not take it seriously. The policy needs to explicitly state the organization's commitment to preventing sexual harassment from occurring and to eliminating harassing behavior if it does occur.

The policy should also describe behavior that is prohibited, both quid pro quo and hostile work environment, so that employees clearly understand what types of behavior are prohibited. It is helpful to give examples of different actions, comments, or physical conduct that is not acceptable as well.

For the policy to be taken seriously, it should spell out the penalties that will befall employees who exhibit harassing conduct.

Because employees who are being harassed are often afraid to come forward, particularly if the harasser holds a powerful position in the organization, the policy must provide a detailed description of the steps victims can take to stop the harassment. It is important that these steps include several alternatives so that employees have an avenue for taking an allegation to someone outside of their chain of command. Very often, this is the human resource department.

It is crucial that the policy explicitly state that any form of retaliation against those who report incidents of sexual harassment will not be tolerated and clearly define the consequences that will occur to anyone who retaliates against a victim of harassment.

Finally, the policy should state the intention of the organization to maintain the privacy of individuals who file complaints about harassment, and a commitment that, to the extent possible, harassment complaints will remain confidential.

Sexual Harassment Procedures An effective procedure for handling allegations of sexual harassment begins by identifying multiple avenues for employees to use in reporting harassment. In particular, employees must be informed of how to report harassment that is perpetrated by their direct supervisors, or what to do if they report harassment to a supervisor who does not take immediate action to protect them.

Continues

Enforcing Sexual Harassment Policies and Procedures   Organizations can demonstrate their commitment to eliminating sexual harassment from the workplace by providing periodic training for employees. This generally occurs at the time new employees are hired and on an annual basis for all employees. It is particularly important that any employees with supervisory responsibility be trained to not only prevent them from becoming harassers, but to recognize the signs of harassment by others and take appropriate steps to eliminate any prohibited conduct. When allegations are made, it is imperative that a full and complete investigation begin within a very short time—two days, or three at the most. If the reported conduct is particularly offensive, the investigation should begin immediately. The longer employers wait before taking action, the more likely they are to find themselves facing large monetary judgments if legal action is taken by the victim. Depending on the nature of the allegation and the position held by the accused harasser, it may be advisable to have the investigation conducted by a third party, usually an attorney. For example, if the CEO is the one accused of harassment, it would be difficult for anyone in the organization to conduct a completely neutral investigation.

If a thorough investigation results in a finding that harassment did, in fact, occur, employers must take action that ends the behavior and protects the victim from future occurrences. Any changes in employment status must be directed at the harasser, not the victim. It may seem like a good idea to move the victim into a position that eliminates contact with the harasser, but courts see this as penalizing the victim and find these actions ineffective.

The effects of harassment on victims can be personally devastating, and work environments in which harassment is allowed to exist affect employees who witness or are aware of harassing behavior even when they are not victims themselves. The resulting negative impact on productivity, as a result of increases in absenteeism and turnover, and lower morale in the workplace, reduces the operating effectiveness of the organization and its ability to meet its goals.

Organizations that do not take affirmative steps to prevent harassment and protect victims when harassment occurs can find themselves facing settlements and penalties that reach into tens of millions of dollars. Each year, the EEOC receives more than 25,000 charges of sex discrimination. In one of these cases, women on a Mitsubishi assembly line in an Illinois factory claimed that they were subjected to a hostile work environment. In 1998, the EEOC reached a settlement with Mitsubishi in the amount of $34,000,000 to resolve the claims.

Establishing an effective program to prevent harassment from occurring in the first place and to deal with allegations quickly and fairly protects both employees and their employers.

Conducting an effective workplace investigation for the first time can be intimidating and overwhelming, so it is helpful to establish a standard plan of action before an investigation is needed. When developing this plan, be sure to include the following activities:

◆ Create a checklist for conducting investigations so you are sure to cover all the bases if the need arises.

◆ Select an investigator who is seen by all parties as neutral in the investigation.

- If possible, have the accuser make a written statement about the incident(s) and sign it; if this is not possible, take careful notes and have the accuser read, date, and sign it. Get the names of any witnesses so that they can be interviewed.

- Interview the accused to get the other side of the story, and get the names of any additional witnesses.

- Interview the witnesses and get their statements.

- Make a determination based on the facts that were gathered.

- Make a written report of the facts and findings for the record.

- Take appropriate action based on the results.

Disciplinary Actions

It would be great if all employees came to work on time every day with no other goal than to do a great job. Unfortunately, this is not always the case, and sometimes organizations must take actions to correct substandard or inappropriate behavior. Many HR practitioners have had the experience of being approached by agitated managers because the managers have reached the end of their tolerance for an employee's misconduct or poor performance. When this occurs, it is easy to become panicked because the manager has already decided to take an extreme action, such as firing the employee, and is demanding that HR process the paperwork to do this. As an HR professional, it is important to remain calm and gather the facts, determine the seriousness of the situation, and help the manager develop an appropriate course of action. Instead of responding to a situation like this by telling the manager, "You can't do that; it's illegal," it's important to find an alternative course of action that is legally compliant and in the best interest of the company. When looking for an appropriate alternative, it is completely acceptable to refer to employment laws and company policies before giving an answer.

When it is necessary, many organizations utilize disciplinary policies that begin with an attempt to correct behavior or performance problems and to provide documentation of steps taken to improve performance prior to terminating an employee. Disciplinary policies help to ensure that employees throughout the organization are treated fairly and consistently.

The typical disciplinary process has five steps:

1. Counsel employees to advise them of the problem   When employees are not performing at an acceptable level or are disruptive to the workgroup, supervisors need to let them know about the problem and describe what the employee should be doing to perform at an acceptable level. This should be an ongoing process that happens informally each day so that employees are always aware of what they need to do to improve performance. (This topic will be discussed in more detail in Chapter 9.)

2. Issue a verbal warning   Sometimes, employees do not respond well enough to performance counseling. When this happens, the disciplinary process moves to the first formal step: a verbal warning. Verbal warnings take the counseling a step further by advising employees of the problem, telling them what level of performance is required, and advising them that failure to improve will result in further disciplinary actions—up to and including termination. Although this is called a verbal warning, the supervisor needs to document in writing the date, time, and topics discussed; any agreements the employee made; and the deadline for improvement given to the employee.

3. Issue a written warning   The next step in the standard disciplinary process is a written warning, also referred to as a performance improvement plan (PIP). This warning is similar to the verbal warning in that the same types of topics are discussed and the employee is once again advised that failure to improve could lead to further disciplinary action—including possible termination of employment. The employee is requested to sign the warning to acknowledge that it has been discussed with the supervisor.

4. Suspension (optional)   Some companies include an unpaid suspension as the next step in the disciplinary process, but it is not always part of the process.

5. Termination   If improvement has not occurred within the time period established by the written warning, the employee can be terminated.

Each organization determines how to implement a disciplinary process that reflects its management philosophy and organizational culture. Some organizations may have three steps; others may have four; and still others may include additional steps, such as final warnings or what are known as "decision days," in which employees are given a day off to contemplate whether or not they want to continue to work for the organization. When decision days are utilized, employees who decide they want to continue working must return to work committed to improving the performance issues and are on notice that the next incident will result in immediate termination of their employment.

The goal of the disciplinary process is to ensure that employees are not surprised by a performance-related termination. Going through these steps, and advising employees early in the process that failure to improve could result in termination, provides the documentation necessary to defend the organization should the employee decide to pursue legal action. Disciplinary processes provide organizations with the documentation necessary to demonstrate that a terminated employee was treated fairly, given an opportunity to correct behavior or improve performance, and warned in writing that the possible consequences of not improving could result in termination. Some HR professionals want to make the disciplinary process a hard and fast rule, but there are times when it may be better for the organization to skip a step or to terminate someone immediately. For example, it may be appropriate to immediately terminate the employment of someone who commits an act of workplace violence or is caught stealing from the organization. In those and similar cases, it is in the best interest of the organization that the employee be removed.

In the case of the agitated manager who wants to fire an employee immediately, it's up to HR to find out the circumstances (is this a performance issue, and, if so, have the problems been communicated to the employee?), what steps in the disciplinary process have already been taken (has the employee been coached, warned, or suspended?), and whether the employee is aware of the seriousness of the situation. Depending on the answers to these questions and on the seriousness of the most recent problem (was the employee late again or did the employee attack a coworker?), it may be appropriate to terminate the employee immediately or to implement the disciplinary process if the problem is performance-related and the employee has not yet been counseled or warned.

Real World Scenario

Employee Rights During Disciplinary Procedures

During the normal course of business, employers sometimes come to suspect that an employee is engaged in activities that are in direct conflict with organization policies or practices. When this occurs, employers must conduct investigations to determine whether or not wrongdoing occurred and who was involved. One step in the investigation process requires employers to talk directly to those who are suspected of violating policies. Of course employers have the right to talk to these employees, but what rights do employees have in these situations? An incident that occurred in a retail store in 1972 illustrates how a typical investigation could progress and where it could go wrong. This episode resulted in a 1975 decision by the United States Supreme Court defining the rights of employees. These are now commonly known as Weingarten rights after the name of the employer involved in the case.

Continues

NLRB v. Weingarten, Inc.   The employees at Weingarten's, a retail chain with operations located in Virginia, were represented by the Retail Clerks Union. Leura Collins was a union member who had been working as a sales clerk for 11 years. For her first nine years, Ms. Collins worked at the lunch counter in one store and, as one of the benefits, received a free lunch each day. Ms. Collins was then transferred to a new position in a different store, working in what Weingarten referred to as its lobby food operations, where take-out food is dispensed to customers. After she had been at the new store for two years, someone reported that Ms. Collins was taking money from the cash register. Weingarten sent an in-house loss prevention specialist (LPS) to the store to determine if this was, in fact, occurring. The investigator observed Ms. Collins at work for two days and determined that she was not taking money. The LPS then identified himself to the store manager and reported the results of his investigation. During this conversation, the store manager informed the LPS that someone reported that Ms. Collins had just purchased food priced at $2.98 but had paid only $1.00 for it. At this point, Ms. Collins was summoned to a meeting with the LPS and the store manager and interrogated about this new accusation.

During the interrogation, Ms. Collins asked several times to have her union representative present, but her request was denied each time. She explained to the LPS and store manager that she had, indeed, purchased some food and paid $1.00 for it, but that the store was out of the small boxes in which it would normally be placed. As a result, she had put the food in a larger box, which was usually used for items costing $2.98. The LPS verified her statements with other employees working in the area and apologized to Ms. Collins for inconveniencing her. At this point, Ms. Collins began crying and told the LPS and store manager that the only thing she had ever taken from the store without paying for it was the free lunch provided to employees working at the lunch counter.

After hearing this, the interrogation began anew, because the store manager and LPS interpreted store policy as not providing free lunches for employees who worked in the lobby food operations. Ms. Collins again requested that her union representative be present and was again refused. During the conversation it became clear that the manager of the department as well as most of the other employees who worked there routinely took lunch without paying for it. The LPS prepared a statement for Ms. Collins to sign, including an acknowledgment that she owed the store approximately $160 for the lunches she had taken. Ms. Collins refused to sign the statement. When the LPS contacted the corporate office, he learned that it wasn't certain whether or not any of the employees in the department at this store had been informed that lunch was not provided as part of their benefits. Based on this information, the LPS once again apologized to Ms. Collins and told her she was free to go.

Even though the store manager had asked her to keep the whole episode to herself, Ms. Collins informed her union representative and as a result, the union filed an unfair labor practice claim with the National Labor Relations Board (NLRB). The case eventually found its way to the United States Supreme Court, which issued a decision giving union employees the right to have a union representative present during any investigative interview if the employee believes that some kind of disciplinary action will occur as a result.

Continues

Weingarten Rights in Non-Union Environments On July 10, 2000, the NLRB issued a decision on employee rights in disciplinary actions occurring in non-union environments. The case involved an employee of the Epilepsy Foundation of Northeast Ohio, who was terminated when he refused to attend a disciplinary meeting without a coworker present. In this case, the NLRB extended protections similar to those of Weingarten to all employees, whether or not they are represented by a union. It's important to note that this decision allows employees to have a coworker present, but does not give them the right to have family members, attorneys, or friends who are not coworkers present. If an employee requests the presence of a coworker, the employer has the following choices:

♦ Allow the coworker to be present.

♦ Conduct the investigation without interviewing the employee.

♦ Let the employee decide to either continue the interview without a coworker present, or to not participate in the investigation at all.

Employers are not required to inform employees that they have the right to have coworkers present during an investigatory interview, but if employees make the request, must respond within the guidelines established by Weingarten and the decision in Epilepsy Foundation of Northeast Ohio.

Resolving Disputes

One of the functions of an ER program is to assist in the dispute resolution process: working with managers and employees or with coworkers who have disagreements. Line managers are responsible for managing their direct reports, so the role of the ER function is to facilitate communication or coach managers through the process, providing assistance as needed. Many times, line managers will approach HR practitioners and ask them to take care of uncomfortable situations (such as an employee's lack of hygiene) or increasing absenteeism. To be truly supportive, practitioners should work with managers to provide the tools necessary for them to feel comfortable addressing these issues with employees directly.

Similarly, when employees come to HR to complain about their managers or about coworkers with whom they are having difficulty, the role of HR is really to provide employees with the necessary tools to handle the situation on their own. Often, employees just need someone who is willing to listen to them and make suggestions for ways to address the problem themselves.

Workplace conflicts sometimes escalate past the point where the parties involved can resolve them without assistance. The worst-case scenario for dispute resolution is costly litigation, so many organizations try to solve problems by using some form of alternative dispute resolution (ADR). The first level of ADR might be an internally facilitated, problem-solving meeting between the parties to the disagreement. In employee relations disputes, these meetings are often facilitated by an HR practitioner. If resolution is not achieved at this level, organizations may utilize other forms of ADR, such as the three described as follows.

Peer Review Panel   A peer review panel is an internal method used to resolve disputes. These panels are made up of management and non-management personnel who receive training on company policies, procedures, and work rules. Panel members listen to the parties to the disputes and then make decisions. These panels can be very effective in resolving problems.

Mediation   Mediation is a form of ADR in which the parties meet with a mediator who is skilled in problem-solving techniques to try to resolve the problem. Mediation is informal, and the decisions are not binding, so either party can continue the dispute to arbitration.

Arbitration   The arbitration process can be binding (if the parties agree to abide by the arbitrator's decision) or non-binding (the dispute can move to litigation for resolution if either party disagrees with the decision).

Administrative Responsibilities

The administrative responsibilities associated with ER include the maintenance of records, handbooks, and personnel files. Records that employers collect about applicants and employees often contain sensitive personal information, and employers have an obligation to maintain these records in confidence. It's important, therefore, that HR practitioners allow access to records only on a need-to-know basis. The types of information that need to be maintained include the following records and documents:

Employee Personnel Files   As you can see from the following graphic, personnel files contain information related to an employee's background and performance. Access to these records should be restricted to the employee, supervisors who need access to the information, and HR staff.

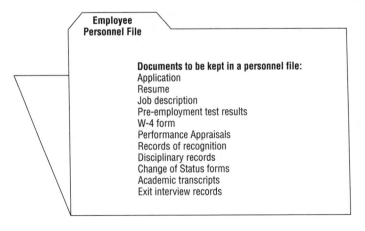

Employee Personnel File

Documents to be kept in a personnel file:
Application
Resume
Job description
Pre-employment test results
W-4 form
Performance Appraisals
Records of recognition
Disciplinary records
Change of Status forms
Academic transcripts
Exit interview records

Employee Medical Files   Because managers may not make employment decisions based on an employee's medical condition, records of employee medical issues should be kept in a separate file and include the documents shown in the following illustration:

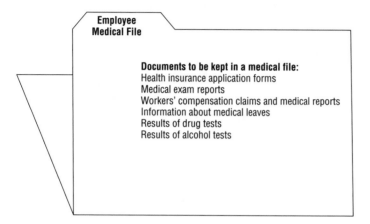

Employee Medical File

Documents to be kept in a medical file:
Health insurance application forms
Medical exam reports
Workers' compensation claims and medical reports
Information about medical leaves
Results of drug tests
Results of alcohol tests

Immigration Documents   Although the law does not require I-9 forms to be maintained separately from employee personnel files, immigration officials can audit them at any time. For this reason, it is a good practice to maintain I-9 forms for all employees in a separate file so that they can be provided easily in the event of an audit.

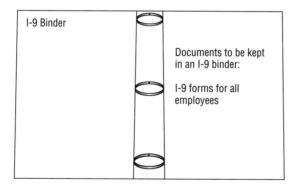

I-9 Binder

Documents to be kept in an I-9 binder:

I-9 forms for all employees

Equal Employment Opportunity (EEO) documents   Employment decisions may not be made based on information collected from employees who self-identify their status as members of protected classes, so it is best to maintain these documents in a binder separate from the personnel files.

In the event that allegations are made of harassment or EEO violations, records related to any investigations that are conducted should be maintained in separate files as well. Unlike the self-identification documents that can be maintained for all employees in a single binder, records of complaints and investigations should be maintained in separate files for each incident.

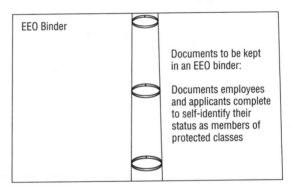

Safety Training Records   The Occupational Safety and Health Administration (OSHA) has the right to inspect and audit records of workplace safety trainings. Similar to the reasons for maintaining I-9 records separately from personnel files, collecting safety training documents in a binder that is easily accessible in the event of an OSHA inspection ensures that they are readily available for review.

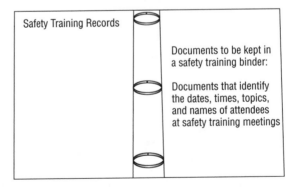

Metrics

ER activities are some of the most difficult to measure because it is rarely possible to tie a particular activity to a particular result. There are, however, ways to determine whether or not the ER program is effective.

Before implementing a new program, HR practitioners can collect information about the current situation (the current turnover rate, for example). After implementation of the program, the same information is collected and, when compared to the original data, provides an indication of whether the program has been effective. Some of the other costs that can be measured include the following:

- The cost of an orientation program with a comparison to tenure in the organization
- The cost of absenteeism
- The cost of counseling employees

These measurements help HRM determine whether or not their ER programs are having a positive impact on organizational goals.

Terms to Know

chain of command	diversity
employee relations	labor relations
on-boarding	organizational culture
retention program	workplace investigation

Review Questions

1. What is an employee relations program?

2. What are the components of an organizational culture?

3. What are some tools typically included in a retention program?

4. What is a mentor?

5. Why do employees form unions?

6. What is the difference between employee relations and labor relations?

7. Why is on-boarding important?

8. Why should I-9 forms be maintained separately from personnel files?

9. What steps should be taken in a disciplinary process?

10. Why is it difficult to measure the effectiveness of ER programs?

Chapter 7

Building the Communication Plan

In This Chapter

* How to develop a communication strategy
* Elements to include in a communication plan
* Advantages and disadvantages of different elements
* What to do with employee feedback
* How to determine whether the communication plan is working

It almost goes without saying that communicating with employees is an integral part of all human resource management (HRM) functions, and it is one of the key elements of an effective employee relations program. Just as communicating with customers, owners, and suppliers is crucial, keeping employees informed about business needs and developments is equally important for organizational success. In particular, the effectiveness of HRM programs is directly related to how well employees are aware of and understand them—whether they are related to performance management, strategic planning, staffing, safety, compensation, training, development, or employee relations.

Strategic Foundation

communication strategy

A communication strategy is a plan that examines different circumstances in which the organization will convey information to employees and identifies communication methods to be used for top-down, bottom-up, and lateral communication in the organization.

The strategic foundation for employee communication plans is almost too basic to have to state: Employees need to know what to do, and employers need to know what is working and what isn't. Establishing an appropriate and effective means for communicating the benefits and expectations of various organization programs, such as performance management or training, ensures that the organization will realize the benefits that were expected when the program was launched. For some, an internal communication plan may seem an unnecessary bureaucratic exercise; after all, people converse all the time without having a plan. Although it's certainly possible to operate a business without a formal *communication strategy*, not thinking about this essential business function can result in missed opportunities, particularly as organizations grow and employees are dispersed around the country or around the world.

An employee communication program can be an easy and cost-effective way to motivate employees and build their enthusiasm for their work. When organization leaders develop operating plans without input from the employees who are responsible for doing the actual work, they can overlook key details that mean the difference between failure and success. There are many opportunities to build on the creativity and good will of employees by soliciting information about process improvements from them or by involving them in the development of organization goals and initiatives. Let's begin by looking at the reasons to create a plan and some of the strategies to be considered when doing so.

Why Create a Strategy?

You may wonder: "Why do we need a strategy for communicating? People talk to each other all the time." It's true that people in organizations talk to each other all the time, even without a plan or strategy. It's also true that sometimes the results are less than ideal, particularly in critical situations when many tasks must be completed in a very short period of time. A plan provides a guide during times when other circumstances rightfully require more attention and concern. It does the organization no good if employees are relying on second- or third-hand information that may or may not be accurate at a time when their cooperation and participation is critical for success. Waiting until a crisis occurs to figure out the best way to disseminate information is likely to result in an uneven result: not everyone who should be included is included, important information isn't included, or the timing may be less than ideal.

In addition to the obvious reasons for communicating with employees (providing information and telling them what results are expected or what assignments need to be completed), there are other goals that might be less obvious but are equally important:

Developing shared understanding of goals   Employees need to be aware of the organization's goals and objectives. Because business moves at such a rapid pace in the global economy, it is easy for senior management to overlook the importance of providing employees with information that affects the way they do their jobs. When employees clearly understand the goals and objectives, they are better able to produce results that contribute to the organization's success. When front-line employees clearly understand what needs to be done, they are more invested in the outcome.

Understanding impact of individual contributions   Employees also need to know how what they do contributes to the goals and objectives of the organization and their individual business units. It's important for them to understand the impact of their actions, both good and bad, on their coworkers (who may have to pick up the slack for individuals who don't pull their own weight) and on customers (who may demand discounts for late deliveries or find another supplier if service is continually below par).

Minimizing effects of misinformation   A communication plan provides a means for clearing up information that may have been misinterpreted or exaggerated by the company grapevine, and establishes a way for employees to get accurate information from official sources.

So what happens in organizations that don't develop an employee communication strategy? Whether the culture is an open one in which management freely shares information with employees, a closed "do-what-I-say-and-don't-ask-questions" atmosphere, or something between those two extremes, a strategy develops based on how the organization interacts with its employees. When the exchange of information "just happens" in this way, the results can sometimes appear inconsistent or haphazard to employees, and this creates a credibility problem for the organization. When employees don't receive "official" information, very often overheard bits are misconstrued by one employee, who shares this misinformation with co-workers, and suddenly a full-blown rumor is spreading throughout the organization. More often than not, rumors bear little or no resemblance to the facts. Left to workers' imaginations, an innocuous change in the organization's goals can morph into a plant closure, major layoff, or corporate scandal. Since it is unfortunately human nature to assume the worst, the rumor mill rarely produces good news.

After inaccurate information takes hold in the workforce, attempts to correct it can be viewed with suspicion, and some employees may never believe the truth when it is finally revealed. More often than not, a lack of communication from the employer is equated with a lack of trust in employees, and the message conveyed (intended or not) is that the organization doesn't value its employees. Employees who believe that the organization doesn't value their contributions are less invested in its success, become demotivated, are uncertain about their future with the organization, and feel vulnerable. When employees feel this way, they generally spend more time talking about their dissatisfaction than they spend actually doing their jobs. As their dissatisfaction with the organization grows, employees begin to care less about doing their jobs well, and this can result in poor service for customers or mistakes that lead to quality-control issues. As a result, productivity can fall, which contributes to other organizational problems and can further lower morale and increase turnover.

No one likes to be the bearer of bad news, and this is true for organizations as well as for individuals. The key to effective communication, though, is to share information early and often, *particularly when there is bad news*. Some employers make the mistake of waiting to share information until they have all the answers figured out. However, employees generally have a pretty good sense about what is really going on, so not being honest with them results in some of the consequences previously discussed. Organizations that share information with their employees build trust and engage them as partners in solving problems. If confidentiality is a concern, it is better to inform employees about a situation, including a reminder about the importance of maintaining the confidentiality with the communication. Of course, there will still be times when some types of information cannot be shared in order to preserve trade secrets or to maintain the viability of ongoing negotiations. To the extent that it is possible, though, including employees in the information loop keeps them motivated and productive and benefits the organization by involving them in solving problems.

Developing the Strategy

During the development stage of a communication plan, an organization examines the different circumstances and situations in which messages are necessary. This process answers five key questions:

- What information needs to be conveyed?
- Who needs to receive the information?
- When should information be disseminated?
- Who should convey the information?
- How will we know if the strategy is effective?

The answers to these questions form the basis of an effective employee communication program.

> **What Information Needs to Be Conveyed?**   It is important to begin by clarifying what information is to be disseminated and defining the results you hope to achieve as a result of the communication. This information is necessary in order to answer the remaining questions.
>
> The answer to this first question helps to frame the presentation of the information and provides a measure for determining whether the information was communicated successfully. In any organization, information is

exchanged for a variety of reasons. Knowing what you want to have happen as a result of any communication helps determine the best process for disseminating the information. For example, is the purpose to bring employees up-to-date on organization goals? Or is it to provide directions, such as what they need to do to participate in the benefits open enrollment period? In some cases, the purpose may be to inspire action from employees or to increase their commitment to organization goals. Management might want to create a sense of urgency among employees to meet a specific deadline or maybe persuade employees that a change in organization goals will make the organization more successful.

Who Needs to Receive the Information?   The audience for the communication will differ depending on the message to be delivered. For example, all employees will need to be informed about the pending merger of the organization, but different information may be necessary for different groups of people. The finance department needs specific information in order to prepare financial information for review and consolidation, while the operations department needs different information about the merger. Many exchanges of information involve only a single business unit. Examining how the information affects interactions with other business units or workgroups determines whether or not employees outside of the business unit need to be informed.

When Should Information Be Disseminated?   The timing of communication, such as the announcement of a corporate acquisition, can be critical. Management may want to advise employees as soon as possible, but other factors (such as sensitive business negotiations) might place limits on when information is released. In some cases, information is disseminated to employees simultaneously with a public announcement. In other cases, information may be less time-critical and can be passed along during regular staff meetings.

Who Should Convey the Information?   Every communication plan should not only identify who the communicators are, but should also contain specific guidelines about the responsibilities they bear in passing the information on to employees. Information that comes directly to employees from top managers, such as the CEO or President, carries the weight and impact of the senior position in the organization. Top managers are best used for communicating major changes or initiatives that affect employees throughout an organization. Most employees, however, feel the greatest amount of trust with their direct supervisor and very often want to know the supervisor's interpretation of information. In many cases, direct supervisors will be the best choice for conveying news to employees.

Communication strategies should also take advantage of informal leaders in the workforce: employees who may not hold positions of authority in the hierarchy, but who are held in high regard by their coworkers. This group of employees can influence how other employees react to information, so utilizing them in a communication plan can benefit employers.

In some circumstances, several individuals may be involved in a particular interaction. For example, an announcement made by the CEO could be followed up with more details from the VP of each business unit, as well as small group meetings between employees and their direct supervisors to discuss how the information affects individual workgroups.

How Will We Know if the Strategy Is Effective? It's critical for communication to work both ways: Not only does management need to provide information to employees, but employees must be able to respond to the information. An effective communication process provides a method for feedback to be directed to someone in the organization who is responsible for acting on it or responding to it.

In some cases, such as a change in production processes, managers will be able to review production output and quality control statistics to know if employees understood the information well enough to implement the process change. If the statistics indicate an increase in the number of products rejected for poor quality, or the number of products produced per employee decreases, it is likely that the communication was not successful.

Operational Responsibilities

With a communication strategy in place, it is possible to develop plans for specific communication needs. There are two closely related components to consider when setting up a communication process in an organization: how the information will be conveyed, and how much it will cost.

The following section discusses a variety of ways to deliver messages to employees depending on the type of information involved and the audience that is to receive it. In determining how best to convey a particular subject, you may want to consider building on the employment brand concept introduced in Chapter 3, "Building a Staffing Plan." Identifying official communication channels in the same way the employment brand is identified can help employees be sure they are getting the most accurate information straight from the source.

One of the most important considerations when selecting a method for a particular communication is how much money is available. Much communication is made without a specific budget. For example, managers often use regular staff meetings to pass on information that affects their individual workgroups. In other cases, as in the announcement of a merger or acquisition that must be made simultaneously throughout the organization, it might be necessary to establish a budget for printing material or for conducting a webcast or teleconference.

Communication Methods

One of the most important considerations in developing a communication process is to allow opportunities for two-way communication, so that information flows both from the top down and from the bottom up. All organizations allow information to be disseminated from the top (management) down (employees). It is equally important to provide a means for information to flow from employees to management, or from the bottom up. This two-way flow of information is important to ensure that organization leaders are fully aware of activity within the organization; it's also important to ensure that employees have an avenue to report problems that occur, such as sexual harassment or other breaches of company policy or legal requirements. In the case of sexual harassment, for example, the establishment of a channel for communicating harassment allegations can provide a legal defense for employers if allegations turn into a lawsuit, as was discussed in Chapter 6 "Building the Employee Relations Program."

Much of the communication in many organizations takes place between individual employees and their direct managers or supervisors in the form of one-on-one meetings or conversations. These meetings provide opportunities for information to be exchanged in both directions and help managers to build rapport and trust with employees. One-on-one meetings are a key element of the performance management program and are discussed in more detail in Chapter 9, "Building a Performance Management Plan."

Top-Down Communication

There are many different ways to convey information, and each is appropriate in different situations. Some methods are simple and inexpensive (such as e-mails), whereas others can be complex and expensive (such as webcasts or road shows). Factors unique to individual organizations must be considered when selecting a method that is appropriate for a specific topic. The following methods are some of the ones more commonly used for *top-down communication*:

top-down communication
The channel of communication in which information flows from the organization to employees.

> **All-hands meetings**   An all-hands meeting, sometimes known as a town hall meeting, is one in which the entire workforce is gathered together to hear the same presentation of information. This communication method almost always includes the involvement of the most senior executives in the organization, and is often led by the CEO. This method for disseminating information is often used to make major announcements and can include a question-and-answer session in which employees are able to ask questions of the CEO or any other organization executive. While these meetings make employees feel valued by the executive team, some employees may be too intimidated to ask questions.
>
> All-hands meetings can be expensive, whether the organization is able to accommodate the entire staff in a single room at one time, utilizes the internet to include staff in multiple locations with a webcast, or sends the CEO

and other executives to locations around the world in a road show to provide the information. In any organization, an all-hands meeting means that operations are shut down while employees attend the meeting, so the expense also includes reduced productivity. In a large, multinational organization, these meetings can be both expensive and difficult to coordinate when employees working in a variety of time zones must be accommodated.

Team briefings   Managers and supervisors generally brief their team members during regular staff meetings, in which they pass on new information released by the executive team or the board of directors. When changes are occurring rapidly, briefings can occur on a more frequent basis to be sure that employees have access to the most accurate and up-to-date information available.

Disseminating information during team briefings has several advantages. Because the relationship between supervisors and direct reports is the most important organizational relationship, and employees can ask questions about their specific situations, briefings can be one of the best ways to share information. Unfortunately, not all managers conduct team meetings on a regular basis, and some managers don't share information willingly. For this communication method to be most effective, some managers might need training to be effective in this setting. In addition, if not managed carefully, team briefings can disintegrate into complaint sessions, so managers must be able to walk the line between allowing employees to vent frustration and persuading them to buy in to changes in the organization.

Newsletters   Like all-hands meetings, newsletters provide ongoing opportunities to promptly reach large numbers of employees in organizations—without the logistical problems and costs of arranging meetings. Newsletters deliver the same message to all employees, regardless of their location or work schedule. To be effective, the purpose of the newsletter must be defined: Does it make announcements and update employees on organization results? Does it look like the annual report to investors? Are there opportunities for employee feedback? Maybe its purpose is to keep employees informed of activities throughout the organization with which they may not be involved on a daily basis. All of these reasons are valid ones for producing a newsletter (and there are many others).

Although they can be less costly than all-hands meetings, newsletters do require input from managers and employees. And because they must be edited and produced by someone, they are not without cost for employers. Newsletters lose their effectiveness when they are issued sporadically, so there needs to be a commitment from management to produce them regularly. Whether newsletters are issued in hard copy or electronically, there is no guarantee that they are read by all employees, and they don't allow for questions to be answered immediately. Providing a section for "Letters to the Editor" from readers is one way to answer questions, although it does not provide an immediate response. It is important to make some type of feedback method available to provide additional information as it is needed. Finally, global organizations must factor into the equation the need to translate newsletters for employees in other countries.

Bulletin boards   Before the widespread use of computers, organizations used bulletin boards in break rooms and other areas in their facilities to disseminate information. These are still in use in many organizations today, especially as a place to post the many notices required by state and federal governments.

Intranets   Intranets are the electronic equivalent of the break room bulletin board, with many additional benefits. To begin with, the intranet has the capability to provide some level of interactivity, providing an easy way for employees to get answers to common questions. E-mail links enable employees to contact appropriate personnel for even more information if it is needed. Intranets can be used to provide a fair amount of detail about HRM programs as well, including access to benefit information and the employee handbook.

E-mail   The advent of e-mail has changed business operations in many ways. It provides a fast, flexible, low-cost method for communication from the top down, from the bottom up, and laterally within organizations. It does require that a level of technology be available so employees can access it, and this may not be readily available in all organizations.

By its very nature, e-mail seems to lend itself to abuse and misuse far more than other forms of communication. One reason for this is its informality, which leads employees to use abbreviations or poor grammar that are not really acceptable in business. It is also very common for employees to say things in an e-mail that they would never dream of saying in a face-to-face conversation, thereby insulting coworkers and causing disruptions in workplace relationships. These issues can be addressed by identifying appropriate techniques for internal and external communication, providing e-mail etiquette tips, or training employees to use the system in a way that conforms with the organizational culture and style.

Another common issue with e-mail is that managers sometimes use it to the exclusion of talking to their employees. While e-mailing is a time-saving and effective means of communication, e-mail should not be used in place of face-to-face communication.

Bottom-Up Communication

bottom-up communication
The communication channel in which information flows from employees up through the organization.

The previous section discussed communication that flows from the organization to employees, or from the top down. It is equally important for a communication process to allow for *bottom-up communication* to occur as well. This channel provides opportunities for management to "take the pulse" of employees and find out whether or not the organization is on track to meet its goals. Providing employees with opportunities to talk to management builds loyalty and reinforces motivation, both of which have a positive effect on productivity. There are some commonly used methods for eliciting feedback from employees, including the following:

open-door policy
A communication method in which management encourages employees to approach any level in the hierarchy with ideas, complaints, or problems.

Open-door policies   An *open-door policy* is a strategy that is often used successfully in organizations to encourage employees to come forward with questions and concerns about issues that are affecting them at work. Whether the issues have to do with work processes, barriers to getting work done, new ideas to improve workflow, or personal issues that are affecting an employee's ability to achieve results, open-door policies can be very effective—but only if management is committed to the policy and willing to follow through on it. Open-door policies provide accountability for decisions made by supervisors and managers, and some may feel threatened when employees are able to go to their boss or their boss's boss with questions or complaints.

Successful open-door policies often include requirements that employees first approach their direct supervisor with questions or complaints before moving to the next level. Open-door policies fail when supervisors and managers don't listen to employee suggestions when they are put forth, when managers don't follow through on suggestions, or when employees are punished in some way for bringing problems to their supervisors' attention. These policies can become burdensome if they are implemented without limits; a single manager, for example, could easily spend an entire day listening to a succession of employees without time to get other work done.

Management By Walking Around (MBWA)
A communication method in which senior executives regularly spend time in production areas, talking with employees about their jobs and answering questions.

Management by Walking Around (MBWA)   *Management By Walking Around (MBWA)* was developed at Hewlett-Packard and first publicized by Tom Peters, who wrote about building successful organizations in his book, *In Search of Excellence* (Warner Books, August 1988). The idea behind MBWA is that managers who get out of their offices and onto the production floor can see the results of their decisions in action and get a feel for how well those decisions are working for the organization. MBWA is a simple and cost-effective way for managers to talk to employees about working conditions and processes, and having the general manager or CEO come to the production floor to talk to them makes employees feel important and valued by the organization. Although MBWA provides opportunities for bottom-up communication, it is time-consuming for executives with a lot on their plate, and some employees may find it intimidating to see the "big boss" on their turf. Employees who do have questions might find that the boss doesn't have an answer immediately available, so it's crucial that a way of providing the information promptly is found when that occurs.

Employee involvement committees   One great way to get employees involved in solving problems is to create an *employee involvement committee* that includes them on a task force designed to solve a particular problem. Participating on a committee gives employees an opportunity to be heard, gives them a sense of control over their work, and increases their level of buy-in to the results. As with committee work in any organization, there are some drawbacks. First, when left to their own imaginations, employees can make some pretty unrealistic proposals. Second, there's no guarantee that what the committee proposes reflects what all employees want. Finally, committee recommendations can be time-consuming and delay implementation of needed changes.

employee involvement committee
Involves employees in solving organization problems.

There are some cautions when establishing committees, though. As was discussed in Chapter 2, "The Impact of Employment Law on HR Practice," the National Labor Relations Act (NLRA) provides employees with the right to bargain collectively about working conditions. It is an unfair labor practice for an employer to dominate an employee group and control its results or recommendations. When establishing employee involvement committees, it's important to be sure that this line is not crossed. In unionized environments, employee involvement committees are even more problematic because the union may see them as an infringement on its right to represent employees.

Brown-bag lunches   A *brown-bag lunch* is an informal way for senior executives to meet with small groups of employees and talk with them about what is happening in the company. It presents an opportunity for employees who would not otherwise have a chance to talk to organization leaders to do so and to ask questions in a less-intimidating situation than an all-hands meeting.

brown-bag lunch
A brown-bag lunch is an informal meeting between a senior executive and a small group of employees who can get to know the executive and ask questions about the organization.

Suggestion programs   Suggestion programs are effective when they are taken seriously by the organization. In many companies, employees find the "suggestion box" to be a source of humor because nothing ever happens based on suggestions that are made. The first rule about a suggestion program, then, is that employers must read and respond to the suggestions. Whether or not the suggestions are viable, it is important for employees to understand why they are not implemented. When appropriate suggestions are implemented, it's important to follow up and let employees know that the change occurred as a result of a suggestion. Allowing employees to make suggestions anonymously may increase their willingness to take risks and make suggestions that go against the status quo and result in significant savings.

Kiosks/hot lines/online forums   Organizations find many ways to utilize technology to provide opportunities for communication, even in environments in which employees do not have access to computers for their daily work. A relatively new development in this area is the installation of computer kiosks in production areas to provide employees with access to the company intranet.

Other opportunities for bottom-up communication are made available with hot lines that can be set up to report malfeasance or harassment situations. Online forums allow employees to post questions that can be answered by other employees or company experts in a particular subject.

All these methods provide a single source for giving or receiving information that is easy for employees to find and for employers to update. They can be used to control rumors during times of rapid change or uncertainty. The downside of these programs includes the fact that management can use them as a reason for not communicating directly with employees about serious issues. To be effective, they must also be updated regularly to maintain credibility with employees; in order to do this, senior executives must be willing and available to provide information for this purpose.

exit interview
Exit interviews are conducted with employees who are leaving the organization to find out about their experiences and why they chose to leave. The purpose is to determine whether changes need to be made to the work environment.

Exit interviews   One way to obtain information from employees (although one might argue that it comes too late) is through the exit interview process. *Exit interviews* provide an opportunity for employees who have decided to leave to provide an honest assessment of their experience in the organization. Even though the information is gathered when employees have already decided to leave, some employees decide to be less than open about their reasons in order to maintain a good relationship with former supervisors. Some organizations have found success by utilizing third parties to conduct exit interviews so that the results remain anonymous. Other organizations conduct exit interviews six months after employees leave and have found that former employees are often more open about their experiences once they have had a chance to gain some perspective. This method makes it possible to obtain information that provides a better assessment of their experiences.

employee survey
An employee survey is a formal process in which employees answer questions about what is working or not working in an organization.

Employee surveys   One of the best ways to find out what employees think is to conduct an *employee survey*. This method allows employees to provide information honestly, anonymously, and without the fear of reprisal because the information is collated with other responses.

Employee Opinion Surveys Valuable Management Tool

By Richard A. Sherwood, SPHR, Managing Partner, Innovative HR Solutions, LLC

While many HR practices are difficult to quantify, most managers realize that there's a direct connection between employee satisfaction and productivity. If employees are the primary focus of any manager's quest for increased productivity, shouldn't they play a role in determining the best workplace solutions? Employers interested in developing a high-performance work team know that they must find out what motivates and satisfies their employees. Employees are typically thrilled when management solicits their opinions. But what's the best way to go about it? The most powerful vehicle to accomplish this goal is an anonymous employee opinion survey.

The Process

Filling out an employee opinion survey is easy for most individuals. The majority of survey formats include simple instructions and use the Likert scale (a 1-to-5 selection response system that consists of a range from strongly agreeing to strongly disagreeing with a given statement). Although the wealth of information uncovered by an employee opinion survey can at times be astounding, it also can serve as the employer's motivation to fix what's been apparent all along. Any company thinking about tapping the benefits of employee brain power should pay close attention to the before and after phases of the process.

Before the Survey   Before writing the survey, spend time thinking about what the survey should specifically emphasize. This might require a focus group or special meetings in which pertinent issues are identified and isolated. Taking extra time on the front end pays off when it results in more relevant survey questions and thus more revealing responses.

After the Survey   Far too often, management sighs in relief once surveys are completed and the data is analyzed and packed away neatly in a report. In fact, a company should see a survey project through to completion by using what it has learned about its employees. It's perplexing to think of the misperceptions that are uncovered by employee opinion surveys. Even more bewildering is the choice some companies make to sit on their new information. Conducting employee opinion surveys carries an inherent risk for management. If managers have no intention of changing their policies after the surveys have been analyzed, they'd be better off not conducting them in the first place. Employee morale tends to deteriorate if no action is taken after they have participated in a survey in which their opinions were supposed to count. Furthermore, any future attempts at soliciting employee ideas and opinions won't be well received because of lost trust and diminished belief in the process.

Continues

The Greatest Information Source

When employees feel satisfied, they are happier overall. Employees who are generally happy are far more productive than those on the other end of the spectrum, or even those who fluctuate back and forth. Many companies report that soliciting their employees' opinions was the best step they could have taken in reducing labor relations issues.

The Ideal Tool

The win-win scenario that can be fostered by an employee opinion survey makes it an important tool for any organization to consider. Ideally, it will only confirm what management already knew. On the other hand, it might uncover issues in the processes that should have been addressed long ago. Done right, employee surveys help employers to see and to act upon what's really occurring in their organizations. It allows them to ferret out false assumptions and to glean valuable observations and suggestions from employees. Just as important, it gives employees an opportunity to make a difference. The benefits of conducting an employee opinion survey are as follows:

- Reduces turnover

- Identifies organization-wide strengths

- Identifies organization-wide issues and solicits ideas for corrective action

- Gathers objective data from which management may develop a meaningful dialogue

- Establishes benchmark data to evaluate future improvements

- Commits executives to a process that brings them closer to employees

- Provides employees with a stake in their employer's success

- Attracts job candidates

- Helps to align compensation and benefit programs to more effectively meet the needs of both employees and management

Case Study #1

One company wanted to abolish an expensive pension plan that had been in place for many years as a sort of silent benefit. Concerned that the plan's abolition might be perceived as an unfair takeaway, management decided that it would first survey employees for their opinions about the plan. They learned that the majority of their employees didn't understand or care about the pension plan. What they really wanted was a 401(k) plan. So, with no disruption, one plan was replaced with the other, and upper management was freed from its fears.

Continues

Case Study #2

A retail operation with $50 million in sales and 300 employees did not offer its employees the opportunity to move laterally or upward in the company, and management suspected that employees were feeling pigeonholed. An employee survey confirmed that employees liked their jobs, yet planned to stay only for a very short period of time because the company's structure lacked opportunity for upward mobility. As a result of the survey, management implemented a new program that included the creation of a job family matrix that provided opportunities for incremental promotions based on performance. Every 6 to 12 months, performance now dictates which employees are promoted or cross-trained. This allows employees to experience job enrichment.

Summary

By conducting an employee opinion survey, the HR professional can obtain valuable information about the company's workforce: determine if its managers are respected, if communication is clear, if the benefits plans are valued, and if the company acts in an ethical manner. Consider the employee opinion survey as an opportunity to enhance the partnership between management and staff.

Lateral Communication

Another important element to include is a protocol for lateral communication between departments. Encouraging employees to share information with each other can reduce duplicated efforts and can lead to process improvements.

Another important consideration for inclusion in an employee communication program is a method to encourage *lateral communication* between employees. This kind of process builds camaraderie within the organization and reduces the negative effects of "silo thinking," in which individuals in different departments have a single focus (based on the work that they do each day) instead of a global focus (based on what is best for the organization as a whole). One way to develop lateral communication is through the formation of cross-functional project teams.

lateral communication
Lateral communication is communication that takes place between employees in different departments within the organization.

A cross-functional project team brings together employees from different business functions, for example, from the production department, marketing, finance, and IT, with the goal of developing a specific product. The project team has responsibility for coordinating all aspects of the development project, and employees work together to solve problems for the project. This process provides opportunities to build understanding between departments and results in an organization that functions better overall in the long term.

Lateral communication allows employees to identify duplicated work efforts and helps to prevent some tasks from being dropped through the cracks. Working together reduces misunderstandings between departments and builds trust between individuals and business units that each does actually know what they are doing. This trust breaks down barriers that can prevent organizations from functioning at the highest level.

Communication Training

Just as some may wonder why it's necessary to have a communication plan, some may wonder why we need to talk about communication training. After all, we all talk to each other all the time. Anyone who has suffered through a seemingly endless and unfocused business meeting, in which nothing is accomplished, has experienced one of the reasons for training employees to communicate. Many organizations provide training for supervisors and managers on conducting effective meetings that add to productivity and do not waste the time of participants.

Some important training programs to provide include those that teach employees how to use the telephone system and the organization's computer network, and how to access the Internet and intranet. During these programs, it's important to inform employees about the organization's policies regarding personal use of the Internet and the telephone system. Although some organizations allow employees to freely utilize these resources for personal matters during the workday, doing so can be seen as an unauthorized use of organization assets and be considered grounds for disciplinary action in other companies. Whatever approach is taken by your organization, it's important for employees to know the difference between uses that are acceptable and unacceptable. If an organization retains the right to search computers or monitor telephone calls, employees should be advised that the equipment they use at work belongs to the employer and, as such, the employer has the right to search it as needed. Informing new employees of this policy when they join the organization and providing them with periodic reminders on a quarterly or annual basis helps to protect both employees and employers.

Managers need to be trained to know what techniques to use in different situations, how to encourage and reward employee input, and when to listen. Employees also must learn effective methods to use to get their message across in a way that gets results.

Some organizations value communication skills so highly that they spend considerable time and money training managers to communicate effectively. Training topics can vary widely and include one-on-one verbal communication, presentation skills, and the ability to communicate effectively in writing. In Chapter 8, "Building Training and Development Programs," I'll talk about different training and development techniques that can be utilized for this purpose.

Administrative Responsibilities

The administrative responsibilities for employee communication programs include activities designed to support the process. Because HRM is involved in staffing changes (new hires, transfers, and terminations), one of the basic administrative tasks in this area is making sure that contact information lists are updated in a timely fashion so that new employees are included in all appropriate communications.

Another related responsibility for HRM is to ensure that staffing changes are communicated throughout the organization. For example, if a staff accountant is promoted to an accounting manager (replacing an employee who resigned), two announcements are appropriate. First, employees need to know that the person now has a new position. Second, if the promoted employee is now responsible for managing budget reports in the new position, it is important to make sure that others in the organization are made aware of this.

From time to time, the HRM function might be required to collect and distribute employment data and other information related to safety concerns, union negotiations, or other HR-related responsibilities to the organization's public relations function for inclusion in a press release, the annual report, or on the organization's website.

Metrics

There are several methods that can be used to measure the effectiveness of employee communication programs. In a previous section, we talked about one of them: employee surveys. There are several other ways of obtaining feedback as well.

One method that can be used is to have direct managers report on conditions in their own workgroups. As these reports are compiled and move up the hierarchy, a picture begins to emerge about whether or not the planned message is getting through to all levels of the organization.

Another method, used quite often in marketing operations, is to interview a focus group. By selecting employees from various business units and levels throughout an organization and interviewing them about working conditions and information they receive, the organization can obtain feedback about the effectiveness of programs and communication in the organization.

Feedback often provides better insight into conditions when it is provided anonymously so that employees feel they can be honest without the fear of reprisal for criticizing their manager or the organization. The most accurate information is obtained when it can be gathered from all employees directly.

Obtaining feedback is necessary for the organization to ensure that it is moving in the right direction, but soliciting information from employees raises an expectation among them that some action will result (of course, they usually assume that the actions taken will solve all of their problems). This situation can be difficult because it's unlikely that a single solution will make everyone happy. It's even worse if no action is taken as a result of the feedback; at the very least, employees should be provided with a report of the results of the feedback.

The feedback process can be expensive and time-consuming for an organization, both when creating the method for obtaining the feedback and when collating and reporting on the results. For this reason, it requires a commitment from senior management to the process and the will to take some action based on the results.

Terms to Know

bottom-up communication

communication strategy

employee survey

lateral communication

open-door policy

brown-bag lunch

employee involvement committee

exit interviews

Management By Walking Around

top-down communication

Review Questions

1. Why is it important to have a communication strategy?

2. What elements should be included in a communication plan?

3. What are some drawbacks of utilizing employee involvement committees?

4. What are the benefits of a suggestion program?

5. What do employers need to do before they conduct a survey?

6. Why are lateral communication processes important?

7. How does an organization know whether the communication program is working?

8. What steps are necessary to implement a communication process for a particular subject?

9. What should be considered when determining the timing of different messages?

10. What is the difference between an all-hands meeting and a team briefing?

Chapter 8

Building Training and Development Programs

In This Chapter

- Organization development
- Change management
- Leadership development
- Management development
- Succession and replacement planning
- Training program design
- Common training topics

The rapid pace of change that occurs in business today as a result of economic fluctuations, government regulations, or advances in technology requires employee skills to be upgraded on a regular and ongoing basis. There are two ways for organizations to respond to this need: hiring employees who already have the skills or assisting current employees to acquire them. The two areas of human resource management (HRM) that cover programs designed to improve employee skills and prepare them for future responsibilities are known as training and development. These two areas are part of the human resource development (HRD) function.

Strategic Foundation

human resource development (HRD)
HRD is the area of human resource management responsible for working with current employees to attain new skills.

Human resource development (HRD) programs positively affect employee morale and productivity in many ways, including improvements to quality in both product and service offerings. HRD encourages continuous improvement among workers, not only by providing information that is useful to specific duties, but also by increasing knowledge that has long-term benefits for the organization. If the organization is presenting itself as a place in which employees are developed to their highest potential, providing training and development opportunities is essential. Doing so demonstrates the organization's commitment to its employees and reinforces the employment brand that is presented to new employees before they join the organization. An organization that creates a culture and employment brand that values employee contributions and aims to retain skilled employees is one that is supported by both training and development programs.

HRD programs include activities in two areas: training and development. Although similar in some respects, these functions have key differences.

Training   Training programs provide solutions for short-term needs and are designed to solve immediate problems. For example, a business that installs a new customer relationship management (CRM) program in its call center needs to train employees so that they know how to use it effectively. This fills an immediate business need.

Development   Development programs provide long-term solutions that are designed to meet an organization's future needs. Development activities can include training that increases knowledge or skills, job assignments in various organization functions to build broader knowledge, formal education (such as that provided by education reimbursement programs or attendance at graduate-level management development programs), and mentoring from a senior executive in the organization. Development programs increase an employee's value to the organization.

In deciding whether or not to implement an HRD program, the choice is not so much "either/or" for employers; it is understanding what results to expect from training activities as opposed to the results obtained from a development program. The fact is that many organizations utilize both types of programs to meet different needs, and most development programs include a training component.

Hire Skills or Train Employees: Making the Decision

When making the decision about whether or not to implement or continue an HRD program, a number of factors should be considered. The first of these considerations is often cost. As with other aspects of HRM, it can sometimes be difficult to tie specific HRD programs to individual organizational goals. As a result, when organizations are looking for ways to reduce expenses,

HRD programs look like a good place to make cuts because it can appear that they are not adding value. In some cases, organization leaders might decide that it is more cost-effective to hire individuals who are already trained rather than provide training and development programs for current employees. Organizations that reduce training and development expenses in an effort to save money generally find that they suffer losses from reduced productivity, which affects profitability and is eventually reflected in reduced shareholder value.

For some organizations, the cost of the program is the deciding factor. Although cost is certainly a major consideration, it is important to include the benefits provided by HRD in the equation by conducting a cost-benefit analysis to demonstrate how HRD programs add value to the organization.

Another important factor to consider is timing. If there is an immediate need for a particular skill, such as that required for an accounting manager, the organization may not have a choice—it may be a business necessity to hire an employee who already has the required skill level. When timing is not an issue, the organization has an option to develop a current employee for the position. For example, if the current accounting manager plans to retire in two years, the organization can identify one or more employees who have the potential to be promoted into the position and establish a development program to prepare them for the new role. When the accounting manager retires, the organization has one or more employees with the necessary knowledge, skills, and experience ready to assume the new role.

It is also important to consider the availability of a particular skill in the labor market when deciding whether or not to establish an HRD program. Some skills are in short supply, and even if money is no object, employees with those skills are in high demand. For that reason, it might be difficult to hire the skills that are needed. In that case, it is to the organization's benefit to select current employees who have the aptitude and determination to develop the skills, and then provide them with the necessary training.

Organization Development

Organization development (OD) is a systematic method for examining an organization's technology, work processes, and overall organizational structure with the goal of improving performance in each of those areas. In addition, OD looks at the way employees operate within an organization in an effort to affect their behavior so that the organization is better able to meet its goals. This process is designed to ensure that the organization's structure and the processes it uses to produce its goods and services continue to be viable and competitive in the future. OD encompasses a wide range of activities known as OD interventions, which are action strategies used to improve the way an organization reaches its goals. There are several interventions that fall under the OD umbrella.

organization development (OD)
OD examines operations to determine whether improvements to technology, work processes, or structure can improve bottom-line results.

OD Interventions

One of the best-known OD interventions is total quality management (TQM), which was first introduced in the 1940s and has been utilized most successfully in manufacturing operations. This intervention directs its attention to customer needs and views all operating activities from the perspective of what will improve the product or service for the customer. During the 1980s, Motorola was instrumental in taking TQM a step further when it developed the Six Sigma program. Six Sigma added detailed guidance designed to make the implementation of quality programs more effective.

Learning organizations, another OD intervention, focus on lifelong learning for employees, continuous process review, and sharing of information that results in operating improvements. Learning organizations provide opportunities for employees to learn within the organization and to utilize this learning in their daily work.

One of the more recent interventions is known as knowledge management (KM), which represents a change in the way organizations retain information that is critical to operations. During the course of doing their jobs, individual employees build a wealth of information specific to their organizations as they go about their daily work. This information is not always related to the mechanics of the job; it might have to do with where to find relevant documents or the history of customer interactions about specific problems. In the past, this information was often lost when an employee left the organization or was transferred into another department. The process of KM provides a way to retain this information for use by others in the organization to increase operating effectiveness.

A good example of KM is the use of customer relationship management (CRM) software. CRM software provides a way for all employees to have access to information about all the interactions with each customer. For example, the sales representative enters the names of decision makers and other contacts for each customer's organization into a database, along with information about the product that was purchased. If the customer has a problem or question and calls customer service for assistance, the customer service representative (CSR) who answers the call knows which product the customer has and is better able to answer questions. Each CSR enters information about questions or problems from the customer (and the information that was provided or actions taken during each call). When the customer calls back again, the next CSR has access to the full history of interactions that have taken place and is better able to serve the customer. In addition, sales reps can view this information prior to making sales calls so that they are better able to address customer concerns.

Organizations spend countless hours devising strategies to improve operating results and often spend a great deal of money on them as well. No matter how well-planned the strategy is, though, its success relies upon the employees who must implement it. A critical element of the OD process, then, is preparing employees for change and giving them the tools they will need to implement it successfully.

Change Management

The function of *change management* is to make it easier for employees to accept organizational changes. Change is difficult for many people because it takes them out of the "comfort zone" to which they have become accustomed and requires that they work in different ways or interact with people they don't know well. To some employees, proposed changes might represent a loss of status or be seen as politically undesirable. When change initiatives fail, it is most often because employees were not adequately prepared for the change. There are several steps that organizations can take to help employees accept and implement change initiatives.

change management
Change management is the means used to help employees deal with change in organizations.

Prepare for change   Change is a fact of life in business today, and organizations need to be proactive in identifying trends that will affect their industry or individual operations. Being prepared for change in this way reduces the trauma that often accompanies changes that are sudden and seem unexpected to employees.

Communicate the change   As discussed in Chapter 7, "Building the Communication Plan," two-way communications are essential in organizations, especially when a change is planned. Including employees who are directly involved in daily operations during the information-gathering stage is one of the best ways to make sure that they will support the change when it is implemented. Communication must happen early and often so that employees become accustomed to the idea of the change; doing so enhances acceptance for the idea and increases the level of commitment to the change.

Plan for change   Prior to announcing the change, it is important to develop a plan that encompasses the goals of the change; explains what the change means to the organization, the industry, and the employees; and identifies the criteria that will be used in measuring the results. The plan should identify and address issues that are of concern to employees so that the employees have a clear picture of how the change will affect them.

Identify the change sponsor   A successful change must have a high-level sponsor within the organization, such as the CEO (if the change is organization-wide) or the head of the business unit implementing the change. Without this level of sponsorship, some employees may not feel they need to cooperate with the change.

Enlist supervisory support for the change   The closest workplace relationship is between individual employees and their direct supervisors. Getting the supervisors on board with the change is the key to success in influencing employees to support the change.

Obtain support for the change from unofficial leaders   In every organization there are a few employees who are viewed as leaders by their coworkers. When these informal leaders support a change process, they can influence their coworkers to accept and support the change as well.

Implement the change   Having taken the previous steps, employees should be aware of the planned change and well on the way to accepting and supporting it. At this stage, success can be further enhanced by making sure that employees have the information and tools that are necessary to implement the new process.

Evaluate the change   During the planning stage, criteria for measuring success were developed. At this point in the process, a comparison of the desired results to what actually occurred helps employees and the organization to identify ways that future change can be improved.

The best plan in the world cannot succeed if employees are unprepared for the changes that they will need to make to the way they operate. A thoughtful implementation plan is key to preparing them to accept and support organizational changes.

Leadership Development

leadership development
Leadership development is the process that organizations use to prepare managers to step into leadership roles.

A key element of success for any organization is the quality and ability of its leaders. *Leadership development* is the process of identifying managers who have the potential to lead the organization and then providing them with wide-ranging opportunities to learn and demonstrate their capabilities. Over the years, many theories have been advanced about whether leaders are born or made, and whether leadership can be learned. These theories range from defining leadership traits, to identifying leadership behaviors and situations, or some combination of these factors. Thousands of books have been written on the topic of leadership theory, and a full discussion of them all is beyond the scope of this book. If you are interested in learning more about them, there is a detailed discussion in my book *PHR/SPHR Professional in Human Resources Certification Study Guide* (Sybex, 2004). Or you can type "leadership theory" into an online search engine or bookseller, or do a search at your local library and find many books that will explain it. What you should take away from reading this book is an understanding of the various leadership styles exhibited by different leaders and the ability to differentiate the types of programs used to develop leaders within organizations.

Leadership Styles

Everyone who has ever worked for someone else has experienced a leadership style of one kind or another. We all remember the great bosses who inspire us to be and do our best, and we also remember the ones who seem to take pleasure in belittling and humiliating the people who work for them. Although HR practitioners are rarely in a position to force managers to treat employees with dignity and respect, the role we play in organizations allows us to advise managers about the benefits to be gained from treating employees with dignity and respect. In some cases, we are invited to coach managers who are having difficulty, either by the managers themselves or by those to whom they report. When coaching managers, it is helpful to know what kind of leadership style they use and how it impacts employees. There are several common leadership styles found in organizations.

Authoritarian   An authoritarian leader is one who issues orders and directs employee activity. Also known as the directive leadership style, it is effective in some instances, such as an emergency situation when actions must be taken quickly. Leaders who utilize this style on a regular basis may be able to increase productivity in the short term, but may find that their employees have low morale, and their departments have higher turnover rates.

Democratic   Democratic leaders are effective when those who report to them are highly skilled, intelligent professionals whose motivation comes from a desire to do the best possible job. Leaders who demonstrate this style must trust that their employees know what to do and how to do it, and make themselves available for assistance as requested.

Laissez-faire   Laissez-faire leaders exhibit virtually no leadership to their work groups. These leaders allow their employees to operate on their own and provide little (if any) guidance. This leadership style is often exhibited by leaders with little management experience or by those who are afraid to be "the boss." In the worst case, workgroups led by laissez-faire leaders are chaotic and unproductive because employees do not have faith in the leader.

Coach   Leaders who operate as coaches with their work teams help individual team members develop the skills that they need to work independently. These leaders make themselves available to provide encouragement and support, answer questions, and, if needed, provide the extra push that is needed to complete an assignment.

The leadership styles utilized by managers in an organization are most successful when the style conforms to the organizational culture. For example, a culture that encourages employees to take risks, make suggestions, and ask questions would not be a match for an authoritarian style of leadership. Likewise, a manager with a laissez-faire style would probably not be very successful in a culture that was very production-oriented. Effective leaders may find themselves utilizing all of these different leadership styles at different times depending on the nature of the situation, the past performance of the employees involved, and the amount of experience of the employees.

Management Development

management development
Management development is the process organizations use to prepare employees for positions of greater responsibility.

There is an ongoing debate about the difference between a manager and a leader. For the most part, it is generally agreed that a leader's role in an organization is to inspire employees to commit to the vision that the leader has for the organization and to support the vision by performing the work they were hired to do in a way that advances that vision. The role of a manager, on the other hand, is to see to it that the work of accomplishing the vision is done by providing the information and tools needed by employees to do their work. *Management development* is the process used by organizations to prepare employees to move into roles where they are responsible for getting work done through others.

Just as leadership theories abound, so do theories about effective management techniques. Most management theories are centered on employee motivation, identifying motivational factors or which techniques to use. These theories, which were developed during the 1950s and 1960s, are taught in business management courses. One of the best-known of these theories is Maslow's Hierarchy of Needs, developed by Abraham Maslow in 1954. According to Maslow, all human beings are motivated by different levels of needs, depending on their circumstances. At the lowest level—physiological—people are seeking to satisfy their most basic needs for food and shelter. At the next level, when people have enough to eat and a roof over their heads, they look for physical and emotional safety. After they feel safe, people are motivated by the desire for social interactions, and look to join communities where they feel accepted. Once people feel that they belong to a group, the next need is for recognition for their achievements and contributions. When people reach the highest level of motivation—self-actualization—they are looking for a creative outlet that allows them to realize the potential they see in themselves.

From a management perspective, you can see that motivating someone who is seeking to fulfill basic needs is very different from motivating someone who is seeking ways to fulfill a need for personal creativity.

Another well-known motivation theory was proposed by Douglas McGregor in 1960. McGregor describes two styles of management, which he called Theory X and Theory Y. Theory X describes managers who view employees as uninterested in work and requiring ongoing direction to get their work done. These managers don't trust employees to work on their own. Theory Y managers, on the other hand, believe that if people are given the choice, they look for challenges to find more satisfying work. Again, you can see how differently managers with each of these views would operate within an organization.

There are a number of other management/motivational theories that form the basis of much of current management practice. These theories are explained in the *PHR/SPHR Certification Study Guide*, as well as in numerous other books and articles about management theory.

Succession Planning

Chapter 3, "Building a Staffing Plan," briefly touched on the concept of *succession planning*. The idea of this practice is to build "bench strength" in an organization so that as employees are promoted or rotated into different jobs, or leave the company, the organization is prepared to fill those positions with employees who have already established a track record with the organization and are familiar with its operating processes. A recent example of the benefits of succession planning occurred at IBM when a senior executive accepted the position of CEO at another company. As a result, three other IBM executives were immediately moved into new positions, creating a seamless transition for the company. Although some adjustments to their changed roles will be necessary, all three of the executives involved are already familiar with IBM operating practices and business strategies, and can continue moving it forward without a lengthy period of adjustment.

succession planning
Succession planning is the process of identifying employees who have the capability to move into leadership positions within an organization.

Replacement Planning

The purpose of *replacement planning* is similar to succession planning: to have back bench strength within the organization so that critical positions can be filled relatively quickly. While succession planning concentrates on higher-level management positions, replacement planning is used at all levels throughout an organization. For example, it can be used as a mechanism to ensure that the accounting department has a backup plan to replace a senior accountant with an employee who is familiar with the responsibilities of that position.

replacement planning
Replacement planning is the process organizations use to ensure that there is sufficient bench strength to fill critical positions at any level in the organization.

Operational Responsibilities

Because development programs focus on the longer-term need to prepare employees for future positions, developing those programs has a strategic focus. On the other hand, training programs are used to fill more immediate needs and so have a more operational focus. Although the training function has a different focus than development, it is equally important for maintaining the skills of an organization's workforce. An effective training program delivers the information that employees need to do their jobs effectively in the short term. Training programs are more technical in nature than development programs and can be implemented for many reasons, including developing new skills, teaching employees how to perform their jobs safely, interacting appropriately with coworkers in the workplace, and utilizing new technology.

The ADDIE Model

The basic steps in a training process are often described by an acronym, ADDIE, which stands for Analysis, Design, Development, Implementation, and Evaluation. The ADDIE process is an instructional design model that provides an outline to follow when developing training programs. The following sections take a look at each of these steps in more detail.

Analysis

needs assessment

Needs assessment is a process used to determine whether or not training is necessary. It identifies who will be trained, what they will learn, how training will be delivered, and when it will take place.

The analysis phase for a training program in this process is arguably the most important. It is during this phase that the need for the training is explored in a process known as *needs assessment*. Beginning the training development process by identifying who will be trained, what information needs to be presented, how it will be delivered, and when it will occur results in a training program that meets specific organizational needs. Because this phase is the key element of creating an effective training program, the process is described in the following detailed sidebar.

 Real World Scenario

Needs Assessment: A Quick Start Method for the Most Important Training Tool

By Phyllis A. Simmons, MA, CSP

A needs assessment is the most critical tool used to set up a training program. It's normally the first step in the development process. Skipping this step is a common pitfall because people think it's too time-consuming or do not understand its value. The needs assessment is a trainer's best friend because it can tell you what people need to learn and provides answers to many key questions, such as:

◆ Which subjects should be taught?

◆ What type of educational activities do employees prefer?

◆ What resources do we currently have in each department?

◆ How often should classes be conducted?

◆ Does any training need to be outsourced?

◆ Are there any language or special learning needs?

Continues

The results will help you see the big picture, and minimize budget and scheduling disasters. It will be time well spent and worth it in the end because you are not making decisions blindly. Using a Needs Assessment Worksheet, as in the following illustration, provides a quick start to obtain a wealth of information in one shot.

Needs Assessment Worksheet
Quick Start

Section 1. General Information		
Date:	Department:	
Manager's Name:	Contact Information:	
Department Description and Hours of Operations:		
Best Training Days and Times:		

Section 2. Target Audience Assessment	
Number of Employees:	Language & Special Needs:

Types of Learning Activities Employees Prefer (check all that apply)

☐ Videos	☐ Demonstrations	☐ Computer-based	☐ Handouts
☐ Discussion	☐ Mock Scenarios	☐ Lecture	☐ Other:

Section 3. Training Information				
Job Position	Job Required Topics	Frequency Needed	Current Training Methods	Resources Available

Section 4. Budget Considerations and Recordkeeping Comments

© 2004 by Phyllis A. Simmons, MA, CSP

Continues

How to Do an Assessment and Use a Quick Start Worksheet

Getting prepared is extremely important. Schedule some time to meet with each department manager to complete the worksheet. Inform the manager ahead of time so the person will know what to expect. Explain the purpose of the meeting and ask the manager to have the following materials available:

◆ Any mandatory classes needed for the department, especially related to technical skills, certifications, licenses and safety—such as First Aid/CPR

◆ Instructional aids and resources used

◆ Current vendors, including costs of classes (if used)

◆ Types of audiovisual equipment available in the department

◆ Preparation to explain the recordkeeping process and show examples. (For example, how does the manager document training and where are the files maintained?)

Section One: General Information

The purpose of section one on the Needs Assessment Worksheet is to gather basic facts about the department and find out what it does. Write a brief statement; for example: "The department sells computer equipment to educational institutions." Include any other information that could affect the implementation process. Use this section to record preferred class times; for example, "No courses the last week of the month due to sales inventory." It's good to note schedule preferences upfront to prevent errors later down the road. *Here are two important tips:*

◆ *If a department has more than one shift, ask the manager about the most effective way to train the other workers. Overtime pay might need to be considered if classes can't be given during the shift time.*

◆ *If you plan to outsource training for a department with multiple shifts, make sure that services can be provided during off-peak hours (6PM to 6AM).*

Section Two: Target Audience Assessment

Section two of the worksheet focuses on the most important people: the participants (or what's commonly referred to as the *target audience*). Training is designed for the learner, not the trainer; concentrate all your attention on the trainees; not on yourself. A common pitfall is not taking the time to learn about the audience. Find out what you can; some information is better than nothing. Remember that people retain more knowledge and find classes more satisfying when activities are tailored to their specific needs. *Here's an important tip: Find out as much as you can about the target audience—especially education levels, age range, gender, language considerations, literacy issues, and special needs of anyone who is physically challenged. This information will help you determine what types of materials are appropriate for the learners.*

Continues

Tailoring Training Activities

Ask a representative number of employees or the manager which learning activities staff members prefer (video, hands-on, lecture, and so forth). Expect to hear at least three to four different answers. Everyone has a different learning style; however, each person will generally fall into one of the four categories listed here:

◆ Visual learners usually prefer videos, diagrams, handouts, posters, and computer-based activities (if computer-literate).

◆ Auditory learners prefer lectures, videos, and discussions.

◆ Hands-on learners prefer scenarios, demonstrations, discussions, visual aids (that they can touch), and computer-based activities (if computer-literate).

◆ Interactive learners like to be personally involved and usually like role-playing, drills, games, demonstrations, discussions, and computer-based activities (if computer-literate).

When possible, use diverse teaching methods to appeal to different learning styles. For example, a course on workplace violence prevention could include showing a video, discussing the subject, and reviewing the company policy. Thus, there would be an activity for everyone.

Section Three: Training Information

Section three of the worksheet helps you capture the essential knowledge and skills needed for each job position (don't forget to include safety). You can use this data later in the development process to set up training calendars, databases, and courses. *Here's an important tip: Find out which materials are currently present in each department. List the results to see what's missing.*

Ask the manager to discuss the knowledge and skills needed for the positions that will be trained. Here's an example of a sales department.

Job Position	Job Required Topics	Frequency Needed	Current Training Methods	Resources Available
Sales	Products and Sales Techniques	Quarterly	Lecture, led by manager	Literature from the sales department
	Customer Service	Annually	Role-play and video, led by manager	Video and company handbook
	Ergonomics	Upon hire and annually	None	Need to purchase videos and handouts or hire trainer
	Office Safety	Upon hire and annually	Computer-based, self paced	CD-ROM

Continues

Section Four: Budget Considerations and Recordkeeping Comments

So, where do you go from here? Section four is reserved for budget consideration notes and statements about the department's recordkeeping process. *Here's an important tip: Don't forget to ask about record-keeping, especially if it pertains to labor, legal, and safety topics that are subject to regulatory audits.* In this case, setting up a documentation system is important and can't be overlooked.

Now that the assessment is complete, use the data as a foundation for the rest of the development process. You now have a road map. The results can be used for many different purposes: to identify gaps, identify the subjects needed, set up calendars, and purchase materials. Most importantly, you will know more about the target audience and tailor the instruction likewise. Customized training results in higher knowledge retention and increased participation, and will make classes more interesting. Remember that a needs assessment is the most important development tool. Trying to create a program without it is like building a house without a set of blueprints.

Design

Throughout the design phase of the ADDIE model, the information gathered during the needs assessment is used to create the specifics for the program. There are five steps to be completed during this phase of program development, as discussed in the following paragraphs.

Task inventory   During this step, the trainer compiles a list of the tasks required by the job by using information gathered during the needs assessment, or by doing further investigation—such as reviewing job descriptions or interviewing supervisors or job incumbents.

target audience

A target audience describes the people who will receive a particular training, It identifies their level of experience, time with the company, and level of expertise in their field.

Target audience   Knowing the *target audience* is crucial for a successful training program. Are those who will be attending new to the job? Or are they seasoned professionals? Is this program designed to be a refresher course? Or will the information be new to those attending the presentation? The answers to these and similar questions will help to make the training more effective.

training objectives

Training objectives are used to focus training programs by describing what trainees will learn and to establish the criteria for evaluation.

Training objectives   *Training objectives* have multiple uses. They are used during the development phase to focus the presentation. They also describe for the trainees what they will learn as a result of the program. Finally, they are used during the evaluation stage of the ADDIE process to determine whether or not the training accomplished what it was intended to do.

An effective training objective includes four elements:

◆ Describes the situation

◆ Describes a behavior that can be measured

◆ Describes the conditions around the behavior

◆ Describes the criteria for measuring success

Course content   The course content is developed using the training objectives as a basis for identifying the materials and presentation methods to be used during the training.

Evaluation criteria   Finally, the design phase establishes the criteria that will be used to determine whether or not the training accomplished its objectives. Ultimately, this means being able to measure not only whether the trainees learned the information during the training session, but also whether they are able to utilize the information proficiently when they return to their jobs and retain it over a period of time.

Development

During the development phase, the information acquired in the course of the design phase is converted into the actual program format that will be used. The trainer develops a plan for the presentation, selects and prepares any materials or activities that will be used, and develops a means for testing the trainees to determine whether they absorbed the information.

Implementation

In the implementation phase of the ADDIE model, the training is delivered to the target audience. In this phase, all the work done previously—from gathering information during the needs assessment, to the creation of training objectives and development of the program—come together. If the preparation work has been done well, the training will meet the needs of the audience and provide them with the information or skills that were identified in the needs assessment.

Evaluation

A crucial step in the training process occurs during the *training evaluation* phase. At this time, the trainees have an opportunity to evaluate the training, and their managers and supervisors have an opportunity to assess the impact of the training on subsequent job performance. There are many different ways to evaluate

training evaluation
The evaluation process determines whether or not the training accomplished the desired results.

training programs; some are more effective than others. In 1959, Donald Kirkpatrick, PhD (currently Professor Emeritus at the University of Wisconsin), identified four levels of evaluation for training programs: reaction, learning, behavior, and results. Let's examine these now to determine when each of them is used most appropriately.

Reaction   An evaluation that measures the immediate response of participants in a training session is known as a reaction evaluation. This level of evaluation is often gathered with the use of a questionnaire completed by participants at the end of the training. Evaluation at this level provides helpful information for the trainer in terms of program delivery, but does not help in evaluating the long-term impact of the training on the organization.

Learning   The next level of training evaluation is known as a learning evaluation. In this method, participants are tested to determine whether or not they gained knowledge as a result of the training program. This evaluation method provides more information than the reaction method, but it does not provide feedback about how (or whether) job performance improved as a result of the training.

Behavior   A behavior evaluation is a follow-up method that is conducted between six weeks and six months after the training occurs to determine whether the information gained during the training is being utilized on the job or not. This evaluation can be made through observations by supervisors or managers, interviews with participants, or the administration of a test or a survey of the participants. This level of evaluation begins to measure whether the cost of the training yielded increased operating results.

Results   The fourth level of evaluation, the results method, attempts to measure the impact of a training on business results. In a business climate focused on cost reductions and results, for many organizations this is the most meaningful evaluation. It is, however, the most difficult evaluation to accomplish because it is sometimes difficult to isolate the impact of a particular training on results because many factors contribute to the bottom line in addition to training.

Common Training Topics

While job-specific training programs are unique to each industry, profession, and organization, the need for some types of training programs cross all those lines. These include new hire orientations, diversity training, sexual harassment, and communication training.

New Hire Orientation

In Chapter 3, I talked about the importance of new hire orientation to the success of new employees. One important aspect of orientation is the training that is provided to new employees, which sets the tone for their experience in the organization, helps them to integrate into the culture, and helps them to become productive team members. The training methods that are used should be designed to build on the natural excitement and enthusiasm that employees experience on their first day in a new job. In addition to more traditional forms of orientation training (such as videos and group meetings) that take place on the first day or half-day of work, many organizations extend orientation programs with the use of "buddy" or "mentor" programs. These programs are designed to guide employees over the first few months, and sometimes through the first year of employment. The ultimate goal of both programs is similar: to assist new employees in their assimilation into the organization. The goals of each program are slightly different.

Buddy programs   The main goal of a buddy program is to make sure that new employees have a smooth transition into the culture and operating procedures of an organization. This goal is accomplished by pairing a veteran employee with a new employee. The buddy's role is to establish an open line of communication and to build rapport so that the new hire feels comfortable asking questions. Buddies might also assist in the process of introducing new employees to coworkers, although the primary responsibility for these introductions lies with the direct supervisor.

Employees selected to act as buddies generally have been with the organization for an extended period of time (one to three years), work in the same business unit or workgroup as the new hire, and are successful in the organization. It is important that buddies have developed an understanding and appreciation for the culture and operations of the organization, and are sufficiently skilled at building interpersonal relationships to create the rapport required to work those who are assigned to them.

Buddy assignments generally last from three to six months, or until the new hire feels comfortable with the new work environment.

Mentoring programs   The goal of a mentoring program is slightly different from that of the buddy method. In addition to easing the transition of new employees into the culture and operations of the organization, a mentor focuses on developing the new employee with an eye toward the longer term. Mentors coach new hires in developing interpersonal or management skills to prepare employees for future responsibilities in the organization. As such, mentoring relationships generally last longer than buddy relationships.

Those selected to act as mentors are generally from a different business unit or work group and are more senior in the organization than those they mentor.

Diversity Training

As the workforce demographic in the United States continues to change, it becomes increasingly important for employers to ensure that all employees are treated fairly and equitably. The role of training in this effort lies in the ability to inform employees about the differences in culture, religion, ethnic origin, and gender of those in the workforce. It is equally important that misconceptions about individuals with physical disabilities be set straight. Providing training that educates employees about the differences between people helps to break down barriers and increase cooperation, and ultimately results in improved productivity for the organization.

Sexual Harassment Training

Although there are few specific legal requirements for conducting trainings designed to prevent sexual harassment (the Equal Employment Opportunity Commission [EEOC] requirement is vague on the specifics), courts have given weight to the nature and frequency of sexual harassment training when employees claim that harassment occurred. In some cases, organizational liability for the unlawful actions of employees has been reduced when the organization provides regular, ongoing training that is designed to eliminate this harassment from the workplace.

In order to reduce an employer's exposure to sexual harassment claims, it is important that all employees be trained on at least an annual basis as to what constitutes sexual harassment and be informed of the organization's policy prohibiting such harassment in the workplace. These programs play an important role in reducing instances of harassment and can lead to improvements in productivity because employees feel that they are safe from harassment, know where to turn for help if they believe they are being harassed, and make clear the consequences of harassment that is found to have occurred.

Communication Training

As was discussed in Chapter 7, an effective communication program is the cornerstone to a productive workforce. An ongoing training program that provides information to managers about conducting meetings and communicating effectively with employees on a day-to-day basis reinforces the need for appropriate communication in the organization. Providing employees with training opportunities that teach them the best ways to communicate appropriately within the organization helps them to better exchange information in more productive ways. Communication training programs concentrate on teaching employees how to build credibility with others, adjust their communication styles so that they are more effective, and learn how to phrase feedback and requests in constructive ways to further understanding within the organization.

An important facet of training in organizational communication is to provide employees with the tools necessary to make appropriate use of written communication vehicles, such as e-mail. Although e-mail is a valuable and time-saving communication method, it lends itself to inappropriate use more often than other types of written communication because of its inherent informality and immediacy. Providing employees with information on the appropriate use of e-mail can reduce misunderstandings and improve productivity.

Another type of communication training that is often made available to employees in larger organizations involves public speaking or presentations. Many people are intimidated by the thought of speaking in front of a group of people. Training, whether in the form of Toastmaster participation or other delivery methods, builds confidence and increases the employee's ability to convey information to groups of coworkers, customers, or others—depending on the needs of the organization.

Time Management Training

Time management training is designed to help employees identify ways in which they can improve their personal productivity. This type of training can be delivered in a variety of ways, including books, videos, online web courses, one-on-one coaching, and classroom presentations. The general goal of the training is to help employees develop a personal method to stay organized so that they can accomplish the many tasks that are expected of them. The tools presented in these trainings include such abilities as handling documents so they are dealt with appropriately, setting up and maintaining a calendar for appointments, and keeping track of tasks by utilizing to-do lists or other tools.

Another element of time management that is often difficult for new managers to master is the art of delegation—and some never seem able to delegate effectively. Developing training programs that are designed to assist managers with this key requirement often improves relationships between managers and their employees. As the manager becomes more effective at delegation (learning how to clearly convey the task or responsibility, what is expected, and the timeline by which it must be completed), employees are better able to produce work that meets the manager's expectations. Managers, knowing that they have communicated their expectations, are better able to allow employees to complete tasks without micromanaging their work.

Administrative Responsibilities

The maintenance of training records is the main focus of training and development program administration. Depending on the type of training, the records may be important for individual employees to demonstrate that they meet the requirements for advancement in the organization, or the subject of legal requirements. Maintaining records that demonstrate that employees have met organizational requirements is fairly simple. It can be done by recording information in an HRIS system or by filing a document in an employee's personnel file. Records that are required to demonstrate legal compliance or to reduce exposure to legal claims need to be maintained differently.

Safety training records As discussed in Chapter 2, "The Impact of Employment Law on HR Practice," the Occupational Safety and Health Administration (OSHA) requires organizations to provide regular safety trainings for employees. To demonstrate compliance with this requirement, organizations need to maintain records of the meetings. A logbook that includes the dates and topics of safety training meetings, along with a list of employees who attended the meetings, is necessary. This is easily accomplished by using a simple sign-in sheet that includes the date and topic, and space for attendees to sign their names. It might also be useful to include a copy of the sign-in sheet in the personnel file of each employee who attended the training.

Certification training records In some cases, employees who operate special machinery or who possess special skills may be required, either by the organization or a government agency, to maintain a current level of knowledge and/or proficiency. For these situations, copies of documents that verify trainings or test results should be maintained in the individual personnel file.

Sexual harassment As previously discussed, providing employees with regular training designed to reiterate and reinforce organizational prohibitions against harassment activity demonstrates for legal purposes the organization's intent to provide a workplace free from harassment. Records of these types of trainings should include the training schedule, a synopsis of the presentation, and a list of attendees. In addition, documentation may be maintained in personnel files.

Metrics

Many of the issues tied to training metrics were discussed in the previous section on training evaluation. It can be difficult to measure the results of a specific training on an organization, business unit, or even on a workgroup because many other factors (such as an economic upturn or industry changes) can affect operating results. Whether the goal of the training is to increase skills, change behavior, or improve performance, being able to quantify improvements that result from training programs helps managers to see the value training adds to the organization's ability to achieve its goals.

Meaningful metrics begin in the design phase of training when course objectives are defined. The objective provides a point against which to measure results. Using either the learning or behavior evaluation methods to test participants prior to delivering the training, and testing them again after the training, make it possible to determine whether or not the goals of the training (as defined by the objective) were achieved.

Terms to Know

change management	human resource development (HRD)
management development	needs assessment
organization development (OD)	replacement planning
succession planning	target audience
training evaluation	

Review Questions

1. What is the ADDIE model?

2. Why are HRD programs important for organizations?

3. What is the difference between OD and change management?

4. What is the difference between a leader and a manager?

5. What is a learning organization?

6. What is Maslow's Hierarchy of Needs?

7. What are the four levels of training evaluation?

8. What is the difference between succession planning and replacement planning?

9. Why is needs assessment the most important component of developing a training program?

10. Why is it important to maintain records of safety training meetings?

Chapter 9

Building a Performance Management Plan

Mention performance management to employees and supervisors, and the first thing that usually comes to mind is the annual performance review process. Annual reviews are almost universally dreaded by supervisors (who must fit them into already stressed schedules) and by employees (who often feel that the results are unfair). Unfortunately, performance reviews are the only piece of performance management that is utilized in some organizations. In truth, though, reviews make up only a small part of a much larger and more valuable process. When done well, performance management can enhance productivity, build relationships, and facilitate ongoing communications between supervisors and their employees.

Strategic Foundation

Performance management (PM) is an integral part of all other human resource management (HRM) functions. To begin with, it can be used to guide an organization toward the achievement of its strategic goals, so it is a key aspect of HR strategy. To employees, the most visible aspect of performance management is its relation to salary increases or promotions, so it is an integral part of the compensation plan. Very often, training and development needs are identified as a result of performance management activities. Finally, many activities that occur as part of the employee relations function are tied to the results of performance management.

NOTE   **Throughout this chapter, the term "supervisor" is used to refer to anyone in an organization who is charged with responsibility for supervising the work of subordinates. In this context, the term covers first-line supervisors, managers, and executives.**

With the growing emphasis in business on tying individual activities to strategic business goals, it's important to view PM in the context of the strategic goals defined by the organization. Organizational success is directly tied to how well individual employees perform, whether it is the performance of the CEO or the most junior employee on the production line. Obviously, the level of impact on the organization varies greatly, depending on the level of responsibility required by the job. A well-designed PM plan keeps employees on track to meet their individual objectives and, by doing so, keeps the organization on track to achieve its goals. The PM plan also helps employees identify what they need to do and provides them with a means for measuring their progress toward achieving their objectives.

Why is it important to measure individual performance? After all, it is time-consuming and can be difficult for supervisors. One answer is that establishing a measurement system (whether for an organization or an individual) helps to focus attention on what is being measured. For example, if an HR department is receiving low marks on service delivery from its customers in the organization, the VP of HR may decide to establish an objective for improving customer service. When employees know that the way they deliver customer service is being monitored for improvement, they will be more focused on improving service delivery, and their supervisors will be more focused on observing and providing feedback to them on ways they can improve their service skills.

Another reason for measuring performance is that it provides the ongoing impetus for continuous improvement within the organization. As one organizational or individual goal is achieved, new goals are set to further grow the organization and challenge employees. This cycle of continuous growth and learning helps organizations to stay abreast of market changes, identify new opportunities, and ensure that employees are ready to tackle these new challenges.

In this context, a PM plan begins with a review of an organization's strategic goals by setting individual objectives designed to support those goals. Effective PM tools set performance objectives for employees at all levels in an organization. These objectives form the basis for focusing employees on what they need to accomplish as individuals in order for the organization to achieve its strategy.

The next section describes how individual objectives are tied to job assignments and used to manage employee performance.

Operational Responsibilities

Now that you have an understanding of the "why" behind PM, let's turn to the "how" and explore the process used to develop an effective plan. Traditionally, the PM process was based on performance standards derived from job descriptions, and it still is in many organizations. In other organizations, supervisors and their employees work together to develop performance objectives that form the basis of the PM plan. Still other organizations utilize a combination of performance standards and employee objectives as the basis for managing performance. Whether the PM plan relies on performance standards, is based on objectives derived from organizational goals, or is a combination of the two techniques, the same principles apply to the process. The following graphic illustrates the PM process:

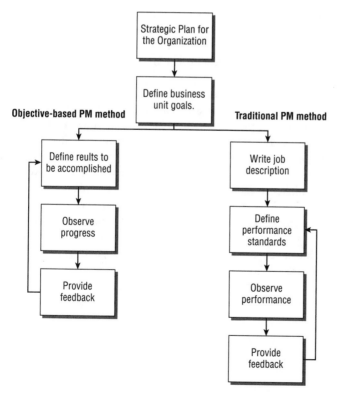

Regardless of the method used by an organization, there are three questions that can help you determine whether your performance management plan is effective:

- Do employees know what they need to do?
- Do employees have a way to measure success?
- Do employees receive feedback on a regular and frequent basis?

The next section takes a look at the role of performance management in answering these questions.

Communicating Performance Expectations

The key to managing performance is to first make sure that employees know what they are supposed to do. In most companies, job duties and responsibilities are communicated with a job description. As discussed in Chapter 3, "Building a Staffing Plan," a job description is based on the results of a job analysis conducted to examine what the employee in a particular job needs to accomplish. A job description consists of essential job functions (those that are most significant for the position) and non-essential job functions (those that are ancillary to the position).

If the job description takes care of informing employees about what they are supposed to do, how do supervisors communicate the level of performance that is expected? After all, there are many different ways that an employee could perform any particular task; some of which meet or exceed the supervisor's expectations, and others of which don't even come close to what is considered acceptable.

Traditionally, the establishment of performance criteria was a unilateral function carried out by management without the input of employees. In the current business environment, this has changed in many organizations as employees have been given a greater voice in defining performance criteria for their duties and responsibilities. As discussed in Chapter 6, "Building the Employee Relations Program," employees who are able to exert some control over their job situations have higher morale, are more loyal to the organization, and are more committed to their jobs. For this reason, building partnerships with employees to develop job performance criteria is a "win-win" situation for the organization and its employees. As mentioned previously, performance criteria can take the form of performance standards or performance objectives. Let's look at how these criteria are developed.

Developing Performance Standards

Performance standards are used to describe the results that the organization expects employees to produce for each function included in a job description. Performance standards do not necessarily need to be contained in a separate document; they can be included as part of the job function statement.

To illustrate how this works, let's take a look at different ways that one of the essential functions typically performed by an accountant could be presented on a job description:

Reconciles bank statements.

This statement describes the function the employee must complete, but it doesn't give an indication of the results that are expected from the activity. A performance standard adds this information to the job function and tells the employee what the supervisor expects will be accomplished:

On or before the third business day of each month, reconciles all bank statements to general ledger accounts, resolves discrepancies, prepares related journal entries, and enters adjusting journal entries into the general ledger.

Based on the information contained in the performance standard, the employee has a much clearer picture of what must be accomplished, what level of performance is expected, and when the task must be completed. In addition, the supervisor has clear, job-related criteria to use in determining whether or not the employee is successfully performing this task. Note, however, that this information does not tell the employee *how* to do the task, but it does clearly communicate the expected *results*. Unless employees are very inexperienced and in a training situation, telling them how to do the job can be demotivating and often results in lower morale.

Developing Performance Objectives

For decades, the use of job descriptions as the preferred method of communicating job duties and responsibilities to employees was considered the "best practice" standard for HRM. In the current business environment, which is characterized by rapidly changing conditions, something of a debate has developed in the business community about the usefulness of job descriptions. Some executives believe that job descriptions place limitations on the ability of their organizations to respond rapidly to changing business conditions. The question becomes, then, how does the organization ensure that its employees know what to do in order to effectively manage performance and ensure that business objectives are achieved? Organizations have come up with a number of unique and creative ways to answer this question by incorporating *performance objectives* into their operations.

performance objectives
Performance objectives are based on organizational and business unit goals and are usually developed jointly by supervisors and employees.

One way that this occurs is that the goal-setting process takes place at all levels in the organization. After the leaders have established strategic goals, the supervisors of individual business units develop goals that are designed to move the unit in the direction established by the strategic goals. When business unit goals are clear, individuals meet with their direct supervisors and work together in an interactive process to develop objectives designed to further the goals of the business unit. These objectives provide the direction employees need to contribute to the organization's achievement of its goals. As organization goals change to respond to changing conditions in the marketplace, the objectives are easily revised to reflect the new direction.

Just as a job description and performance standards must clearly communicate what employees need to accomplish and how they will know if they are successful, performance objectives must also communicate this information clearly. In his book, *The Practice of Management* (written in 1954), Peter Drucker described a method for creating meaningful goals and objectives, known as the SMART method. This method continues to be used because it communicates everything employees need to know about their objectives. The SMART (Specific, Measurable, Action-oriented, Realistic, and Time-based) method creates goals and objectives with the following characteristics:

Specific   A specific goal is one that is not open to interpretation about what the employee must do.

Measurable   A measurable goal includes objective criteria that can be used to determine whether or not it has been achieved.

Action-oriented   An action-oriented goal describes the activities that must be performed.

Realistic   A realistic goal is one that is achievable. Setting goals that require employees to "stretch" their abilities provides a challenge that many employees enjoy because it encourages them to improve their skills and abilities. Unachievable goals tend to act as demotivators for employees, sometimes causing them to give up without trying as hard as possible.

Time-based   A time-based goal is one that imposes a specific time frame for achievement.

Objectives that are developed in this way provide both a description of what the employee needs to do and the results that need to be achieved.

Managing Performance

Providing employees with information that tells them what is expected gives them the tools they need to do their work. At the same time, it gives their supervisors the information necessary to observe employees' work and provides them with constructive feedback designed to help employees improve. After employees know what they are supposed to do and the results they are expected to achieve, it is easier for supervisors to manage their performance.

Probably the greatest obstacle to effective performance management is the fact that people usually want to avoid confrontations at all costs. This is particularly true of some supervisors who are torn between having pleasant relationships or being friends with the employees who report to them and holding those same employees to expected standards. To these supervisors, this seems like an "either-or" choice. In reality, there is no need to make the relationship one that is confrontational. When supervisors understand how to manage performance in an immediate and constructive way, the fear of confrontation is often eliminated.

One of the most common mistakes that supervisors make in the PM process is that they tend to overlook minor mistakes and problems because they don't want to risk a negative interaction with an employee. As a result, employees don't realize that the work they are doing is not satisfactory and don't have a chance to improve their performance. For the supervisor, this can mean an increasing level of frustration with the employee because the work continues to be below standard. This is one reason that the performance appraisal process is viewed so negatively by many employees. Often, the first time an employee learns that performance improvements are needed is during a review, making the review an unpleasant experience for everyone involved. In the worst case, these situations become so untenable that a supervisor wants to terminate an employee, even though the employee has never been told that there is a problem.

In an effective performance-management process, supervisors are trained to provide instant feedback to employees for good work as well as for work that needs improvement. When these performance conversations take place on a daily basis, they become customary to both employees and supervisors, and are seen as "no big deal." In this context, when negative feedback is communicated, it is part of an ongoing process of continuous learning and improvement instead of an unpleasant confrontation. Effective PM requires supervisors to provide employees with both negative and positive feedback on a regular basis. When employees receive regular positive feedback, they are more open to receiving negative feedback when it is necessary. PM helps employees to know that their work is perceived fairly by their supervisors. For the supervisor, providing necessary negative feedback when performance issues are relatively minor makes these interactions less intimidating and confrontational because they usually occur before performance problems become serious.

Benefits of Ongoing Performance Management

Implementing a continuous PM process in an organization can be met with resistance from supervisors who already feel overburdened with responsibilities. As with any change initiative, the best way to convince supervisors of the need for PM is to describe the benefits they will see as a result of the process.

Numerous workforce surveys demonstrate that one of the most often heard complaints made by employees is that they receive little or no feedback about their performance from their supervisors. Utilizing continuous PM is an effective way to satisfy an employee's need for feedback. At the same time, it satisfies the supervisor's need to determine whether or not the workgroup is on track to achieve the operating results required for organizational success.

When employees receive regular feedback, they are able to incorporate it immediately into the performance of their duties. As a result, operating results show a trend of continuous improvement that increases organizational productivity. Increased productivity reduces operating expenses and improves bottom-line profits for the organization.

A direct benefit to supervisors who practice continuous PM is that as the capabilities of their employees increase, employees are able to take on duties requiring a higher degree of skill. This allows supervisors to delegate work that might previously have been beyond the ability of their employees to perform. As the level of complexity of tasks that can be delegated increases, supervisors are able to increase their own effectiveness by spending more time on functions that have a higher payoff for the organization.

Because employees crave feedback which is often lacking in their employment relationships, supervisors who establish a reputation for providing regular feedback and development opportunities for their employees are able to attract and retain high-quality performers to their business units. As the caliber of employees increases, productivity is enhanced, and the supervisor is seen as an effective leader in the organization. For the supervisor, this can mean opportunities for growth in the organization.

Finally, a continuous PM process provides structure for documenting poor performance. For employees who are not performing at an acceptable level, the use of regular, ongoing feedback provides the documentation needed for the disciplinary procedures discussed in Chapter 6, particularly when the feedback can be verified with contemporaneous notes taken during each conversation.

Elements of a Performance Management Program

After the decision to implement continuous PM is made, it is very important to provide supervisors with the tools and training they will need to effectively manage performance.

As previously discussed, the first step in PM is to make sure that employees know what they are supposed to do, most often by providing a job description. From the job description, performance measurement criteria are established, usually in the form of performance standards or objectives. Providing employees with this information helps to ensure that they will perform successfully.

The next step in the PM process is for the supervisor to observe employee performance. There are a number of ways to do this, and the method of observation will vary depending on the nature of the work being performed. For example, the supervisor of a customer service representative working in a call center might observe performance by listening in on service calls to determine how well the employee is performing. On the other hand, a construction foreman could observe a carpenter's performance both by watching the carpenter work and by examining the results of the work, such as a wall or a staircase. A CFO might review spreadsheets or reports produced by a financial analyst in order to observe the work produced.

Observations can be made by individuals other than the supervisor. For example, most of the work done by outside sales representatives takes place out of the view of a supervisor. Customers, on the other hand, have a direct experience of how well the rep is doing the job. The sales manager can observe the work of a rep by talking to customers to find out how well the rep is representing the organization. In addition, the sales manager will review the sales records, which show whether or not the rep is accomplishing sales goals.

Observing the work being done allows the supervisor to develop a basis for providing feedback to the employee. Situations might occur in which it is appropriate to give immediate feedback, such as when a construction foreman notices that the wall a carpenter is building is uneven. Pointing this out and working with the carpenter to straighten the wall is one form of feedback. Immediate feedback should not be limited to negative situations. Catching an employee in the act of doing something above and beyond what is required provides an opportunity for supervisors to provide spontaneous positive feedback, which is a cost-effective way to build employee morale.

Another way to give feedback to employees is by meeting one-on-one with them on a weekly or monthly basis, depending on the nature of the work and the experience level of the employees. Although face-to-face meetings are ideal, they might not always be possible, particularly when the individuals involved are geographically separated. In those situations, feedback can occur via telephone, or if necessary, by using e-mail. Whichever method is used, the goals of one-on-one feedback sessions are the same: for the supervisor to offer constructive comment on performance, and for the employee to provide an update on progress, ask questions, or make suggestions. The supervisor should make note of topics discussed and instructions given, including performance observations—both positive and negative. These written notes form the basis for more formal performance reviews when they occur, whether that is quarterly, semi-annually, or annually.

What kinds of constructive comments should the supervisor provide? To begin with, feedback should be specific and based on facts, not on opinions or judgments. For example, if an accountant submitted a financial report that was poorly formatted and included mathematical errors, the supervisor might provide feedback similar to this:

> *This report is a mess! I can't understand what it says, and the amounts in the total column don't add up. I'm really disappointed that you would turn in work that is so sloppy.*

This feedback is not constructive. It isn't specific, and it attacks the accountant. Instead, the supervisor could deliver the feedback in this way:

> *I'm having a problem understanding this report. It's not clear to me which of these numbers are direct expenses and which are indirect. I also found a mathematical error in the total column. Let's talk about how to present the information more clearly and accurately. Tell me what steps you will take to make that happen.*

This feedback is constructive: It's specific, based on facts, and doesn't attack the accountant. In addition, the supervisor is involving the accountant in the process of correcting the errors instead of dictating how to correct them. This provides an opportunity for development so that the employee will be able to produce reports more accurately in the future.

One-on-ones should provide an opportunity for two-way communication. Just as supervisors provide feedback for employees, employees should be able to ask questions, request guidance on projects, and be encouraged to talk about challenges they are facing while working on their assignments. This open, two-way communication builds strong employment relationships and contributes to increased productivity.

Another way to provide feedback is to conduct a "post-mortem" meeting when a project concludes. These meetings include all the members of the project team and provide an opportunity to discuss what worked and what didn't work during the project. This information can be utilized to improve work processes and increase productivity for future projects. It involves employees in developing more effective ways to complete their assignments and helps them to develop skills in communicating and negotiating with coworkers.

Finally, the feedback process provides a natural opportunity to discuss development opportunities that the supervisor has in mind for the employee, as well as opportunities that the employee is interested in pursuing. As supervisors work more closely with the employees who report to them, opportunities to delegate projects, rotate assignments within the workgroup, and assign more challenging work will become available. These opportunities help to keep employees interested in their jobs and prepare them for future responsibilities—a win-win situation for everyone involved.

 Real World Scenario

Performance Management Tips and Pitfalls

By Alice Elliott, SPHR

It is important to send one message—performance—throughout your organization by incorporating it into as many things as possible. Constructive, day-to-day conversations about work increase organizational productivity and are an important part of performance management, so all employees should be encouraged to give feedback daily. Employees become comfortable with performance conversations with practice and experience. Performance management is often initially introduced to employees through the performance appraisal system and reinforced through both formal training and the day-to-day coaching they receive when problem solving with their managers. As employees learn performance management, they embrace it. It saves time and lets everyone know where they stand.

A common complaint in organizations without a performance culture is that employees don't know where they stand or what is expected. Performance management eliminates that problem, and as a result productivity and morale go up. As an organization becomes conversant with the best practices of performance management, morale climbs. Everyone knows where they stand and what they must do to be a high performer. The following sections provide tips for good performance management and warn about some of the pitfalls that produce poor performance management.

Tip: Performance management begins in the interview

An excellent opportunity to reinforce the language of performance is during the interview process. A helpful thing to do is to train the interview team to conduct behavioral interviews. Ask the manager to pick his interview team and provide everyone with a copy of the position description. During the preinterview strategy meeting discussed in Chapter 2, "The Impact of Employment Law on HR Practice," ask each person what the new hire needs to do in the position to be successful immediately and over a six month period. Ask them to discuss and agree on the skills needed and the soft competencies they want.

Continues

Provide the team with some sample questions that are phrased in a behavioral manner. For example, if the interviewers want to make sure that candidates can work in a team, a series of sample questions could include the following: "Tell me about a project at your last company in which you worked in a team. What was the project? How big was the team? What would your teammates say that you did that was helpful to the team? What would they say that you did that you could improve on?"

Advise interviewers that the candidate should give specific examples and not opinions. A poor answer would be: "They think I am great." The next question from the interviewer should be: "Give me an example of what you did that they thought was great."

All behavioral interview questions are basically questions geared to understand performance—it's important to avoid asking for opinions from the person.

When the team meets for post-interview feedback, ask each team member to state the question they asked and the answer they received and then give their summation. This prevents an interviewer from saying "I think he will be a good team member" without any concrete reasons that can be cited from examples in the person's background.

Beginning an employment relationship by having candidates talk about their prior performance experience sets the framework for continuing to talk about performance with them on a day-to-day basis. It is also an easy way to help employees become comfortable with talking about performance in a matter of fact manner.

Pitfall: Thinking that everyone understands how performance management works

A pitfall that HR sometimes falls into is thinking that everyone understands how to manage performance because HR gave two classes during the year: one class on the appraisal process and one class on performance management. Although both classes are important and give a common language for everyone to use, performance management needs to be practiced daily. Just as we would not expect to learn to read by going to class for two hours a year and then never practicing it the rest of the year, we should not expect employees to know how to practice performance management without ongoing coaching.

Tip: Use the language of performance management

Performance language is about what one is doing on the job, not about opinions. HR can be especially helpful in the coaching process with both managers and individual contributors. The fact is that many organizations are so busy that formal classes never happen. There are always a few employees who fill out their performance appraisals without reading the instructions, let alone attending a class on how to complete them.

Tip: Teach everyone how to give constructive feedback

Coaching managers and employees to give constructive feedback is often a natural result of the problem-solving process about an employee issue. When a manager says that he has a problem employee, it is an opportunity to ask for specifics and to show the manager how to communicate the specifics to the employee in a constructive manner.

Continues

For example, suppose that a manager says that John has a bad attitude. The follow-up questions should be: "What is John doing that shows a bad attitude? How is the work product?" Sometimes the manager cannot articulate the problem immediately. HR can guide the manager by asking for examples. As the examples emerge, the manager can then talk to the employee about the specific behaviors that need to improve without the label of "attitude." It may be that the manager will say to the employee, "When you sigh when asked to do a task and take a day to get back to the requester, the requester does not get the work they were expecting from you on a timely basis. They also feel it is unpleasant to ask you for work." This helps the employee to understand the issue that needs to improve. If necessary, HR can then guide the manager through the disciplinary procedure without having the employee feel attacked and labeled.

Tip: Teach employees how to get feedback from managers

Coaching individuals to handle issues with their bosses is just as important as coaching managers to provide feedback. Many times, employees feel their bosses are "unfair" or do not give them respect. Again, the same process can be followed. By asking what the boss is doing, HR can guide the employee into the specific issues and then suggest ways to approach the boss about those issues.

Pitfall: Becoming part of the complaint instead of remaining the guide

Do not join employees in their feelings. It is important to hear what they feel, but to continue to drive to an understanding of the business issues (performance) and not participate in a complaint session.

Pitfall: Speaking for the employee

Do not tell the boss about the conversation. The employee and boss must have a good working relationship; that means they both must talk about the work/performance issues between themselves. HR has failed when it does the talking for the employees.

Tip: Teach employees how to exchange performance feedback with coworkers

Last but not least in the coaching process is coaching peers, which can be the most challenging. If regular coaching does not work, HR may need to work with the two peers and guide them through their issues. Again, it is important to steer them away from personal or emotional comments and drive the conversation to the performance issues.

Performance Appraisals

The *performance appraisal* process is fraught with negative emotions for many employees and their supervisors. Often, part of the reason is that supervisors do not provide ongoing feedback to employees during the normal course of work. By the time the review rolls around, the supervisor's level of frustration has risen to a high level, and the employee feels completely blindsided by information that could have resulted in improved performance if it were communicated in a more timely way.

performance appraisal
A performance appraisal is a regularly scheduled event, generally occurring once per year, in which employees meet with their supervisors to discuss performance during the preceding review period.

Performance appraisals, also known as reviews or evaluations, are a way of checking in periodically so that employees and their supervisors are on the same page. When this occurs as one part of a performance management process in which regular, ongoing conversations about performance are taking place, the review itself becomes just another conversation about performance, and it is less unpleasant for both parties.

Selecting a Review Method

There are many different performance appraisal methods available for use by organizations. Descriptions of some of the more common formats follow:

Ranking   The ranking evaluation method is useful in smaller organizations, but it becomes increasingly less effective and unwieldy as the employee population increases. When using the ranking method, supervisors list employees from the highest-level performer to the lowest.

Rating   In the rating evaluation method, supervisors are provided with a rating scale, either numeric (1–5) or based on phrases (such as "exceeds expectations," "meets expectations," or "does not meet expectations"). The scale is defined so supervisors and employees know what each rank represents.

critical incident review
In a critical incident review, a supervisor maintains a log of incidents, good and bad, that occur during the year in order to write a narrative review of an employee's performance during the review period.

Critical Incident   The *critical incident review* is a narrative method of evaluation in which supervisors make notes during the review period (typically, a timeframe of one year). When it is time for the review, the supervisor refers to these critical incidents and provides the employee with a written narrative of performance during the year.

360° Reviews   The 360° review method is most frequently used for supervisory and management personnel. In this method, the individuals being reviewed are rated by subordinates, customers, vendors, and peers in addition to their supervisor. The intent of this method is to provide multiple sources of information to the individuals so that they can improve their performance.

The Appraisal Process

Selecting a review method is an important step in designing an appraisal process, but there are other, equally important issues to consider. Decisions must be made about timing and fairness, and a plan for training supervisors should also be developed. The timing of the review process should reflect the organization culture and goals. The process must be viewed as fair by employees, and supervisors must receive training on the best ways to conduct appraisals.

Timing   When establishing or revising an appraisal process, a decision must be made on when and how often formal appraisals will be conducted. As to when, there are two standard approaches: anniversary reviews and focal reviews. The decision on how often appraisals occur is related to the review schedule selected by an organization.

Anniversary Review   As the name implies, *anniversary reviews* are scheduled on the anniversary of the employee's date of hire. In many organizations that use an anniversary review schedule, newly hired employees receive their first formal appraisal six months after their hire date, and subsequent appraisals are conducted annually on that date. Many supervisors find an anniversary review schedule easier to manage, particularly when they supervise a large number of employees. This schedule allows them to spend more time with each individual, making it easier to manage the process within the context of their other responsibilities. Supervisors are less likely to base employee appraisals on comparisons to other employees because they are focusing on individuals. The anniversary schedule can also be easier for HR departments to manage because they are not inundated with hundreds or thousands of reviews to process at one time.

anniversary review
An anniversary review is an appraisal conducted on the anniversary of an employee's date of hire.

There are some disadvantages of using the anniversary review schedule, though. In organizations that tie performance standards to operating goals and objectives, it might be difficult for supervisors to assess how well an employee whose review occurs early in the goal period will achieve those goals in the future. When salary increases are based on the results of the performance review, this review cycle also requires supervisors to plan increase amounts carefully to ensure that funds are available for high performers whose reviews occur later in the budget cycle.

Focal review   In a *focal review* schedule, all performance appraisals are administered at one time during each review cycle, regardless of individual dates of hire. This process has a number of advantages. To begin with, the appraisal date can be set to coincide with the organization's strategic and budget planning cycle. For employees, this means that performance is judged based on the achievement of goals during the entire review cycle, so performance can be judged more equitably. The focal review schedule provides supervisors with the ability to assess varying levels of contribution by different employees more easily. When salary increases are based on the results of performance appraisals, a focal review cycle also makes it easier to distribute the increases more equitably.

focal review
A focal review is a schedule in which appraisals are conducted for employees throughout the organization on the same date.

While focal review schedules have a number of advantages, there are also some drawbacks to consider when deciding whether or not to implement this schedule in an organization. One drawback is that it can be difficult for supervisors to review all employees at the same time because it requires a substantial time investment. It is also possible for supervisors is to base individual appraisals on comparisons between employees instead of on job standards. For HRM, the focal review schedule can impose a significant administrative burden when hundreds or thousands of appraisals must be completed in a short period of time.

Appraisal frequency   Organizations utilizing an anniversary review schedule conduct formal appraisals on an annual basis. In a focal review process, however, the schedule can vary depending upon how goals are established. For example, organizations that define quarterly goals for employees may conduct formal reviews on a quarterly basis. Other organizations may require reviews on a semi-annual or annual basis.

The decision on frequency should be based on the organization's strategy and culture and designed to support the achievement of goals and objectives.

Fairness   As you know from Chapter 2, equal opportunity legislation requires employers to base decisions about any of the terms and conditions of employment on job-related criteria. This includes decisions that are related to the performance appraisal process. Chapter 3 described a number of common biases that can affect the interview process, and many of them can have a negative impact on the fairness of the appraisal process as well. It is important for supervisors to be aware of these biases and avoid them to the extent possible.

Central tendency   During the appraisal process, some supervisors are reluctant to identify employees who are performing at a very high or very low level. As a result, these supervisors tend to assess the performance of all employees as "average." This creates problems for employees at both ends of the spectrum. For high performers, an average review is a demotivator that can lower their morale and motivation. As a result, their performance and productivity suffer, or they may decide to leave the organization. For low performers, an average review creates three problems. It does not provide them with an opportunity to improve their performance, so they believe that their work is acceptable. When the supervisor later decides to terminate the employee for poor performance, the formal documentation gives no indication that there was a problem. This becomes a serious problem if the termination results in any type of legal action. Finally, other employees in the work unit are always aware of poor performers. When they do not perceive any consequence for poor performance by coworkers, they begin to wonder whether the supervisor knows what is going on, and the supervisor begins to lose credibility. Employees who are performing at an acceptable level can become demotivated when this happens, and both morale and productivity suffer as a result.

Halo/horn effect   When supervisors focus their evaluations of individuals on a single incident that occurred during the review period, the halo/horn effect is at play. For example, a supervisor who does not maintain a critical incident log or record of individual employee performance during the review period might remember only a single event that had either a very positive or very negative result. When the halo/horn effect is at work, a supervisor will evaluate an employee who made a single mistake in an otherwise error-free performance and then characterize them as a poor performer.

Recency   One of the most common errors in performance appraisal occurs as a result of the recency bias. This bias occurs when supervisors use only the most recent performance results as the basis for an evaluation. Employees who have the misfortune of making errors or missing deadlines within a few weeks of the appraisal may find that their otherwise stellar performance during the rest of the review period is ignored. Again, the use of a critical incident log or other means of recording performance throughout the period will assist supervisors to avoid recency errors.

One criticism that is sometimes made about the performance appraisal process is that it relies on judgments made by a single individual—the supervisor—and is therefore subject to errors based on bias and other concerns. One result of this can be a belief by employees that some supervisors hold employees to a different standard with the result that a high rating given by one supervisor means something different than a high rating by a different supervisor. This is known as *inter-rater reliability*, and it is based on the concept that different raters, or supervisors, rate the same employee's performance differently. The impact this has on an appraisal process can be minimized by providing supervisors with standard definitions of performance levels to increase the consistency of evaluations throughout the organization.

Inter-rater reliability
Inter-rater reliability is the term used to describe the different ratings that often result when different supervisors rate the same employee.

The performance appraisal process is a critical HR function which is unfortunately poorly administered in many organizations. The process must be seen as fair in order to serve its ultimate dual purposes of encouraging employees to continue delivering positive results and correcting the results of employees whose results are less than ideal.

Preparing for the appraisal   Because many supervisors find the performance appraisal process to be a difficult one, advance preparation can be advantageous. In organizations that encourage the use of ongoing performance management processes (discussed earlier in this chapter), this is much easier because information is collected on an ongoing basis. Completing the following tasks in advance will help the actual performance meeting to go more smoothly.

Collect relevant information   The supervisor should begin by collecting relevant information. One source for information is the critical incident log if one has been maintained throughout the review period, but this should not necessarily be the only source of information used in the review. In addition to observations made by the supervisor about performance, it's important to find out how employees are serving those with whom they work on a regular basis. This does not necessarily require the use of a 360° process (which is generally utilized for supervisory, management, and executive personnel), but it does mean that the supervisor needs to talk to coworkers, customers, vendors, and others with whom the employee comes in contact on a regular basis in order to make a fair determination about overall performance. Obtaining this information can help to reduce concerns about inter-rater reliability and builds credibility with regard to the overall fairness of the review process.

Provide specific examples   When preparing the review, it is essential that the supervisor provide specific examples to assist the employee's learning process. Instead of saying only that the employee did a great job (which will no doubt make the employee feel good, but doesn't identify the results or behavior that made the performance great), a statement that the employee consistently submitted accurate reports requiring little or no revision on or before the deadline describes exactly the kind of behavior that the supervisor wants to encourage.

Employee self-evaluation   Another task to be completed prior to the review is an employee self-evaluation. The format used for self-evaluations is sometimes identical to the appraisal format used by the supervisor, but it is possible for the forms to be different. In either case, employees completing a self-evaluation should have an opportunity to address issues similar to those used by the supervisor. Self-evaluations often provide supervisors with insights into how employees see their roles in the organization and help to direct the supervisor's review in a direction that is most useful to employees.

Conducting the appraisal   The appraisal meeting should be conducted in a setting that allows for privacy, with enough time allotted so that both the employee and supervisor are able to express and discuss all their concerns. In addition, to the extent that it is possible, the meeting should take place at a time when interruptions are less likely to occur.

The goal of the appraisal meeting is to enhance performance and productivity, so it's important for the supervisor's comments to be presented according to the guidelines for providing feedback discussed earlier in this chapter. Whether the comments are positive or negative, the employee should leave with a clear idea of what needs to be done and some thoughts on how to improve. Even employees who are stellar performers can benefit from constructive suggestions for further improvement.

If the organization bases appraisals on performance standards, the supervisor should discuss each area that is being reviewed, beginning with a review of the original standard. After that, the supervisor should provide employees with an assessment of how their performance met, exceeded, or fell short of those expectations. When performance objectives based on strategic goals are used, the discussion should begin with a review of the objectives, followed by an assessment of whether or not the employee met, exceeded, or fell short of the goals. It's important that this be a two-way discussion— employees must be able to express their concerns about obstacles that were overcome or prevented them from performing at the highest level.

In either type of program, the formal appraisal meeting also provides an opportunity for supervisors to discuss future growth opportunities with employees. This discussion can lead into the establishment of goals and objectives to be achieved during the next review cycle. When possible, these future goals and objectives can be designed to provide development opportunities for employees.

At the end of the appraisal meeting, the employee is asked to sign the review, not necessarily indicating that they are in agreement with all the contents, but that they have received a copy of the document. The employee signature can be useful later to confirm that the employee had knowledge of the key points of performance, both positive and negative, and therefore should understand both successes achieved and areas for which improvement for the position is needed. This information becomes critical as documentation for any future performance-related termination.

In some states, a signature of the review is also useful to employees because it entitles them to receive a copy of the document from the personnel file.

Following up after the appraisal   Whether an organization has a formal performance management program requiring ongoing employee feedback or not, the appraisal can serve as a starting point for supervisors to build this kind of feedback into their daily interactions with employees.

Administrative Responsibilities

As with many other HRM functions, the performance management process produces documents which must be managed appropriately. Not surprisingly, there is debate in some organizations as to where performance documentation should be located: in files maintained by the direct supervisor or in the official personnel files maintained by the HR department. The short answer is that the original documents should be maintained in the HR department because HRM is more familiar with legal retention and confidentiality requirements. HRM is usually charged with the responsibility of ensuring the availability of all employment documents in an organization, and performance appraisals are no exception. Maintaining these documents in a centralized location increases the likelihood that they remain confidential and are available when needed for future employment decisions.

Since Title VII and other equal opportunity legislation require that all documents relative to any employment action be maintained for at least three years, it is important that the appraisal documents also remain available for review as needed for legal actions.

Documentation of performance becomes critical when disciplinary actions are taken. For example, when an employee has been counseled for poor performance, received verbal and written warnings, and been told that performance needs to improve or termination is a possible outcome, if these actions are not properly documented it is difficult for the employer to justify an otherwise legitimate termination.

Terms to Know

anniversary reviews	performance appraisal
critical incident review	performance objectives
focal review	performance standards
inter-rater reliability	

Review Questions

1. True or false: Performance management is an annual task.

2. Why is performance management important?

3. How is a performance standard developed?

4. How is a performance objective developed?

5. How do strategic organization goals affect individual employee work?

6. What is a SMART goal?

7. What is a common mistake made by supervisors in the PM process?

8. When is the best time to introduce employees to the PM process in an organization?

9. What is the halo/horn effect?

10. What kinds of tasks should be completed before doing an employee review?

Chapter 10

Strategic Human Resource Management

As the role of HR has changed, greater emphasis has been placed on the need for practitioners to "be strategic" and have "a place at the table" with management. Even practitioners who are entering the HR field must be able to identify how the functions, programs, and activities they provide to an organization contribute to its success. So, while you are processing benefit paperwork, placing a job advertisement, counseling employees, or developing a training program, it is important to keep in mind that ultimately, the HR role requires practitioners to be aware of and understand the mission and goals of their organizations. The purpose of this chapter is to look at how the functions covered in previous chapters fit into the management of organizations.

Strategic Management

Strategic management is a term used frequently in the business world, but what does it mean exactly? According to the dictionary, a *strategy* is a careful plan or method. In a business context, *management* refers to the functions necessary to run a successful business: planning, organizing, directing, controlling, and coordinating. In its broadest and most generic sense, strategic management is the term used to describe the practice of developing plans, organizing operations, directing employees, controlling outcomes, and coordinating work processes to achieve a desired result.

Planning   Planning is the crucial first function for effective organizational management. The next section discusses different aspects of the planning function in more detail.

Organizing   During the process of organizing, managers identify the tasks and activities needed to achieve the results developed in the planning process. Each function is then divided into manageable groups; authority is delegated to group leaders, managers and supervisors; and lateral and vertical interactions are clarified. Organizing is also more fully described in a subsequent section.

Directing   Managers perform this function when they work with their employees. This management function involves activities in the areas of employee relations, communication, development, and performance management.

Controlling   Managers operate in the control function when they ensure that operating results conform to plans established during the planning function.

Coordinating   Managers act in the coordinating role when they bring people and resources together at the right times and in the proper sequence to achieve desired results.

In order to provide the level of service and accountability that is a growing requirement for human resource management (HRM), practitioners need to understand the strategy developed by organization leaders and be able to demonstrate how daily HRM activities support and contribute to the achievement of those goals.

Strategic Planning

To better understand the strategic planning process, let's begin with a brief overview of what goes into creating a plan. This section is designed to provide practitioners with a base to help them develop an understanding of the strategic plans that are specific to their own organizations. While a general understanding of the planning process is helpful in this regard, the key to successfully supporting an organization's goals requires the ability to speak the same language as the senior management team. To do so requires an understanding of the organization's specific strategy and goals, and the role that the organization plays in the broader industry of which it is a part.

During the planning process, organization leaders look at various internal and external factors in order to answer four basic questions:

◆ Where are we now?

◆ Where do we want to be?

◆ How will we get there?

◆ How will we know when we arrive?

The answers to these questions form the basis for developing a strategy that leaders believe will provide the best operating results for the organization. A plan is only as good as the information used to create it, so it is important to gather as much relevant information as possible for the planning process. Over the years, academicians and management consultants have developed many tools to help answer these questions. One of the most common is known as a *SWOT analysis*, which looks at the strengths, weaknesses, opportunities, and threats facing the organization.

SWOT analysis
A SWOT analysis is a tool that looks at the strengths, weaknesses, opportunities, and threats facing an organization.

Strengths are *internal* issues that help the organization achieve its goals. These issues include factors such as a highly skilled workforce, recently modernized machinery and equipment, or a high level of technology available to the workforce. These things make it easier for the organization to compete successfully in the marketplace

Weaknesses are *internal* issues that might impede the organization in its quest to achieve its goals. Weaknesses can include factors such as difficulty in attracting and retaining employees with the necessary level of skill, old equipment or machinery that is expensive to operate, and a lack of technology in the organization. These factors tend to make it more difficult for an organization to compete successfully.

Opportunities are *external* issues that could be helpful to the organization, such as positive economic conditions, weak competition, or high consumer demand for the organization's products.

Threats are *external* issues that work against the organization in the marketplace. These issues can include such things as a new strong competitor in the marketplace, an economic recession, or increased government regulation.

By collecting and analyzing information in each of these areas, the management team has access to information that makes it possible to formulate a strategic plan with a full range of available information. Access to this type of information makes it easier to develop a plan designed to address various situations in a way that benefits the organization.

Based on the information collected during a SWOT analysis, the management team is able to formulate an operating strategy. In most organizations, the operating strategy consists of the following five basic elements:

Vision Statement A *vision statement* is a concise inspirational statement that communicates what the organization does, discusses why it does it, and describes what success will look like when it is achieved. For example, the Coca-Cola Company vision statement says:

> *The Coca-Cola Company exists to benefit and refresh everyone it touches.*

This vision statement communicates (to investors, employees and the general public) what the leaders of the organization expect to achieve as a result of selling their products.

Mission Statement The *mission statement* gets more specific and is often designed to guide employees toward accomplishing the vision.

For example, the mission statement for the Ritz-Carlton Hotels, which they call "The Credo," states:

> *The Ritz-Carlton Hotel is a place where the genuine care and comfort of our guests is our highest mission.*
>
> *We pledge to provide the finest personal service and facilities for our guests who will always enjoy a warm, relaxed, yet refined ambience.*
>
> *The Ritz-Carlton experience enlivens the senses, instills well-being, and fulfills even the unexpressed wishes and needs of our guests.*

As you can see, this statement provides clear expectations for the level of service employees are to provide.

Values A number of organizations identify core *values* that describe how people in the organization work together and interact with those outside the organization as well. Microsoft EMEA (Europe, Middle East, and Africa) created the following value statement to guide its employees:

> *Achieving our mission requires great people who are bright, creative, and energetic, and who share the following values:*
>
> *Integrity and honesty.*
>
> *Passion for customers, partners, and technology.*

Open and respectful with others and dedicated to making them better.

Willingness to take on big challenges and see them through.

Self critical, questioning, and committed to personal excellence and self improvement.

Accountable for commitments, results, and quality to customers, share-holders, partners, and employees.

Corporate value statements help guide managers during the selection process for new employees. For all employees, corporate values provide a standard for acceptable behavior in the workplace.

Strategic goals   After the leaders have examined the opportunities and challenges both inside and outside of the organization and identified their vision and mission, they must set specific *strategic goals* that are designed to move the organization toward achievement of the mission. Creating goals based on the SMART model (specific, measurable, action-oriented, realistic, and time-based) discussed in Chapter 9, "Building a Performance Management Plan," helps to ensure that the goals will be clearly understood by employees. By their very nature, SMART goals contain a basis for measurement that makes it possible to determine whether or not the goals were achieved.

A strategic goal for a construction company might be: "Increase remodeling sales by five percent during the next fiscal year."

Tactical goals or objectives   After strategic goals for the organization have been established, the leaders of each of the functional areas (human resources, production and operations, sales and marketing, information technology, and finance) determine what must be done in their areas to contribute to the achievement of the strategic goals.

In the case of the construction company goal, the marketing director might develop a *tactical goal* such as: "Within 30 days, develop a profile of home-owners who comprise the target market for remodeling work."

The strategic plan for an organization, then, consists of the strategic goals developed by the organization leaders and the tactical goals developed for each of the functional areas. These plans provide a guideline to be used in fulfilling the vision and mission.

Organization Structures

The structure of an organization influences how rapidly it is able to respond to changing needs. In most cases, the structure selected strongly influences the way the organization operates on a daily basis, which in turn strongly influences the culture. Most organization structures are based on the concepts of centralization, decentralization, and span of control.

Centralized In *centralized* structures, power and authority are concentrated at high levels in the organization. Many decisions must be made in accordance with an established approval process in which decision-making authority is clearly defined for each level.

Decentralized *Decentralized* structures distribute power and authority throughout the organization so that decisions are made at or very near the level closest to where the work is being done.

Span of control
Span of control is the number of employees who report to one manager or supervisor.

Span of control *Span of control* refers to the number of employees supervised by a single manager or supervisor. In general, the greater the demands that are placed on supervisors, the fewer employees they are able to supervise. Some circumstances limit the number of employees reporting to a single supervisor. This is known as a narrow span of control, and can result from situations such as the following:

◆ Work that is complex and requires diverse processes

◆ Work that requires a high level of coordination

◆ Employees who are geographically dispersed

◆ A large number of administrative requirements placed on the manager

◆ Environments in which there is a high level of change

Conversely, a wider span of control (more employees reporting to the supervisor) is possible under the following conditions:

◆ Experienced, well-qualified employees

◆ Work processes that are clearly defined

◆ Jobs that are designed with built-in checks and balances

There is no "one-size-fits-all" structure that works for all organizations. Organization structure needs to reflect how the business operates, so the best structure is one that is appropriate for the size of the organization, the type of product or service that is produced, and the work processes involved. Some structures that are seen frequently in American businesses are explained in the following sections.

Traditional Structures

Traditional structures are usually seen in organizations with many layers of management and often require multiple levels of approval to make changes. As a result, it can take many months to transform an operating procedure to respond to market changes. By the time the approval is received, it is possible that the need for that particular change no longer exists, meaning that the organization has lost an opportunity to increase its market share. Traditional organizations are generally geared toward a "command-and-control" atmosphere, in which much of the communication in the organization flows from the top down. The following organization chart illustrates a typical traditional structure.

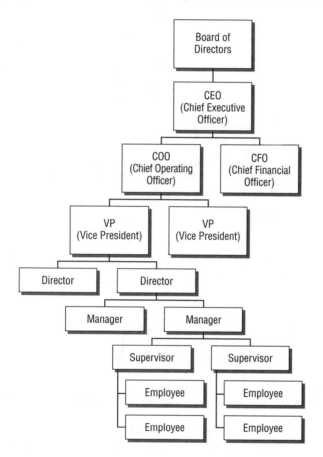

Organic Structures

Organic structures (also known as flat structures) have fewer levels of management and less bureaucracy than traditional structures, and are generally able to respond more rapidly to changes in the marketplace. These organizations are more fluid, and are characterized by open communications that flow not only up and down the organization, but laterally among peers as well. Flat structures are used to best advantage with smaller organizations. For that reason, some large organizations are organized into smaller entrepreneurial groups to take advantage of this type of structure, as seen in the following illustration.

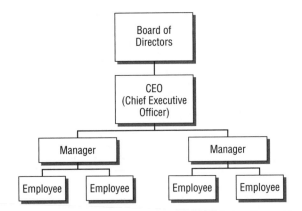

Functional Structures

In a *functional structure*, each of the five business functions has its own reporting structure, led by a senior executive who reports to the CEO or COO, as seen in the following illustration.

Business functions are further identified as either line functions or staff functions. A *line function* is one that has responsibility for operating results, such as production, operations, sales, or marketing. A *staff function* is one that provides support for managers with line responsibilities, such as human resources, information technology, or finance.

Divisional Structures

The *divisional structure* is best used in organizations that are conglomerates (made up of entities that have little or no relation to each other) such as General Electric Corporation. GE is made up of 11 business units, in industries as widely diverse as entertainment, financial services, health care, and energy. A divisional structure would organize these units as illustrated in the organization chart.

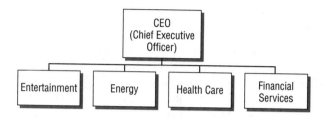

Customer Structure

In a *customer structure*, an organization that produces a variety of different products or services for customers with very different needs might decide to structure itself according to the different product lines it offers. For example, Dell Computer produces personal computers, peripheral equipment, and network systems for individuals and businesses. One structure that could be used in this business might look like the following illustration.

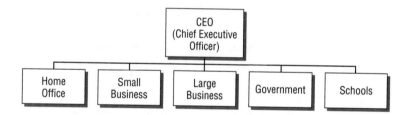

Geographic Structures

An organization with operations dispersed around the country or around the world might find it advantageous to use a decentralized *geographic structure*, led by senior executives for each region or geographic area.

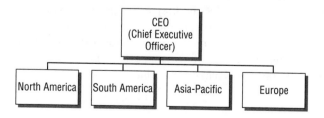

Each geographic area can then be organized in the way that best suits the needs of that region, whether it is uses a customer, product line, or functional structure.

Matrix Structures

A *matrix structure* is designed to increase communication between functional areas within a product line or customer structure. In a matrix organization, employees have responsibilities to supervisors in two different areas. For example, an accountant might report to both the Controller and the Marketing Director for a particular product line. The following illustration shows how this might look.

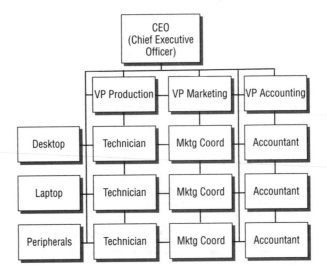

The purpose of this structure is to provide greater communication between employees assigned to the same product line, regardless of their job duties. In the previous illustration, the production, marketing, and accounting employees working on the desktop product have a responsibility to the manager of the product line. In addition, they are responsible to the managers of their functional areas as well. The advantage of this system is that employees are able to work together more closely to produce desktop products. At the same time, they have the support and technical expertise of the managers in their respective functional areas. One downside the use of matrix organizations is the difficulties that ensue when employees report to two different managers. This can create frustration for employees whose managers make conflicting demands.

The structure of an organization is based on many factors. When establishing an organization for the first time, or when major changes in strategic direction occur, a review of the organization structure might be in order. This review should take place when HRM is developing the strategic HR plan to ensure that the best structure for achieving organization goals is utilized.

Organization Life Cycles

Just as understanding an organization's strategy and structure is important for HRM, it is also important to know which stage of the business life cycle it falls into. There are a number of different models describing organization life cycles, with as few as four or as many as eight stages. Life cycle models that describe more than four stages break one or more of the basic stages into more specific phases. The basic stages of the business life cycle are the following:

Startup   During the *startup* stage, the organization is generally understaffed as the founders struggle to obtain funding, hire employees, and develop the product or service. At this stage, employees tend to wear many hats and work closely with the founders. When hired, employees are already fully competent in their professions, and little training or development is necessary. At best, compensation and benefits during the startup phase meet the market, but often lag it. In many cases, employees receive moderate base pay, which is supplemented by profit-sharing bonuses and stock options. During a startup phase, HRM most often is reactionary rather than proactive, with programs and activities taking place as needs arise.

Growth   As organizations grow, the organization might continue to struggle financially in order to meet customer demands. At this *growth* stage, the founders are no longer able to adequately supervise all the employees, so a layer of management begins to develop. As employees who are used to regular access to senior leaders find that this access is no longer available to them, morale problems might develop. Jobs are better defined during the growth phase and there is less need for employees to perform multiple functions. For HRM, recruiting becomes the dominant requirement to fill the necessary jobs, and as a result, compensation and benefits must now be more competitive with the labor market. It is at this stage that HR policies and plans begin to develop. Training and development activities also become necessary to assist in retaining employees.

Maturity   As organizations mature they reach a level of stability not generally seen in previous stages. In the *maturity* stage, HRM programs are more fully developed and formal. The compensation and benefit programs might begin to lead the market in order to attract the best candidates, and executive compensation plans are developed. Training and development programs are expanded to provide growth opportunities for employees.

Decline   An organizations in the *decline* stage has passed its peak, often as a result of changes in market conditions and a reduced demand for its products or services. Declining organizations are more bureaucratic and resistant to change, making it more difficult for leaders to turn the decline around and bring the organization back to profitability. As demand declines, organizations must reduce operating costs, and this often leads to reductions-in-force. HRM needs in a declining organization center on change management, employee relations, and initiatives designed to increase productivity.

To respond to changing organizational needs, it is important for HR practitioners to understand the various stages of the business life cycle. For example, leaders of an organization in the startup stage will be more interested in getting the job done than in establishing policies and procedures. An attempt to implement a policy initiative at this stage is not likely to be seen as necessary or as the best use of time and resources. Attempting to establish formal HR policies under these conditions might leave an impression with leaders that the HR practitioner doesn't see the "big picture" or understand the organization's needs.

With this basic understanding of organizational planning, structure, and life cycles, let's look now at strategic HR management.

Strategic HR Management

The role of an HR practitioner can be both rewarding and frustrating. Many people enter this profession because they like working with people—and that is certainly a component of many HRM jobs. The fact is that the modern HRM function requires much more from practitioners. Because HRM does not have an operational role in many organizations, much work must be accomplished by influencing the decision-makers. The ability to exert influence effectively is directly related to the level of credibility HRM has built within an organization.

The most successful HRM practitioners know that doing the basics well and providing excellent customer service to employees and management is crucial in order to be taken seriously as strategic partners. To be truly effective, HR practitioners must deliver basic tactical and administrative services at a very high level of proficiency, whether that means counseling employees, administering benefit plans, or performing one of the other basic HR functions. Over time, a record of quality results and accessibility builds credibility in an organization. A history of quality delivery on the basics opens the door for HRM to influence the decision-making process and have an impact on the organization.

As has been discussed throughout this book, it is crucial for HR practitioners to understand their particular businesses in order to develop and deliver programs and services that are aligned with corporate strategy and goals. Practitioners must be able to speak the language of business in this regard, backing up recommendations with accurate facts, costs, and benefits.

HRM must demonstrate that it is accountable for achieving results. The best way to do this is to develop a method for measuring HR activities and programs because if something can be measured, it can be controlled and managed. Once a baseline measurement is established, subsequent periodic measurements hold HRM accountable for delivering results in those areas. While many HRM activities are difficult to measure in a meaningful way (for example, the results of employee counseling sessions), it is important to develop a measurement method. Measurements might be made in the form of performance standards for the HRM department, as well as for individual practitioners. In this situation, SMART goals are an effective solution. Some areas of HR lend themselves more easily to the use of metrics, and some of them have been discussed in preceding chapters.

Finally, HRM must be able to deliver accurate information (in the form of reports and/or analysis) when it is needed. This becomes much easier with the use of a *human resource information system (HRIS)*, a database that collects a wide variety of information about employees that is easily accessible when reports are necessary. In a subsequent section, there is a discussion of the process to follow when selecting an HRIS software application.

Let's look more closely now at the process used to develop a strategic HR plan that is tied to, and supports, an organization's strategic goals.

human resource information system (HRIS)

A human resource information system (HRIS) automates recordkeeping and reporting for many HRM requirements, including benefit administration, performance appraisal programs, and government reports.

HR Planning

During development of the strategic plan, HR practitioners must work with the managers of the other four functional areas, as well as with organization leaders, to ensure that the programs and services provided by HRM are in alignment with the needs of the organization. The strategic HR plan begins with a review of the organization's vision, mission, values, and goals to determine what needs to be contributed from each functional area of HRM.

During development of the strategic HR plan, the same four questions that are asked during development of the organization's strategic plan need to be answered for each HRM function:

◆ Where are we now?

◆ Where do we want to be?

◆ How will we get there?

◆ How will we know when we arrive?

This analysis identifies the HRM issues related to planned organizational changes and pinpoints any policy, process, and tactical adjustments needed in each area. When the organizational strategy requires building and enhancing current operations, the strategic HR plan might be used to "tweak" HR programs and services. On the other hand, a major shift in direction for the organization will likely require major changes in one or more HRM functions. The strategic HR plan will, of course, relate to the specific needs of individual organizations. Let's look now at some issues that will probably need a periodic review to keep pace with organization, industry, or environmental changes.

As previously stated, the most important aspect of HR planning is that it reflect and be designed to support the organization's strategic goals. HR practitioners must therefore work closely with the managers of other business functions who have budget responsibility for those functions. The managers of each functional area determine the resources for technology, materials, and human resources that will be necessary to achieve their part of the overall organization strategy. HRM takes the information regarding the skills and numbers of employees needed and surveys the labor market to determine the availability and cost of individuals who possess the necessary qualifications. From this information, strategies for successfully attracting and retaining qualified employees are developed.

Staffing   The HR plan identifies the skills and levels of experience required for each position, and then identifies the labor market where individuals with the necessary qualifications are to be found. This information is used to identify the appropriate recruiting strategies and hiring practices that work best to attract those individuals. The staffing plan also evaluates various methods for filling the needs by examining alternative staffing methods, such as hiring temporary workers, outsourcing nonessential functions, and telecommuting.

For example, if the organization decides to create a new line of business, the staffing plan must be reviewed to ascertain whether the skills needed for this new work exist in the organization. If not, the best way to ensure that the skills become available must be determined, whether that means providing training for current employees or hiring new employees who possess those skills. As part of this assessment, HRM also needs to determine how available the skills are in the labor market.

Training   The HR plan also anticipates the types of training programs that might be needed to upgrade the skills of current employees. It should also include a plan to provide legally mandated training such as safety meetings and sexual harassment prevention.

Development   In accordance with the organizational culture and goals, the HR plan should outline development opportunities within the organization, provide a succession and replacement plan, and identify the organization's program for individual career development.

Employee Relations   The HR plan addresses organizational culture and identifies areas in which change might be necessary to conform to new organizational needs, or to reinforce organizational values and expectations with the employee population. If the strategic plan calls for staff reductions, the HR plan should include programs designed to deal with the impact that it will have on morale and productivity in the remaining workforce.

Performance Management   A performance management program is a key component of an HR plan. The HR plan outlines steps for managers to follow to maximize productivity, and increase employee morale and retention. In addition, the plan describes the performance appraisal process for the organization.

Compensation and Benefits   Compensation strategy is another key element of the HR plan. Whether the organization plans to lead, meet, or lag the market in its compensation practices is defined and provides guidelines for managers to follow when hiring or promoting employees. If, for example, the organization's goal is to develop cutting-edge technology, the compensation strategy will be to lead the market in compensation in order to attract and retain employees with the highest possible skill levels.

Metrics   Previous chapters included a section that identified some suggestions for ways to measure the effectiveness of specific HRM functions. The HR plan should identify the metrics that will be used in each HR function to demonstrate the effectiveness of programs in that area so that adjustments can be made if necessary.

Administrative Changes   Finally, the HR plan needs to address operating issues within the HRM function and identify opportunities for improving service and streamlining operations.

Now that some of the most important areas for inclusion in an HR plan have been described, how exactly does an HR practitioner go about gathering the information needed to develop the plan? One key source is the organization's strategic plan, which helps HRM identify where it needs to go. A helpful tool used to evaluate how well HRM is meeting current organizational needs is known as an HR audit.

HR Audits

An *HR audit* is conducted to determine how well the HRM function is complying with legal requirements and meeting organizational needs. Audits should be conducted on an annual basis to identify areas in which changes are needed due to changes in the law as well as to address strategic goals.

HR audit
An HR audit is the method used to evaluate how the HRM function complies with legal requirements and meets organizational needs.

An audit begins with basic identification information about the organization: the number of employees, states of operation, and any global operations that are part of the organization. This information is used to identify the laws that apply to the organization and what the organization should be doing to comply with each of them.

If metrics are in place, the audit evaluates how well current HRM programs are meeting organizational needs. If metrics are not yet in place, the audit is an appropriate place to identify which metrics will provide the best information about HRM contributions to the organization.

As part of an audit, it might be appropriate to conduct an employee survey to find out whether or not HRM programs are providing the services that employees need. A survey also identifies any areas in which the services provided by HRM staff fall short of employee expectations. Depending on the size of the organization, a separate survey for management might be conducted to determine how well HRM is supporting operational goals. In smaller organizations, this might be done informally when the leader of the HRM function meets with the leaders of other functional areas.

HR audits also review policies, processes, and procedures to ensure that they are legally compliant and do not provide an unnecessarily bureaucratic burden on management and employees. At this time, it is important to make sure that policies and procedures are still valid—as operating objectives and needs change, some procedures might no longer be relevant. To maintain effectiveness and credibility, any outdated procedures must be revised or eliminated as appropriate to reflect current operating needs.

The audit then examines each HR function (staffing, compensation, employee relations, safety, training, development, communications, and performance management) to make sure that it is operating in a way that best serves current organization strategy. As organization goals change, it is important for HRM functions to change as well in order to contribute to organizational effectiveness.

Finally, the audit examines internal HRM structure and processes to ensure that they continue to be appropriate for organizational needs. For example, as organizations grow, it becomes necessary to automate recordkeeping with the use of an HRIS. For efficiency, HRIS and payroll processing systems are often integrated to reduce the time spent on data entry and to improve accuracy.

HRIS Systems

HRIS systems provide many benefits for HR practitioners. As previously mentioned, they reduce the time that is spent on repetitive data entry tasks and increase the accuracy of information available for reporting and analysis. A well-designed system also provides easy access to reports of information for government agencies and for the organization. One of the most effective uses of an HRIS is the ease with which it is possible to produce the information necessary for annual EEO-1 reports required by the EEOC. They also collect information that can be accessed for management reports, such as benefit utilization, compa-ratios, and performance appraisal summaries.

Selecting an HRIS that is appropriate for a particular organization can be difficult because there are thousands of different products to choose from—at all levels of complexity and cost.

So, what criteria should be used to select a system?

To answer this question, it is appropriate to begin by examining what is needed. Some questions to ask include the following:

◆ What information needs to be included?

◆ Will the system interface with the payroll system or other organization systems?

◆ Who will have access to the HRIS?

◆ Will it need to run on a network? Or will it be used on a single computer?

◆ Is the organization centralized or decentralized?

◆ What level of technology is available within the organization?

◆ Does the organization have a single facility? Does it have multi-state operations? Does it have global operations?

◆ What information will need to be extracted from the system? What reports will be required? Does the system simply need to collect the information? Or does it need to produce specific reports?

◆ What are the cost limitations for the system?

◆ What process is currently being used to maintain information? How much time does it take? How accurate is it? How will an HRIS reduce time and increase accuracy?

Knowing what the HRIS is expected to provide is the first step in identifying the specifications to be used in evaluating different systems.

Policies, Procedures, and Work Rules

As organizations grow larger and more diverse, it becomes increasingly difficult for senior leaders to involve themselves in day-to-day operating decisions. As this decision-making authority is delegated to managers at lower levels in the organization, it is important to provide guidelines that ensure consistency between business units and work groups so that similar situations are handled similarly by different managers. This consistency is beneficial because it reduces the organization's legal exposure for claims of discriminatory treatment. On the other hand, overly restrictive policies can be seen as obstacles by managers who are responsible for achieving the operating results necessary to meet organizational goals.

Organization guidelines can be categorized in three ways: as policies, procedures, or work rules.

Policies *Policies* are broad guidelines developed to inform managers and supervisors of the ways senior management intends for the organization to operate. These guidelines must be responsive to current operating conditions and reflect legal requirements of federal, state, or international laws as appropriate.

Procedures While policies provide a broad guideline, *procedures* are designed to inform managers and supervisors about established methods for handling specific situations.

Work rules A *work rule* is both more specific and more restrictive than a procedure, setting conditions for handling individual situations.

Policy:	The organization reimburses employees for tuition expenses.
Procedure:	Managers may approve tuition reimbursement for business-related courses.
Work rule:	Employees must submit proof of satisfactory course completion prior to receiving reimbursement.

HR practitioners must be diligent about reviewing policies, procedures, and work rules on a regular basis to ensure that they are contributing to the ability of the organization to meet its goals and are not creating obstacles to effective operations. Managers often complain that HR policies are irrelevant and unrealistic given their current operating reality. When this happens, managers sometimes simply ignore the policies and act on their own to make sure that they are able to meet their goals. HR practitioners complain about this, but the fact is, if the complaints come from managers throughout the organization, HRM must work to bring the policies in line with organizational needs.

Effective policies and procedures reflect current operating conditions and provide consistency within organizations. In addition, it is important that they be clear and easily understood by employees at all levels throughout the organization. The best policies are sensible and based on business needs so that employees perceive them as fair. Finally, it is essential that employment policies, procedures, and work rules be communicated to employees so that they clearly understand organizational expectations and are able to act accordingly. Many organizations utilize employee handbooks to communicate this information to employees.

Employee Handbooks

In many organizations, the employee handbook serves several purposes. First and foremost, it is an effective tool for communicating human resource policies and procedures and provides an easy reference tool for employees. Second, the employee handbook is often used to reinforce organization values and culture by including a narrative description of its history and mission. Third, handbooks promote consistency and equitable treatment throughout the organization by informing employees about performance and behavioral expectations.

When is it appropriate to create an employee handbook? The answer varies, but generally it is necessary to develop one when an organization reaches between 5 and 15 employees. Even in companies of this size, a handbook is useful in communicating information about payroll and benefits, along with the organization's philosophy, mission, and culture.

One very important policy to include in the handbook is an "at-will" employment statement. As you recall from Chapter 2, "The Impact of Employment Law on HR Practice," employment-at-will is a common law doctrine that means employees and employers are both free to end an employment relationship at any time, for any reason. By including a statement to this effect in the handbook, employers indicate that they do not intend to create an employment contract based on any of the policies or procedures contained in the handbook. Even when an at-will statement is included, employers sometimes inadvertently include policies or statements that can be interpreted by a court as express or implied employment contracts. For this reason, it is a good idea to have any handbook or revisions reviewed by an employment attorney prior to distribution.

Successful handbooks are created as part of a team effort. Generally drafted by the HRM function, the handbook should be reviewed by senior managers to ensure that the policies and practices it describes reflect the intentions of the organization.

Global HRM

For many years, large corporations have conducted some of their operations in different countries around the world. With the technological advances that have taken place in the recent past, it is now not unheard of for small and medium-sized businesses to operate globally as well. Although the subject of global HRM is far too complex and diverse to cover in any detail within the confines of this book, it is important for HR practitioners to understand some of the key concepts related to this growing business reality.

expatriates

Expatriates are employees who originate from the home country.

inpatriates

Inpatriates are employees who originate from any country other than the home country and work in the home country.

host-country nationals (HCNs)

Host-country nationals are employees who are citizens of the country in which a corporation operates a plant or office.

third country nationals (TCNs)

Third-country nationals are employees from a country other than the host or home country.

ethnocentric

An ethnocentric strategy is a global staffing strategy in which key management positions are filled by expatriates.

polycentric

A polycentric strategy is a global staffing strategy in which home country positions are filled with expatriates, and positions in the host country are filled by host-country nationals.

There are a number of factors to consider when building an international workforce, beginning with determining how to recruit employees. There are four options to consider when making this decision:

♦ The home or parent country is the domicile of the company, where its corporate headquarters are located. Employees who originate from the home country are known as *expatriates*, or parent-country nationals (PCNs).

♦ Employees who come from any other country to work in the home country are known as *inpatriates*.

♦ The host country is the country wherein the corporation is operating, or is planning to operate, a business unit. Employees originating from the host country are known as *host-country nationals (HCNs)*.

♦ Employees from any country other than the home or host country are known as *third-country nationals (TCNs)*.

One of the first decisions to make with regard to international staffing assignments is which staffing strategy to utilize. There are four basic strategies:

The *ethnocentric* approach is one in which all of the key management positions are filled by expatriates. The benefits of an ethnocentric approach include the capability of the organization to maintain control of its business units and ensure that business is conducted in accordance with corporate mandates. Communication with the home office is made easier because the expatriate is familiar with the organization's culture and business practices. International assignments also provide opportunities to develop individuals who are part of the succession plans for senior management roles. This approach is often taken during the start–up phase of a business unit to ensure that organization standards are established and maintained, or when there is a real or perceived lack of management talent available in the host country labor market. Although this approach encourages a cohesive culture throughout the organization, it focuses on the home country/parent organization and doesn't take into consideration local customs and business practices. This lack of consideration can lead to misunderstandings and create ill will between the local government and the company.

A *polycentric* approach fills corporate positions in the home country with expatriates, whereas management positions in the host country are filled by home-country nationals. This approach can have a positive impact by showing commitment to the host country and generating goodwill for the business, but it does not afford upward mobility for top managers in the host country. The business benefits because it is less expensive to hire local employees—even at top dollar—than it is to fill international positions with expatriates. However, it can also limit communication between business units in the different locations and result in animosity between the home and host country business units due to differences in cultural practices and compensation levels between countries.

A *regiocentric* approach takes a somewhat larger operational view than does the polycentric strategy, covering a trade region such as the European Union and having managers move between business units in different countries in the region.

The *geocentric* approach seeks to place the best-qualified person into each position, regardless of their country of origin. As a result, the business builds an international management team whose members are able to move into and address issues in any geographic area.

There are three main issues to consider when making the decision about how global operations are staffed: cost, foreign business practices, and cultural acclimation.

Cost The cost of sending employees to work in a foreign country can be substantial, sometimes as much as twice the annual salary they would earn in similar positions in the home country. The costs are calculated by factoring in family moving costs, expenses required to minimize the cultural adjustment for employees and their families (such as subsidies for schooling costs, taxes, and housing), and any pay adjustments needed to keep the employee's salary "whole" to retain their pay equity within the company.

Foreign business practices The way business is done in foreign countries can be significantly different from the way business is done in the United States. Candidates for expatriate jobs must receive training on the culture and practices of the country to which they will be assigned to be successful in their positions and to avoid unintentionally insulting those with whom they are working. It is important as well as to provide training on laws governing U.S. business practices in foreign countries, particularly the Foreign Corrupt Practices Act (FCPA), which prohibits American businesses from proffering bribes to obtain contracts or encourage foreign bureaucrats to get things done in a timely fashion.

Cultural acclimation Cultural acclimation can be difficult—not only for the employee, but also for the employee's spouse and children—and often results in the resignation of the employee or insistence on a transfer back to the home country. Another issue that can make a successful transition difficult is that, although women are accepted in business leadership positions in this country, cultural difficulties can be encountered in other countries with fewer women in leadership positions in the workforce. This issue alone can become a huge conflict, with equal employment opportunity requirements to provide equal access to training and upward mobility at odds with the ability to do business in a country unaccustomed to dealing with women in powerful positions.

---

regiocentric

A regiocentric strategy is a global staffing strategy in which managers move between business units in regional areas, such as Europe or South America.

geocentric

A geocentric strategy is a global staffing strategy in which the best-qualified employees are selected for a position, regardless of their country of origin.

After the company has decided which approach best suits its strategic goals and culture, there are many complex issues to be addressed by HR. There are a myriad of laws, customs, and local practices to be dealt with that often conflict with home-country practices, and it is important to understand the impact of these issues when evaluating international workforce needs. Even solutions that seem on their face to make good business sense may be inherently problematic. For example, it may seem that few problems will occur when host-country nationals are placed in positions in their own countries. While cultural issues within that country may be reduced, conflicts related to the organizational culture can still arise unless the host-country national spends time as an inpatriate working in the home office to become acclimated to the organization's business practices.

It may be possible to alleviate some of the cultural and organizational clashes by utilizing experienced third-country nationals who are familiar with the organization culture and business practices to set up a new business unit in a neighboring country. This can be an advantageous solution for the business because it is less expensive than relocating an expatriate.

Metrics

Previous chapters concluded with some ideas for incorporating measurement into the practice of HRM. HR metrics is a growing field of study, and there are several excellent books available on the topic. One of the most useful is *How to Measure Human Resources Management* by Jac Fitz-Enz (3rd ed., New York City, NY: McGraw-Hill Trade, December 2001).

Table 10.1 summarizes a few commonly used metrics and explains how they are used.

Table 10.1   Commonly Used Metrics

HRM Function	Metric	Purpose
Staffing	Cost-per-hire	Measures total recruiting costs. This metric is calculated by collecting data for all costs related to hiring for a defined accounting period (such as a month, quarter or year) and dividing the total costs by the total number of hires during the same period of time. Expenses included in this calculation are sourcing (advertising and job posting, etc.), interviewing (time spent by each interviewer), testing expenses, recruiter fees or salaries, related administrative wages or salaries, travel expenses, and relocation costs.

Table 10.1   Commonly Used Metrics *(continued)*

HRM Function	Metric	Purpose
Staffing	Replacement Cost	Measures the total cost of replacing an employee. This metric is calculated by collecting data for all costs related to hiring for a defined accounting period (such as a month, quarter or year) and dividing the total costs by the total number of employees replaced during the same period of time. Costs included are for advertising and posting jobs, recruiter fees or salaries, the cost of interviewer time, expenses for temporary employees who fill in during the search, training the replacement, and lost productivity.
Staffing	Time-to-fill	Measures the proficiency of the staffing function. Time-to-fill measures the number of days between the date approval for filling the position is received and the date an offer is accepted.
Staffing	Yield ratios	Measure effectiveness of recruiting methods. Appropriate yield ratios are selected based on organization needs. Some common yield ratios include: # of qualified applicants divided by # of total applicants # of offers made divided by # of qualified applicants # of offers accepted divided by # of offers made
Compensation	Compa-ratio	Measures how well managers administer salary policy. Individual salaries are divided by the midpoint of the range.
Safety	Days since last injury	Measures effectiveness of safety procedures. Each day without a work-related injury is added to the total. The count starts at zero whenever an injury occurs.

Table 10.1 Commonly Used Metrics *(continued)*

HRM Function	Metric	Purpose
Safety	Number of worker comp claims	Measures effectiveness of safety procedures. Calculated by adding all new worker compensation claims to a total for the period (month, quarter or year).
Safety	OSHA recordable case rate	Measures injury rate against a baseline established by OSHA. The formula also appears in Chapter 5.
Employee Relations	Turnover	Measures the rate at which employees leave the organization. In the absence of outside influences (such as an economic downturn), the turnover rate is an indicator of employee satisfaction. If turnover is low, employees are generally satisfied with their working conditions in the organization. A high turnover rate can indicate poor management skills, lack of training, inadequate screening during the selection process, lack of competitiveness with salary and benefits, or other internal problems. To calculate turnover, the total number of employees leaving the organization during the period (month, quarter, or year) is divided by the average number of total employees during the period (number of employees on the first day plus number of employees on the last day divided by 2).
Employee Relations	Employee Satisfaction Survey	Measures how satisfied employees are with the organization. Employee satisfaction surveys provide management with a snapshot of how well management practices and HRM programs are meeting the needs of employees. Surveys are most often conducted using a questionnaire, often by a third party to ensure confidentiality.

Table 10.1   Commonly Used Metrics *(continued)*

HRM Function	Metric	Purpose
Training	Training Cost-per-Employee	Measures the investment in developing employee skills. This metric is useful in tracking how much the organization is investing in its employees. It can be used in conjunction with turnover rates to determine if increasing training contributes to retaining employees. To calculate training cost per employee, all training costs (salaries of training personnel who develop the program or the cost of pre-packaged programs, lost productivity costs, salaries of employees attending the training, presentation costs, travel expenses, etc.) are divided by the total number of employees in the organization.

Terms to Know

ethnocentric	inpatriates
expatriates	polycentric
geocentric	regiocentric
host-country nationals (HCNs)	span of control
HR audit	SWOT analysis
human resource information system (HRIS)	third-country nationals (TCNs)

Review Questions

1. What are the five functions of management?

2. What four questions are answered by a strategic plan?

3. What is the difference between a vision statement and a mission statement?

4. What is the difference between a decentralized and a centralized organization?

5. When is a wider span of control most appropriate?

6. In what situation would a divisional organization structure be most appropriate?

7. What are the benefits of using a matrix structure?

8. What are some of the changes that take place in the growth phase of the organization life cycle?

9. What is the difference between a policy, procedure, and a work rule?

10. What are some of the advantages of implementing a polycentric global staffing plan?

Appendix A

Answers to Review Questions

Chapter 1

1. What is the role of human resource management in an organization?

   Answer: HRM provides programs and services for the people in the organization. These programs must be tied to the goals of the business and provide assistance to other functional departments (IT, sales/marketing, finance/accounting, and operations/manufacturing) to meet their goals.

2. What does it mean for HR professionals to "be strategic"?

   Answer: HR professionals operate strategically when they can tie daily tasks and activities to the overall goals of the business, such as recruiting employees who have the specific skills needed by the business to achieve its goals.

3. How is HRM restricted in an NPO organization?

   Answer: Funding is often in short supply, which limits the capability of the organization to attract and retain the most highly qualified individuals for their positions.

4. What sets HR apart as a profession?

   Answer: There are five characteristics that set HR apart as a professions: a defined body of knowledge, a code of ethics, ongoing research into the body of knowledge, a national organization to represent the interests of the profession, and a program for certifying members of the profession.

5. What are some things for HR to consider when establishing operations outside the United States?

   Answer: Local laws and customs as well as U.S. laws governing operations outside the country must be considered when establishing operations in other countries.

6. Why do HR professionals need to understand other organizational functions?

   Answer: HR professionals are required to provide programs and services that serve the needs of individuals in other functional areas. For that reason, we need to know the unique requirements of these functions and what they have in common.

7. What areas of HR are subject to legal requirements?

   Answer: Virtually all areas of HR practice must consider either some federal, state, or local legislation—as well as common law practices that apply to situations in each area.

8. Describe the administrative aspect of HRM.

   Answer: In an administrative capacity, HR professionals are responsible for ensuring organizational compliance with legal requirements and for maintaining records that are required for operational as well as legal purposes.

9. Describe the operational aspect of HRM.

   Answer: In an operational capacity, HR professionals perform day-to-day activities such as recruiting, training, counseling, or interviewing.

10. What is the difference between training and development programs?

    Answer: Training programs provide skills that employees need in their current positions, whereas development prepares employees for additional responsibilities in a future role.

Chapter 2

1. What is a protected class?

   Answer: A protected class is a group of individuals that has been discriminated against in the past and is protected from further discrimination by Title VII, the ADEA, or the ADA. There are currently seven protected classes: race, color, religion, national origin, sex, age, and disability.

2. What are common law doctrines?

   Answer: Common law doctrines developed over time as the result of court opinions and rulings that are used to guide subsequent decisions in the courts. Common law is often seen in the areas of contracts and civil actions. The common law doctrines of interest to HR practitioners include employment-at-will, defamation, and constructive discharge.

3. Define a BFOQ.

   Answer: A BFOQ, a bona fide occupational qualification, is an exception provided by Title VII for jobs that require a specific religion, sex, national origin, or age as a reasonable necessity for normal operations of a business.

4. Describe the difference between disparate impact and disparate treatment.

   Answer: Disparate treatment is the negative result of an action or practice that is designed to discriminate against members of a protected class only because they are members of that protected class. Disparate impact occurs when an action or practice appears to be neutral but has a negative consequence on a protected class. Disparate impact can be intentional or unintentional.

5. True or False: An employer must hire a disabled individual who applies for a job, even if that person is not the best qualified for the position.

   Answer: False. Title VII and other equal employment opportunity laws such as the ADA do not require employers to hire individuals who are not qualified for the job.

6. What requirements must be met before an employee qualifies to take a FMLA leave?

    Answer: The employee must work for an organization with 50 or more employees in a 75-mile radius and been employed with the company for at least 12 months, working a minimum of 1,250 hours during that time. The leave can be granted to care for a spouse, son, daughter, or parent; or when the employee has a serious illness and cannot perform job duties.

7. True or False: All employers with more than 100 employees must have an affirmative action plan.

    Answer: False. An AAP must be completed only by organizations employing 50 or more employees when they have federal contracts of $50,000 or more. All employers with 100 or more employees must complete an EEO-1 report and file it with the EEOC by September 30 of each year.

8. What four elements did the Supreme Court identify as necessary to prove a prima facie case of discrimination in the *McDonnell Douglas Corp v Green* case?

    Answer: A prima facie case of discrimination occurs when the complainant is a member of a protected class, has applied and was qualified for a position when the employer was seeking applicants, was rejected despite being qualified, and after rejecting the candidate, the employer continues to seek applicants with the same qualifications.

9. An employer requires the office receptionist to attend a special training on Saturday morning to learn to operate a new telephone system. The employer does not have to pay the receptionist for the time spent at the training. True or False?

    Answer: False. Because the employer is requiring attendance at a job-related training class, the receptionist must be paid for the time.

10. An employer suspects that an employee is talking to coworkers about forming a union. The employer decides to change her work assignment so that she is isolated from her coworkers. Is this an unfair labor practice?

    Answer: Yes. The employer might have committed two ULPs with this action: The first is to interfere with her right to form a union; the second is to assign her to an unpleasant task.

Chapter 3

1. What arguments can you use to convince management of the necessity for a staffing plan?

    Answer: A staffing plan is a guideline describing the steps management takes to define jobs and hire qualified people to fill them. Using a staffing plan helps management determine what skills are necessary and avoid hiring mistakes, either those that occur when jobs are badly defined or those that occur when a person is hired without the skills needed to do the job.

2. What information can you obtain with a turnover analysis?

    Answer: A turnover analysis is a measurement that helps employers to identify areas where employees are leaving at a higher rate than in other areas in the company. It can also be an indicator of low morale.

3. Describe the importance of job descriptions and how they are used in organizations.

    Answer: Job descriptions are important documents for many HR functions. They serve as a point of communication between managers and their employees. They are a source document for the development of a recruiting strategy and search for qualified candidates. They can protect the company in ADA situations. Job descriptions are also useful in performance management and appraisal, and are an indicator of training and development needs.

4. What is an essential job function and why is it important?

    Answer: An essential job function is one that is the reason why a position was created. Identifying functions that are essential to particular jobs separately from those that are nonessential enables employers to engage in an interactive discussion of reasonable accommodations when requested by disabled employees.

5. What are job competencies?

    Answer: Job competencies are characteristics broadly defined that are needed for success in a particular job.

6. What are the methods used to obtain information during a job analysis?

    Answer: The methods used to collect information during a job analysis are questionnaires, interviews, task inventories, and observations.

7. Why should physical and mental requirements be included on a job description?

    Answer: Physical and mental requirements are included on job descriptions to help employers identify areas in which they may provide reasonable accommodation to disabled employees.

8. How can an employer benefit from developing an employment brand?

    Answer: An employment brand is one way for an employer to set itself apart from other organizations competing for qualified employees. A positive brand, such as those that result in designation as a one of *Fortune* magazine's "Great Places to Work," attracts employees to the organization.

9. What are alternative staffing methods?

    Answer: An alternative staffing method is one that does not involve hiring a full-time employee. These methods include part-time employees, job-sharing situations, telecommuting, temporary employees, independent contractors, PEOs, and outsourcing.

10. What is the difference between an open-ended and a close-ended question? When is each appropriate?

    Answer: A close-ended question requires a response that provides a fact but does not encourage the candidate to explain or add other information. These questions are appropriate when an interviewer wants to confirm information that appears on a resume, an application, or comes from another source. An open-ended question is one that lends itself to a description by the candidate of a situation and can be used to find out how a candidate approaches problems. Effective interviewers use both types of questions during an interview.

Chapter 4

1. What is the purpose of a compensation strategy?

    Answer: The compensation strategy ties decisions about the form and implementation of employee compensation to organization goals. It is used to align individual employee goals with corporate objectives and can encourage employees to develop skills that the organization needs for future success.

2. What is a performance-based compensation philosophy?

    Answer: A performance-based compensation philosophy rewards employees based on the level of the contribution they make toward achieving individual, workgroup, or organizational goals.

3. What is a total rewards program?

    Answer: Total rewards include all forms of compensation: monetary (base pay, variable pay, equity, and benefits) and nonmonetary (intrinsic and extrinsic rewards).

4. What is indirect compensation?

    Answer: Indirect compensation includes all benefits that the employer pays for on behalf of employees. This compensation includes voluntary benefits such as various forms of insurance, paid time off, wellness programs, work-life benefits, and retirement plans—along with any other benefits the employer provides.

5. How are job descriptions used in the compensation function?

    Answer: Job descriptions form the basis for job evaluations, which determine how much individual jobs are worth to the organization.

6. Why are wage and salary guidelines important to the compensation plan?

    Answer: Wage and salary guidelines are used by managers throughout the organization to ensure that the plan is implemented in a fair, equitable, and consistent manner.

7. How is job worth determined?

    Answer: Job worth is a function of the value placed on a job by the organization and how much the job is worth in the labor market.

8. What is the point method?

    Answer: The point method is a commonly used means of job evaluation. It is based on compensable factors that are developed for all jobs, weighted, and assigned points. The points are totaled, and jobs with similar total points are placed in the same salary ranges.

9. What are the limitations of the ranking method?

    Answer: The ranking method is based on subjective judgments that make it hard to defend if employees disagree with its results. Its use is also restricted to smaller organizations because it is not feasible to rank many thousands of jobs in order from most- to least-valuable to the organization.

10. Why is the midpoint of the salary range important?

    Answer: The midpoint of the salary range is important because it represents the market rate for jobs in the range. It is also the basis for calculating the amount by which an organization will lead, meet, or lag the market.

Chapter 5

1. How does a safe, healthful, and secure workplace benefit an employer?

    Answer: Employees are more productive when they work in a safe and secure environment. This kind of workplace lowers costs that are related to absenteeism, turnover and poor product quality.

2. What is the difference between OSHA and NIOSH, and why are they important to employers?

    Answer: OSHA, the Occupational Safety and Health Administration, is responsible for creating and enforcing safety standards in American workplaces. NIOSH, the National Institute for Occupational Safety and Health, is a branch of the federal Centers for Disease Control (CDC). It conducts research into workplace health issues, working with businesses and labor organizations to develop ways to prevent injury and illness in the workplace. These organizations are important to employers because the standards they set protect workers from job-related injuries and illnesses, thereby reducing medical and workers' compensation costs for employers.

3. What is a chemical hazard?

    Answer: A chemical hazard is caused by a substance that can cause burns, respiratory ailments, or illnesses including cancer when employees are exposed to it. Depending on the type of substance, exposure can occur as a result of inhaling the substance, ingesting it or absorbing it through the skin.

4. What is a physical hazard?

    Answer: A physical hazard can be caused by an electrical current, too much noise, exposure to radiation, or to excessive vibrations in the workplace.

5. What is a biological hazard?

    Answer: A biological hazard is the result of exposure to bacteria, molds, dust, or other industrial substances that cause illness, injury, or death to workers exposed to them.

6. Why should employers be concerned about substance abuse?

    Answer: Substance abuse increases employer costs due to absenteeism, poor product quality, medical expenses, and workers' compensation claims. Substance abusers also create morale issues for other employees who must pick up the slack created when abusers are unable to adequately complete their work.

7. What steps can employers take to reduce the level of job-related stress for their workers?

    Answer: Many of the steps employers can take to reduce job-related stress are actions that lead to improvements in the relationship between employees and employers. These improvements include providing clear communication about assignments and describing the results that are expected, allowing employees to exercise some level of control over their work routines, and providing an avenue for feedback between managers and their employees. In addition, employees who spend excessive amounts of time at work should be encouraged to pursue personal goals, spend time with their families, and engage in physical exercise. All these actions have been shown to reduce stress.

8. What are the benefits of an employee assistance program?

   Answer: An EAP is one of the most cost-effective benefits available to employers. These programs provide a variety of counseling and support services to employees for issues that are personal or job related. These programs include legal advice, financial counseling, mental health counseling, and crisis support, among other services.

9. What do employers need to consider prior to implementing a drug testing program?

   Answer: Employers must consider several factors before they begin testing employees for drug use. These factors include ensuring that the program will be implemented fairly and equitably, deciding which employee groups will be tested, and determining how frequently testing will occur. In addition, if employers decide to require drug tests for all new hires, they might require potential employees to take a drug test only after an employment offer has been made.

10. Why should employers create safety and health plans?

    Answer: Aside from the fact that many employers are required to create these plans based on federal or state OSHA requirements, there are solid business reasons for developing them. First, in the event of an accident, emergency, or disaster, people have a tendency to panic. A written plan helps employees to focus on the steps they need to take to protect themselves and their coworkers. Second, including employees in the development of the plan gives them an opportunity to voice their concerns about safety and health issues and participate in creating solutions to those issues. This cooperation increases buy-in to the safety and health procedures that employers establish. Third, these plans help to ensure consistent reporting of accidents or other incidents so that management can identify developing hazards. Finally, these plans create a mechanism for providing safety training to employees.

Chapter 6

1. What is an employee relations program?

   Answer: An ER program includes activities designed to manage workplace relationships.

2. What are the components of an organizational culture?

   Answer: Organizational cultures are affected by many elements, including the management style and philosophy of organization leaders, level of employee involvement that is encouraged, diversity, chain of command, and tone set by senior managers.

3. What are some tools typically included in a retention program?

   Answer: Retention programs typically provide employees with opportunities for advancement, public recognition, challenging and rewarding work, training, and mentoring. Many retention programs also include flexible work arrangements so that employees can maintain a balance between their work and private lives.

4. What is a mentor?

   Answer: A mentor is an individual who generally is outside an employee's normal reporting relationship. Mentors provide employees with career guidance and offer advice on how to deal with organization policies, politics, and workplace relationships.

5. Why do employees form unions?

   Answer: Employees generally form unions when they are mistreated, feel overworked, or perceive that they are not valued or appreciated by the organization.

6. What is the difference between employee relations and labor relations?

   Answer: Employee relations consists of relationships between employees and employers; labor relations adds a third party to the mix: the union.

7. Why is on-boarding important?

   Answer: On-boarding provides extended support for new employees to ensure that they have what they need to be successful in the job and in the organization.

8. Why should I-9 forms be maintained separately from personnel files?

   Answer: I-9 forms must be available for inspection by immigration officials when they conduct an onsite visit. Maintaining the forms separately from personnel files ensures privacy for employee information and easy access for inspection.

9. What steps should be taken in a disciplinary process?

   Answer: Depending on the severity of the reason for the disciplinary action, there are typically five steps in the process: counseling, verbal warning, written warning, suspension, and termination. The number of steps depends on the organization's culture and management philosophy.

10. Why is it difficult to measure the effectiveness of ER programs?

   Answer: Unlike some other HRM functions such as safety or compensation, ER programs are not tied to specific organizational outcomes. Instead, they can be one of many reasons for the success or failure of an organization to meet its goals.

Chapter 7

1. Why is it important to have a communication strategy?

   Answer: A communication strategy or plan provides a guideline to follow when communicating different types of information to employees.

2. What elements should be included in a communication plan?

   Answer: An effective plan identifies five key elements: what type of information is shared, who needs to receive it, when it is communicated, who communicates it, and identifies how the organization will determine if the communication was successful.

3. What are some drawbacks of utilizing employee involvement committees?

   Answer: Based on the National Labor Relations Act (NLRA), employers must use caution when establishing employee involvement committees because they can be considered employer-dominated labor organizations (which are considered an unfair labor practice). Aside from that, recommendations from employee involvement committees may be unrealistic and costly; not necessarily reflective of the general employee population; or time-consuming, causing delays in implementing needed changes.

4. What are the benefits of a suggestion program?

   Answer: Suggestion programs can be effective if they are taken seriously by the organization. They provide an anonymous way for employees to suggest changes to operations or processes. This anonymity can encourage employees to take risks and it can result in significant savings.

5. What do employers need to do before they conduct a survey?

   Answer: Before conducting a survey, employers need to decide what information they want to collect. Making this decision results in questions that are more focused and relevant to the issues, which provides better responses.

6. Why are lateral communication processes important?

   Answer: Lateral communication processes provide a means for employees in different business units or support functions to gain an understanding of other functional areas of the business and learn how they all work together to benefit the organization.

7. How does an organization know whether the communication program is working?

   Answer: There are several ways for the organization to know whether the communication program is working. First, MBWA allows managers to see first-hand what is happening in the organization. Second, employee surveys provide insight into how employees view the workplace. Third, focus groups can be used to solicit information about operational effectiveness.

8. What steps are necessary to implement a communication process for a particular subject?

   Answer: In order to implement a communication process, you must determine how the communication will be made and what budget is available.

9. What should be considered when determining the timing of different messages?

   Answer: The nature of the communication is the major consideration for timing. It may be necessary to make an internal announcement simultaneously with a public announcement, in which case timing is critical. In other situations, the timing may be less crucial and can be made during a quarterly all-hands meeting or in a newsletter.

10. What is the difference between an all-hands meeting and a team briefing?

    Answer: A team briefing takes place in individual work groups in which a supervisor passes on information from higher levels in the organization. An all-hands meeting takes place when senior executives meet with all employees directly to share information, make announcements, and answer questions.

Chapter 8

1.   What is the ADDIE model?

     Answer: ADDIE is an acronym used to describe the five phases of instructional design: analysis, design, development, implementation, and evaluation.

2.   Why are HRD programs important for organizations?

     Answer: HRD programs encourage employees to continually improve the skills and abilities that help the organization grow and achieve its goals. They also attract qualified employees and retain them in the organization.

3.   What is the difference between OD and change management?

     Answer: OD examines various aspects of organizational operations to determine how they can be improved, and develops plans for doing so. Change management is the process used to ease the transition for employees to the new way of operating.

4.   What is the difference between a leader and a manager?

     Answer: A leader's role is to define the organization's vision and inspire employees to follow; a manager's role is to ensure that daily operations are focused on goals and that employees have the information and tools they need to complete their work.

5.   What is a learning organization?

     Answer: A learning organization is focused on continuous review of organizational processes, sharing of information that is needed to improve operations, and ongoing learning for its employees.

6.   What is Maslow's hierarchy of needs?

     Answer: Abraham Maslow described five levels of needs that motivate individuals. They are physiological, safety, social, belonging, and self-actualization. According to Maslow, individuals at different levels in their lives can be motivated by satisfying needs that correspond to that level.

7.   What are the four levels of training evaluation?

     Answer: Training is evaluated at four levels: reaction (the most basic), learning (includes a test for participants), behavior (determines if training continues to be effective after a period of time), and results (attempts to measure the effect of the training on operating results).

8.   What is the difference between succession planning and replacement planning?

     Answer: Succession planning is focused on preparing managers for leadership positions in the organization; replacement planning is utilized at all levels throughout an organization to ensure that critical positions are filled in a timely fashion.

9.   Why is needs assessment the most important component of developing a training program?

     Answer: A needs assessment gathers the information that will be used throughout the development of the training program. It identifies who needs to be trained, what they need to learn, which tools will most effectively communicate the information, how the training will be conducted, and how often the training will be needed.

10. Why is it important to maintain records of safety training meetings?

    Answer: OSHA requires organizations to conduct safety trainings on a regular basis, and organizations must be able to demonstrate that they have complied with this requirement.

Chapter 9

1. True or False: Performance management is an annual task.

   Answer: False. Performance management is an ongoing process that takes place on a daily basis.

2. Why is performance management important?

   Answer: Performance management is important because it communicates to employees what they are supposed to do and what successful performance looks like. This information enables employees to be more productive and valuable to the organization.

3. How is a performance standard developed?

   Answer: A performance standard is based on a job function listed in a job description. The standards describe what successful performance of the function looks like.

4. How is a performance objective developed?

   Answer: Performance objectives are developed jointly with supervisors and employees. They are based on the strategic goals of the organization and the business unit, and help employees identify how their work contributes to organization success.

5. How do strategic organization goals affect individual employee work?

   Answer: Strategic goals set the direction for the organization. All the work done by employees at all levels in the organization must be focused on achieving the strategic goals for the organization to succeed.

6. What is a SMART goal?

   Answer: A smart goal (or objective) is specific, measurable, action-oriented, realistic, and time-oriented. Objectives that contain this information are easier to measure than those that do not contain the same information.

7. What is a common mistake made by supervisors in the PM process?

   Answer: Many supervisors are reluctant to discuss negative performance issues with employees because they are afraid of confrontation. This results in increasing frustration for the supervisor when the employee continues to perform in the same way. When the information is finally communicated to the employee, the supervisor is often extremely frustrated, while the employee has not been given the opportunity to improve the performance.

8. When is the best time to introduce employees to the PM process in an organization?

   Answer: The PM process should begin in the job interview by conducting behavioral interviews that are designed to find out whether or not the employee has the skills and experience to perform well within the organization.

9. What is the halo/horn effect?

   Answer: The halo/horn effect occurs when supervisors focus an evaluation on a single incident, good or bad, that occurred during the review period, rather than considering the sum of all the work throughout the review period.

10. What kinds of tasks should be completed before doing an employee review?

   Answer: Prior to the appraisal meeting, the supervisor should collect relevant information about work completed by the employee during the review period including feedback from coworkers, customers, vendors, and others. The supervisor should also compile specific examples of positive and negative results and behaviors that occurred. In addition, supervisors should ask their employees to complete and submit a self-evaluation.

Chapter 10

1. What are the five functions of management?

   Answer: Planning, organizing, directing, controlling, and coordinating.

2. What four questions are answered by a strategic plan?

   Answer: Where are we now? Where to do we want to be? How will we get there? How will we know when we arrive?

3. What is the difference between a vision statement and a mission statement?

   Answer: A vision statement is a short statement designed to inspire employees to follow the vision of the leader. A mission statement provides a more full and specific description of what the organization plans to accomplish.

4. What is the difference between a decentralized and a centralized organization?

   Answer: In a decentralized organization, power is delegated to lower-level managers and supervisors who have authority to make decisions at the local level because they are closest to daily operations. A centralized organization is one in which power is held closely at the top of the organization to maintain tighter control of costs, or operating details.

5. When is a wider span of control most appropriate?

   Answer: A wider span of control, in which one supervisor supervises a larger number of employees, works best when employees are well-qualified and experienced, when work processes are clearly defined, or when jobs are designed with built-in checks and balances.

6. In what situation would a divisional organization structure be most appropriate?

   Answer: The best use of divisional organization structure occurs when a very large corporation consists of a variety of operations that bear little or no resemblance to each other.

7. What are the benefits of using a matrix structure?

   Answer: A matrix structure is most advantageous when operations require a high level of interaction between employees from different business units, such as operations, marketing, and finance. This structure is designed to make it easier for team members to work together while maintaining a level of supervision on technical issues.

8. What are some of the changes that take place in the growth phase of the organization life cycle?

   Answer: During an organization's growth phase, the management team begins to develop, a level of management begins to develop, more employees are hired, and jobs become better defined. HR policies and the employee handbook become more formalized.

9. What is the difference between a policy, a procedure, and a work rule?

   Answer: A policy is a broad guideline, a procedure describes established methods for handling specific situations, and a work rule sets conditions for specific situations.

10. What are some of the advantages of implementing a polycentric global staffing plan?

    Answer: A polycentric global staffing plan is one of the least expensive ways to staff operations in other countries because employees generally work in their country of origin.

Appendix B

FairPay Exemption Regulations Effective August 23, 2004

As you recall from Chapter 2, "The Impact of Employment Law on HR Practice," the Fair Labor Standards Act (FLSA) establishes criteria used to determine which employees are exempt from the requirements for payment of overtime and other requirements of the law. In March 2003, the Department of Labor (DOL) proposed changes to the criteria used to determine the exemption status for employees in white-collar positions. As this book goes to print, it is likely that these proposed changes to the regulations proposed will go into effect on August 23, 2004. Efforts are still under way to rescind the regulations, so it is possible that further changes might be made in the future.

Due to the uncertainty about which regulations will be effective when this book is printed, I included the current regulations in Chapter 2, but I also present readers with the new regulations in this appendix. This is to provide readers with the best possible information while the regulations are being challenged.

The following information can be obtained from the DOL website at www.dol.gov/esa/regs/compliance/whd/fairpay/main.htm. This page provides links to detailed information for each of the white-collar exemption categories, as well as to general information about exemption requirements.

White Collar Exemption Status

Under the new regulations, employees in executive, administrative, professional, computer, and outside sales positions continue to be exempt from the FLSA requirements for payment of minimum wage and overtime pay. To be considered exempt, employees must be paid on a salary basis of no less than $455 per week ($23,660 per year). In addition, the duties performed by employees in these positions must meet specific exemption tests established by the regulations.

As you recall from Chapter 2, the old regulations provided two tests for each category: the short test and the long test. When formulating the new regulations, the DOL attempted to make the rules less confusing by eliminating one of the tests.

Let's begin with information that applies to all the white-collar exemption categories: the definition of *salary basis*, *fee basis*, and an explanation of permissible deductions from pay.

Salary Basis

The DOL describes a *salary basis* as the regular payment of a predetermined amount on at least a weekly basis. FLSA regulations allow salaried employees to be paid less frequently than weekly. Employers may not reduce this salary amount as a result of fluctuations in the quality or quantity of an employee's work. Similarly, an employer may not make deductions from an employee's weekly salary when work is not available for the employee.

Fee Basis

In some cases, exempt employees in the administrative, professional, and computer categories can be paid a fee for completion of a single job, regardless of the amount of time needed to complete the work. Fees are most often paid for unique projects or jobs that do not recur. Fee payments are acceptable as long as the payment meets the minimum salary of $455 per week.

Salary Deductions

The FLSA requires employees to be paid their full salary for any week in which the employee performs any work, *regardless of the number of days or hours worked*. An exempt employee who does not perform any work during a week does not need to be paid for that week. There are limited situations in which FLSA allows deductions from the pay of exempt employees. The following list describes these situations defined by the FLSA:

- When employees are absent from work for one or more full days for personal reasons (other than sickness or disability).

- When employees are absent from work for one or more full days due to sickness or disability, if the deduction is made based on a bona fide sick leave policy or practice.

- When employees are paid for jury duty, receive witness fees, or are paid for military service, the employer can deduct those amounts from the salary.

- When employees commit significant violations of safety rules, employers can assess and deduct penalties from their salaries.

- When employees violate rules governing workplace conduct, unpaid disciplinary suspensions of one or more full days can be made.
- During the first or last week of employment, if the employee does not work the full week, the employer can pro-rate the salary for that week.
- When employees take unpaid leave under the Family and Medical Leave Act (FMLA), employers can pro-rate the salary.

Employers who have an "actual practice" of deducting amounts from salaried employees under any conditions other than those listed previously risk losing the exemption status for all employees in that position. If unallowable deductions are made inadvertently, and the employer reimburses the employee for the difference, exemption status is not lost.

Exemption Categories

Positions that are classified as exempt must meet the requirements described in one of the following white-collar exemption categories:

Executive Exemption   Exempt executives are paid at least $455 per week on a salary basis.

The executive exemption is used for employees whose primary duty is to manage an organization, a department, or a subdivision of an organization. To be exempt under this category, the employee must be responsible for the supervision of at least two full-time equivalent (FTE) employees and have the authority to hire, fire, promote, or change the status of employees, or to make recommendations for employment actions that are given particular weight.

Administrative Exemption   Exempt administrative employees are paid at least $455 per week on a salary or fee basis.

The administrative exemption applies to employees whose primary duty is to perform office or nonmanual work related to the management or general business operation of the employer or its customers. These employees must exercise discretion and independent judgment on significant matters.

Professional Exemptions   Exempt professionals are paid at least $455 per week on a salary or fee basis.

There are two types of professional exemptions: learned professional exemptions and creative professional exemptions.

Learned Professional Exemption   A learned professional's primary duties require advanced knowledge or learning in a field of science or learning and to perform work that is predominantly intellectual and requires the consistent exercise of discretion and judgment.

The advanced knowledge required by this exemption is usually obtained by a prolonged course of specialized intellectual instruction.

Creative Professional Exemption   The work done by exempt creative professionals must require invention, imagination, originality, or talent in a recognized field of artistic or creative endeavor.

Computer Employee Exemption   Exempt computer employees must be paid *either* at least $455 per week on a salary or fee basis *or* at least $27.63 per hour on an hourly basis.

Only computer employees performing work as computer systems analysts, computer programmers, software engineers, or other similarly skilled work in the computer field can be exempt. To be classified as exempt, computer employees must perform specific techniques and procedures related to systems design and analysis, fully described on the DOL website at www.dol.gov/esa/regs/compliance/whd/fairpay/fs17e_computer.htm.

Outside Sales Exemption   The primary duty of an exempt outside sales employee must be making sales or obtaining contracts for services or facilities. In addition, outside sales employees must regularly work away from the employer's place of business.

Highly Compensated Employee Exemption   Employees whose total annual compensation equals or exceeds $100,000 per year (including payments of at least $455 per week on a salary or fee basis) and who perform office or nonmanual labor are exempt from FSLA requirements if they perform at least one of the duties described in the executive, administrative, or professional categories described previously.

Nonexempt Employees

The FLSA does not allow exemption for employees who work in blue-collar jobs, performing manual labor that requires the completion of repetitive tasks by using their hands, physical skill, and energy. The FLSA specifically requires payment of minimum wage and overtime to employees who perform work in production, maintenance, and construction; and similar occupations such as carpenters, electricians, mechanics, plumbers, iron workers, craftsmen, operating engineers, longshoremen, construction workers, and laborers. There is no exemption for highly compensated employees when they perform this type of work.

Another group of employees for whom exemptions specifically do not apply are those who work as police officers, firefighters, paramedics, and others in first-response positions. This policy applies to all employees in these job categories, regardless of the rank or the amount of money they are paid.

Appendix C

Resources

There are literally thousands of references available for every aspect of human resources, so it's just not possible to include every great resource here. The resources we have included are those that add dimension or different perspectives to the information presented in this book. The following compilation may also be helpful if you are considering pursuing the PHR certification track by HRCI.

NOTE Should you choose to pursue your certification in Human Resources, we suggest the *PHR/SPHR: Professional in Human Resources Certification Study Guide*, also by Sybex, as further reading.

A word about the Internet There is a wealth of information available on the Internet that is current and easily accessible. The best way to access this information is through a search engine such as Google (www.google.com) or Ask Jeeves (www.ask.com). If you haven't used a search engine before, you can get instructions on how to search by clicking the Help button on each search page. When you type in the phrase you want to research, you will get a list of websites to check out.

Professional associations Professional associations are often a great source of information about current trends in a particular practice area. Some of these are member-only sites, but even those very often have useful information available to nonmembers.

As mentioned earlier, there are many HR sources available. The inclusion of these materials is not an endorsement of the information contained in them. They are provided only as suggestions for further reading should you feel the need for more detail in one of these areas. For ease of use, the list is organized according to particular areas and topics.

NOTE At the time of publication, the URLs included below were operational; given the changing nature of the World Wide Web, some of them may have been changed or no longer exist.

Strategic Management

Resources included with Strategic Management cover general human resource books and resources for other business disciplines that HR professionals interact with on a daily basis.

Books   Chase, Richard B., F. Robert Jacobs, and Nicholas J. Aquilano. *Operations Management for Competitive Advantage*, 9th ed., New York City, NY: McGraw-Hill/Irwin, 2001.

Fitz-Enz, Jac. *How to Measure Human Resources Management*, 3rd ed., New York City, NY: McGraw-Hill Trade.

Gardner, Christopher. *The Valuation of Information Technology: A Guide for Development, Valuation, and Financial Planning*, New York City, NY: John Wiley & Sons, Inc., 2000.

Hiam, Alexander. *Marketing for Dummies*, New York City, NY: John Wiley & Sons, Inc., 1997.

Kaplan, Robert S., and David P. Norton. *The Balanced Scorecard: Translating Strategy into Action*, Boston, MA: Harvard Business School Press, 1996.

Mathis, Robert L., and John H. Jackson. *Human Resource Management*, 10th ed., Cincinnati, OH: South-Western College Publishing, 2000.

Tracy, John A. *How to Read a Financial Report*, 5th ed., New York City, NY: John Wiley & Sons, Inc., 1999.

Professional Associations   American Institute of Certified Public Accountants, www.aicpa.org

American Management Association, www.amanet.org

American Marketing Association, www.marketingpower.com

The Human Resource Planning Society, www.hrps.org

The Institute for Management of Information Systems, www.weball.org

The Institute of Operations Management, www.iomnet.org.uk

The International Association for Human Resource Information Management, www.ihrim.org

Society for Human Resource Management, www.shrm.org

Strategic Management Association, www.smsweb.org

Workforce Planning and Employment

These resources are some of the many related to planning for workforce recruiting and employment.

Books Ahlrichs, Nancy S. *Competing for Talent: Key Recruitment and Retention Strategies for Becoming an Employer of Choice*, Palo Alto, CA: Davies-Black Books, 2000.

Bechet, Thomas P. *Strategic Staffing*, New York City, NY: AMACOM, 2002.

McCarter, John, and Ray Schreyer. *Recruit and Retain the Best: Key Solutions for HR Professionals*, Manassas Park, VA: Impact Publications, 2000.

Smalley, Larry R. *On-The-Job Orientation and Training*, San Francisco, CA: Jossey-Bass, 1999.

Steingold, Fred S. *The Employer's Legal Handbook*, 5th ed., Berkeley, CA: Nolo Press, 2003.

Truesdell, William H. *Secrets of Affirmative Action Compliance*, 5th ed., Walnut Creek, CA: The Management Advantage, Inc.2001.

Professional Associations American Staffing Association, `www.staffingtoday.net` (look for the issue papers)

Employee Relocation Council, `www.erc.org`

International Labour Organization, `www.ilo.org`

International Public Management Association for Human Resources, `www.ipma-hr.org`

Human Resource Development

These resources provide additional information about developing talent within organizations.

Books Anderson, Dean, and Linda Ackerman Anderson. *Beyond Change Management: Advanced Strategies for Today's Transformational Leaders*, San Francisco, CA: Jossey-Bass/Pfeiffer, 2001.

Becker, Brian E., Mark A. Huselie, and Dave Ulrich. *The HR Scorecard: Linking People, Strategy, and Performance*, 1st ed., Boston, MA: Harvard Business School Press, 2001.

Fitz-Enz, Jac. *The ROI of Human Capital: Measuring the Economic Value of Employee Performance*, New York City, NY: AMACOM, 2000.

Grote, Dick. *Discipline without Punishment: The Proven Strategy That Turns Problem Employees into Superior Performers*, New York City, NY: AMACOM, 1995.

Knowles, Malcolm S., Elwood F. Holton, and Richard A. Swanson. *The Adult Learner: The Definitive Classic in Adult Education and Human Resource Development*, 5th ed., Houston, TX: Gulf Publishing Company, 1998.

Philips, Jack, and Ron D. Stone. *How to Measure Training Results: A Practical Guide to Tracking the Six Key Indicators*, 1st ed., New York City, NY: McGraw-Hill Trade, 2002.

Senge, Peter M. *The Fifth Discipline*, 1st ed., New York City, NY: Currency/Doubleday, 1994.

Kline, Peter, and Bernard Saunders. *Ten Steps to a Learning Organization*, 2nd ed., Arlington, VA: Great Ocean Publishing, 1998.

Professional Associations   American Society for Training and Development, www.astd.org

Compensation and Benefits

Additional information about compensation and benefit issues and processes is available in the following resources.

Books   Beam, Burton T., Jr., and John J. McFadden. *Employee Benefits*, 6th ed., Chicago, IL: Dearborn Trade Publishing.

Berger, Lance A. (Editor), and Dorothy R. Berger (Editor). *The Compensation Handbook*, 4th ed., New York City, NY: McGraw-Hill Trade, 1999.

Plachy, Roger J., and Sandra J. Plachy. *Building a Fair Pay Program: A Step-by-Step Guide*, 2nd ed., New York City, NY: AMACOM, 1998.

Professional Associations   American Payroll Association, www.americanpayroll.org

Employee Benefit Research Institute, www.ebri.org

International Foundation of Employee Benefit Plans, www.ifebp.org

International Society of Certified Employee Benefits Specialists, `www.iscebs.org`

World at Work (formerly American Compensation Association), `www.worldatwork.org`

Employee and Labor Relations

Books   Brounstein, Marty. *Coaching and Mentoring for Dummies*, 1st ed., New York City, NY: John Wiley & Sons Publishing, Inc., 2000.

Costantino, Cathy A., and Christina Sickles Merchant. *Designing Conflict Management Systems: A Guide to Creating Productive and Healthy Organizations*, San Francisco, CA: Jossey-Bass, 1996.

Holley, William H., Kenneth M. Jennings, and Roger S. Wolters. *The Labor Relations Process*, 7th ed., Cincinnati, OH: South-Western College Publishing, 2000.

Grazier, Peter B., *Before It's Too Late: Employee Involvement…An Idea Whose Time Has Come*, Chadds Ford, PA: Teambuilding, Inc., 1989.

Kaye, Beverly, and Sharon Jordan-Evans. *Love 'Em or Lose 'Em: Getting Good People to Stay*, San Francisco, CA: Berrett-Koehler Publishers, Inc., 1999.

Larkin, T.J., and Sandar Larkin (Contributor). *Communicating Change: Winning Employee Support for New Business Goals*, 2nd ed., New York City, NY: McGraw-Hill Trade, 1994.

Loughran, Charles S. *Negotiating a Labor Contract: A Management Handbook*, Washington, DC: BNA Books, 1992.

Delpo, Amy, Lisa Guerin, and Janet Portman. *Dealing with Problem Employees: A Legal Guide*, 2nd ed., Berkeley, CA: Nolo Press, 2001.

National Labor Relations Board, Office of the General Counsel, *A Guide to Basic Law and Procedures under the National Labor Relations Act*, Washington, DC: U.S. Government Printing Office, 1997 (can be downloaded from `www.nlrb.gov/publications/basicguide.pdf`).

Spitzer, Dean R., *Supermotivation: A Blueprint for Energizing Your Organization from Top to Bottom*, New York City, NY: AMACOM, 1995.

Professional Associations   Employment Management Association, `www.shrm.org/ema`

National Public Employer Labor Relations Association, `www.npelra.org`

Occupational Health, Safety, and Security

These are some of the many resources available for workplace health, safety, and security issues.

Books   Bible, Jon D., and Darien A. McWhirter. *Privacy in the Workplace*, Westport, CT: Greenwood Publishing Group, 1990.

Blanco, James A. (Editor), et al. *Business Fraud: Know It and Prevent It*, Huntington, WV: Humanomics Publishing, 2000.

Fay, John J. *Contemporary Security Management*, 1st ed., St. Louis, MO: Butterworth-Heinemann, 2001.

Geller, E. Scott. *The Psychology of Safety: How to Improve Behaviors and Attitudes on the Job*, Boca Raton, FL: CRC Press, 1996.

Levy, Barry S. (Editor), and David H. Wegman (Editor). *Occupational Health: Recognizing and Preventing Work-Related Disease and Injury*, 4th ed., Philadelphia, PA: Lippincott Williams & Wilkins, 2000.

Mitroff, Ian I., et al. *The Essential Guide to Managing Corporate Crises: A Step-by-Step Handbook for Surviving Major Catastrophes*, New York City, NY: Oxford University Press, 1996.

Professional Associations   National Association of Safety Professionals, www.naspweb.com

National Safety Council, www.nsc.org

The American Society of Safety Engineers, www.asse.org

Glossary

administrative role   HRM is responsible to develop company policies that enhance the organization's capability to meet its goals and be in compliance with federal, state, and local employment laws and regulations.

alternative staffing methods   Alternative staffing methods, which are used to staff an organization without hiring regular full-time employees, include temporary employees, part-time employees, independent contractors, PEOs, and outsourcing.

anniversary review   An anniversary review is an appraisal conducted on the anniversary of an employee's date of hire.

body of knowledge (BOK)   A BOK defines the information that is common to the practice of a profession. The HR BOK requires knowledge of strategic management; workforce planning and employment; human resource development; compensation and benefits; employee and labor relations; and occupational health, safety, and security.

bona fide occupational qualification (BFOQ)   A BFOQ is an exception allowed by Title VII when a business can demonstrate that a practice is necessary to maintain normal business operations.

bottom-up communication   The communication channel in which information flows from employees up through the organization.

brown-bag lunch   A brown-bag lunch is an informal meeting between a senior executive and a small group of employees who can get to know the executive and ask questions about the organization.

chain of command   The structure that identifies the level of authority, scope of responsibility, and accountability for different positions in an organization.

change management   Change management is the means used to help employees deal with change in organizations.

code of ethics   A code of ethics establishes guidelines for professional conduct.

communication strategy   A communication strategy is a plan that examines different circumstances in which the organization will convey information to employees and identifies communication methods to be used for top-down, bottom-up, and lateral communication in the organization.

compensable time   Compensable time is time for which an employer is required to pay nonexempt employees.

constructive discharge   Constructive discharge is conduct by an employer that makes the work environment so hostile and unpleasant that an employee quits.

cost-benefit analysis   A cost-benefit analysis collects all available information about the costs of an HRM proposal, identifies benefits such as cost savings and reduced turnover, and projects whether the proposal will be cost-effective.

critical incident review   In a critical incident review, a supervisor maintains a log of incidents, good and bad, that occur during the year in order to write a narrative review of an employee's performance during the review period.

direct compensation   Direct compensation includes salaries or wages, incentive awards, bonus payments, sales commissions, and other monetary compensation paid directly to employees.

disparate impact Disparate impact, which can be intentional or unintentional, occurs when an employment practice that is applied equally to all individuals has a disproportionate adverse effect on members of a protected class.

disparate treatment Disparate treatment occurs when members of a protected class are intentionally treated differently from other individuals.

diversity An equal opportunity practice in which individuals from a wide variety of backgrounds and protected classes are included in an organization.

emergency response plan (ERP) Describes what actions will be taken in the event of different emergencies or disasters that can occur at the workplace, including fires, floods, severe storms, and earthquakes; as well as incidents of workplace violence or terrorist attacks.

employee involvement committee Involves employees in solving organization problems.

employee relations (ER) The functional area of HRM related to managing workplace relationships

employee survey An employee survey is a formal process in which employees answer questions about what is working or not working in an organization.

employment brand An employment brand is used to describe the unique characteristics about an organization and what makes it a good place to work. It helps HRM to focus its recruiting strategy.

entitlement philosophy An entitlement philosophy is one in which salary and promotion decisions are based on length of service; this philosophy is exemplified by a union environment.

ergonomic injury An injury related to the physical design of the work place or task.

essential functions Essential job functions are those tasks, duties, and responsibilities that form the basis for the job's existence.

ethnocentric An ethnocentric strategy is a global staffing strategy in which key management positions are filled by expatriates.

executive order (EO) An executive order is issued by the chief executive of a federal, state, or local government entity (for example, the president, governor, or mayor).

exempt job An exempt job meets one of the four tests for exemption from the Fair Labor Standards Act requirements: executive, professional, administrative, or outside sales.

exit interview Exit interviews are conducted with employees who are leaving the organization to find out about their experiences and why they chose to leave. The purpose is to determine whether changes need to be made to the work environment.

expatriates Expatriates are employees who originate from the home country.

express contract An express contract is a verbal or written statement by an employer or company representative, such as "You have a job here for life" that might create an employment contract.

external equity External equity compares jobs in the organization to other similar jobs in other organizations to make sure that the organization's wages and salaries are sufficient to attract the qualified employees it needs.

focal review A focal review is a schedule in which appraisals are conducted for employees throughout the organization on the same date.

general duty standard The OSHA standard requiring all employers to provide a safe and secure workplace for employees.

geocentric A geocentric strategy is a global staffing strategy in which the best-qualified employees are selected for a position, regardless of their country of origin.

green-circle rates   A green-circle rate refers to a job incumbent whose salary falls below the minimum of the range for the salary grade.

host-country nationals (HCNs)   Host-country nationals are employees who are citizens of the country in which a corporation operates a plant or office.

hostile work environment   A hostile work environment can be created by a coworker, customer, vendor, or visitor to the workplace as well as by supervisors or managers. It is an environment in which individuals are exposed to taunts, comments, or physical conduct that would be considered offensive by a reasonable person.

HR audit   An HR audit is the method used to evaluate how the HRM function complies with legal requirements and meets organizational needs.

human resource development (HRD)   HRD is the area of human resource management responsible for working with current employees to attain new skills.

human resource information system (HRIS)   A human resource information system (HRIS) automates recordkeeping and reporting for many HRM requirements, including benefit administration, performance appraisal programs, and government reports.

human resource management (HRM)   HRM is the management function responsible for all activities related to workforce needs in organizations, including attracting and retaining qualified employees, ensuring that the organization operates within legal requirements, and maintaining a workforce that serves the organization's needs.

implied contract   An implied contract is conduct by an employer that can create a contract, such as the consistent use of a progressive discipline policy.

indirect compensation   Indirect compensation is a type of monetary compensation that consists of benefits paid by the organization on behalf of employees, such as medical insurance, workers' compensation, or mandated benefits.

injury and illness prevention program (IIPP)   Also known as a safety and health management plan. Describes the work environment, known hazards and actions that have been taken to report and correct them, as well as methods used to facilitate communication about safety and health issues between employees and management.

inpatriates   Inpatriates are employees who originate from any country other than the home country and work in the home country.

intellectual property (IP)   An intangible asset that includes inventions, customer lists, software code, and business processes unique to the operation of a business.

internal equity   Internal equity places a value on the worth of each job to the company. This value is based on the content of the job, its level of responsibility, and how much impact the decisions in the job have on organization results.

inter-rater reliability   Inter-rater reliability is the term used to describe the different ratings that often result when different supervisors rate the same employee.

job analysis   A job analysis gathers information about various aspects of a job, including reporting relationships, interactions with others, exemption status of the position, qualifications, work environment, and KSAs needed to perform the job successfully.

job competencies   Job competencies are broadly defined characteristics that allow an individual to be successful in a job.

job description A job description is a written document that is produced as the result of a job analysis. It contains information that identifies the job, its essential functions, and the job specifications or competencies that enable an individual to be successful in the position.

job specifications A job specifications section of a job description describes the KSAs needed by an individual in order to perform successfully in the job.

job stress Occurs when employees do not have the capabilities and/or resources to accomplish their job requirements and cannot control the circumstances in which they must operate.

knowledge, skills, and abilities (KSAs) KSAs are the qualifications that are needed by an individual in order to perform successfully in the position.

labor relations Describes the relationship between employers and employees who are represented by unions.

lateral communication Lateral communication is communication that takes place between employees in different departments within the organization.

leadership development Leadership development is the process that organizations use to prepare managers to step into leadership roles.

Management By Walking Around (MBWA) A communication method in which senior executives regularly spend time in production areas, talking with employees about their jobs and answering questions.

management development Management development is the process organizations use to prepare employees for positions of greater responsibility.

needs assessment Needs assessment is a process used to determine whether or not training is necessary. It identifies who will be trained, what they will learn, how training will be delivered, and when it will take place.

nonexempt job A nonexempt job is any job that does not qualify for exemption from requirements of the Fair Labor Standards Act.

on-boarding The process of welcoming new employees to the organization, integrating them into operations, and ensuring that they have the support they need to be successful.

open-door policy A communication method in which management encourages employees to approach any level in the hierarchy with ideas, complaints, or problems.

operational role The operational role is one of the three roles HRM plays in organizations. In the operational role, HR practitioners perform day-to-day tasks such as recruiting, counseling employees, and coaching managers—among many others.

organization development (OD) OD examines operations to determine whether improvements to technology, work processes, or structure can improve bottom-line results.

organizational culture The atmosphere, values, and beliefs shared by individuals at all levels within an organization, following the example of senior management which sets the tone for other employees.

OSHA recordkeeping requirement Most employers with 11 or more employees are required to maintain records of workplace illnesses and injuries during the year, and to post a summary of these incidents between February 1 and April 30 of the following year.

performance appraisal A performance appraisal is a regularly scheduled event, generally occurring once per year, in which employees meet with their supervisors to discuss performance during the preceding review period.

performance objectives Performance objectives are based on organizational and business unit goals and are usually developed jointly by supervisors and employees.

performance standards   Description of the results that the organization expects employees to produce for each function included in a job description.

performance-based philosophy   A performance-based philosophy is one in which salary increases and promotions are awarded to those employees who contribute to the achievement of organization goals.

polycentric   A polycentric strategy is a global staffing strategy in which home country positions are filled with expatriates, and positions in the host country are filled by host-country nationals.

prima facie evidence   A Latin term used to describe evidence that clearly shows a violation of an employment law.

professional certifications   A professional certification indicates that an individual has met requirements established by a national certifying body for that profession.

protected classes   Protected classes are groups of individuals identified by equal employment opportunity legislation as having been subjected to discrimination in the past.

quid pro quo harassment   Quid pro quo is a Latin term meaning "this for that." Quid pro quo harassment is a term used to describe harassment in which a supervisor or manager asks for favors in exchange for favorable employment actions. It is usually used in reference to sexual harassment.

reasonable accommodation   A reasonable accommodation is an accommodation to the work environment or job duties that allows a disabled individual to successfully perform the essential functions of a job.

red-circle rate   A red-circle rate occurs when a job incumbent makes more than the maximum of the salary range.

regiocentric   A regiocentric strategy is a global staffing strategy in which managers move between business units in regional areas, such as Europe or South America.

replacement planning   Replacement planning is the process organizations use to ensure that there is sufficient bench strength to fill critical positions at any level in the organization.

retention program   Retention programs provide employees with opportunities that encourage them to remain with the organization.

risk assessment   Identifies possible external threats and internal vulnerabilities, assesses the possible costs and impact on business operations, and develops plans to prevent or reduce the effects of an incident if it occurs.

span of control   Span of control is the number of employees who report to one manager or supervisor.

staffing plan   An HRM guideline that outlines the process of the way an organization recruits, hires, retains, promotes, and terminates employees.

strategic role   The strategic role is one of the three roles HRM plays in organizations. The strategic role identifies organizational goals and develops HR practices and programs that contribute to the achievement of those goals.

subject matter expert (SME)   A subject matter expert is someone who has both training and experience in a specific function or line of work.

succession planning   Succession planning is the process of identifying employees who have the capability to move into leadership positions within an organization.

SWOT analysis   A SWOT analysis is a tool that looks at the strengths, weaknesses, opportunities, and threats facing an organization.

tangible employment action (TEA)   A TEA is any action taken by an employer that significantly changes the status of an employee.

target audience   A target audience describes the people who will receive a particular training. It identifies their level of experience, time with the company, and level of expertise in their field.

third country nationals (TCNs)   Third-country nationals are employees from a country other than the host or home country.

top-down communication   The channel of communication in which information flows from the organization to employees.

total compensation   Total compensation includes all types of direct cash compensation employees receive.

total rewards   Total rewards include monetary compensation (direct and indirect) and nonmonetary compensation.

training evaluation   The evaluation process determines whether or not the training accomplished the desired results.

training objectives   Training objectives are used to focus training programs by describing what trainees will learn and to establish the criteria for evaluation.

unfair labor practice (ULP)   A ULP is any action that prevents or interferes with the rights of employees to organize or bargain collectively.

unlawful employment practice   An unlawful employment practice is any employment practice that has an adverse impact on members of one or more protected classes in any of the terms and conditions of employment.

variable pay   Variable pay is tied to specific performance goals and includes sales commissions, bonuses, and incentives.

workplace investigation   A workplace investigation is conducted when allegations or suspicions of misconduct come to the attention of the organization. These investigations occur when claims of sexual harassment are made, after an accident occurs in the workplace, or when management suspects that other misconduct has occurred.

workplace security   Activities designed to protect business assets from loss.

workplace violence   Occurs when individuals who lack the ability to control their actions become overly stressed and react to a situation with physical violence.

Index

Note to the reader: Throughout this index **boldfaced** page numbers indicate primary discussions of a topic. *Italicized* page numbers indicate illustrations.

Project Management Skills for all Levels

Project Management JumpStart™

by Kim Heldman, PMP • ISBN: 0-7821-4214-1 • US $24.99

For those interested in beginning or exploring a career in project management, coverage includes:

- The basic skills of a project manager
- Creating project schedules and determining project budgets
- Communication and negotiation skills

PMP®: Project Management Professional Study Guide, 2nd Edition

by Kim Heldman, PMP • ISBN: 0-7821-4323-7 • US $59.99

A comprehensive package to prepare for the PMP certification exam, this Study Guide provides:

- Detailed coverage of all PMP Exam Process Groups
- Refreshed content that make project management concepts clearer and easier to comprehend
- Companion CD with Testing Software, Flashcards for PCs, Pocket PCs, and Palm Handhelds, Two Bonus Practice Exams, and the Entire Book in PDF

PMP®: Project Management Professional Workbook

by Claudia Baca, PMP; Patti Jansen, PMP • ISBN: 0-7821-4240-0 • US $34.99

A one-of-a-kind book that will give you hands-on experience as you prepare for the PMP exam, this workbook provides:

- Clear introductions that put the exercises in context and explain the importance of key project management skills
- Dozens of exercises designed by two veteran project managers to correlate directly with PMP objectives
- Cross references to the PMP Study Guide for additional instructional content

PMP®: Final Exam Review

by Kim Heldman, PMP • ISBN: 0-7821-4324-5 • US $29.99

To ensure you're truly prepared for the exam, this book contains:

- Four complete practice tests
- Complex scenario questions with detailed explanations
- Companion CD with testing software and flashcards for PCs, Pocket PCs, and Palm Handhelds

PMP®: Project Management Professional Certification Kit

by Kim Heldman, PMP; Claudia Baca, PMP; Patti Jansen, PMP
ISBN: 0-7821-4325-3 • US $109.97

A 3-in-one product, this kit includes:

- PMP®: Project Management Professional Study Guide, 2nd Edition
- PMP®: Project Management Professional Workbook
- PMP®: Final Exam Review

$124.97
Value
Save $15!

SYBEX®

www.sybex.com

TELL US WHAT YOU THINK!

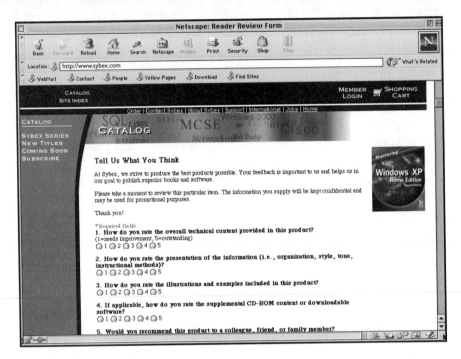

Your feedback is critical to our efforts to provide you with the best books and software on the market. Tell us what you think about the products you've purchased. It's simple:

1. Go to the Sybex website.
2. Find your book by typing the ISBN or title into the Search field.
3. Click on the book title when it appears.
4. Click **Submit a Review.**
5. Fill out the questionnaire and comments.
6. Click **Submit.**

With your feedback, we can continue to publish the highest quality computer books and software products that today's busy IT professionals deserve.

www.sybex.com

SYBEX Inc. • 1151 Marina Village Parkway, Alameda, CA 94501 • 510-523-8233